Who Killed
The Essex Boys?

By Alex Duggan.

Chapters.

Chapter 1.
Being There.

"The only good grass is the grass that works for me."
The Long Good Friday.

I

Chances are you already know something about the murders. Whether it's the truth, that's for you to decide. On the night of 6th December 1995, Tony Tucker, Pat Tate, and Craig Rolfe, sat in a Range Rover in Workhouse Lane, Rettendon; a small village in the county of Essex. At some point all three were shot in the head at point blank range, and then shot again. There were no witnesses, no forensic evidence, but plenty of suspects. In January 1998 at the Old Bailey two men were given life sentences for the murders. Both protested their innocence. They still do. The case has gone on to create numerous books and films, all with different answers as to what really happened. The story was that Mick Steele and Jack Whomes had argued with the Essex boys over a consignment of bad cannabis, and that was the cause of the shootings. In this book I cannot prove if Steele and Whomes are innocent, I have not seen all the evidence to be able to make that decision. Instead, I will ask one question: was it proved beyond all reasonable doubt that they did it?

From the time when Jack the Ripper was drinking in the Ten Bells pub in the 1880's, right up to the Blitz in 1940, the east end of London had rarely changed. Drugs were around even then. The women in Whitechapel were mostly addicted to alcohol, but cocaine and heroin were freely available, if you had the money. The second world war took its toll on the cockneys; and what Hitler couldn't finish, the town planners did. Yet again, the working class who had been promised homes fit for heroes, but got high rise flats instead. The government decided to clear the east end and created new towns, such as Basildon in Essex. The perfect place for a young Michael Steele to grow up, and nick stuff. Born in 1942, young Michael knew what is meant to face death when from his pram he watched the V1 and V2 rockets drop from the sky. His mum gladly took the move out to Essex, hoping one day she would end up with a bungalow near the coast.

The fifties were a time of austerity for Mick; no one had anything worth taking. The rich remained in their country houses, whilst the rise of the black community who came over to find work in the cities was dwarfed by the number of Irish labourers; who followed the motorways and set up homes along the routes. Patrick Tate and Anthony Tucker were born in these council estate suburbs. Southern Essex was just a short journey into the west end if you wanted to earn money; and east of Essex was the docks, where you could obtain anything for the right price. And just a few miles off the coast a cargo ship had been turned into a "Pirate" radio station. Radio Caroline would be played as Steele learn how to drive. Jack Whomes was born before the Beatles had their first hit. He was brought up in Canning town, until his brother was stabbed, and the family moved out to the sticks.

When the Profumo affair broke in 1963, people reading the News of the World choked on their sausages as they heard about salacious sex orgies which had taken place in some of the best country houses in England. Lady Astor from the Cliveden estate in Maidenhead, who in her time must have held some magnificent balls, was there when Stephen Ward introduced his young friend Christine Keeler to the Minister of war, John Profumo. Ward also introduced Keeler to Soviet spy Yevgeny Ivanov, and this was a threesome too far in the Governments eyes. The British establishment needed a scapegoat. They chose Ward. The police spent thousands of hours and took hundreds of statements trying to get something on him. Eventually they threatened Christine Keeler with prison for the offence of perjury if she did not cooperate. She mentioned that when she and Mandy Rice Davies had lived at Ward's flat, she had slept with some of his friends, because she wanted to, and some of them gave her money to spend on food and clothes, because they wanted to. On one occasion Ward asked for help to pay for the phone bill, as they used it more than him; and the girls handed over a little bit of money that they had in their purse. That was enough to charge him with living off immoral earnings.

When the case reached the Old Bailey, all of Ward's establishment friends disappeared. Although it was common knowledge the trial was a stitch up, and with no real evidence to charge Ward, the establishment continued with the case. The defence claimed that the police had been told to get Ward and then went out to find the evidence. The judge didn't care, and told the jury they should find him guilty. Ward said that when it was over, the truth would finally come out. The night before he was convicted, Ward took a load of drugs and went into a coma. He died a few days later of what was described as "an overdose of sleeping pills." At the time no foul play was suspected. But later evidence suggested that he could not have taken the quantity of pills he did over such a period of time as he would have fallen asleep. The only possibility was that someone had kept feeding him the pills even while he was unable to move. But those little details didn't matter. The establishment believed that justice had been served, and so refused to re-examine the case. Lord Profumo was never arrested, and never officially questioned about sharing any Government secrets that may have passed on to the Russians during his pillow talks with Christine Keeler. He was later given a CBE for services to his country. Hidden amongst all the evidence were stories about marijuana, and now the rich and famous were smoking joints with criminals. A year later Michael Steele moved to London, and got his first conviction.

He was working in the capital when in 1965 Freddie Mills, former world champion boxer was found shot dead in his car in Soho. A rifle was standing up on the seat next to him. The police listed it as a suicide, but it is now believed that he had been murdered by a London Crime Cartel that had links to corrupt police officers. At the time, every club paid protection money to criminals. In turn, part of it went into the pockets of detectives who worked the area. There was a rumour that Mills was going to go public about the situation. The names of Reg and Ronnie Kray were mentioned as being involved; but at the time they had been linked with Lord Boothby, and various other members of parliament in a possible blackmail allegation. The establishment was happy to put working class criminals away, but not their own kind; and the police were never going to arrest the police. They said that Mills had blown his brains out, and then simply placed the gun down next to him; ignoring the fact that another shot had been fired at the car by the same weapon. It would be a few years later when a supergrass would expose what was happening between the police and crime cartels.

Codenamed Operation Countryman, a covert police team uncovered detectives taking large bribes by criminals in order for them to look the other way for armed robberies, drug raids, and even murder. Politicians could do whatever they liked, as long as they were in the same freemasons lodge as the chief Inspector. Detectives would also deliberately fuck up a live investigation for the right price. This had been going on in London throughout the late sixties and early seventies. Although over two hundred and fifty officers were required to resign because of the operation, and many police officers were arrested, not one single person was ever charged with any offence. Parliament has never released the findings of the investigation. It is kept safe under the Protection of Public Interest Immunity Act, which states that the Home secretary can block any police investigation being made accessible to the public if they believe it would be damaging to the public interest. In simple terms, politicians made up a law in which they can decide what is right or wrong, and can keep things secret forever, without having to give a reason why.

Whilst all this was going on, Darren Nicholls was born on the same day London Bridge was sold to an American who believed he was buying Tower Bridge. We don't know if Mick Steele had a hand in that; but year later Lorraine Rolfe met John Kennedy from Basildon and started an affair. After falling in love, Kennedy, the old romantic, decided to beat Lorraine's husband's head to a pulp whilst she was asleep in bed next to him. When she woke up, it was like a scene from The Godfather. They put the body in the driver's seat of a car and parked it in a lane to try and make it look like a robbery. The police knew something was wrong as soon as they saw that there was no blood on the upholstery, and the dead man was still in his pyjamas. As the Krays were given life sentences for the killing of two other criminals, Lorraine Rolfe went to Holloway prison, where, she gave birth to a son called Craig.

II

There is a scene in the film Layer Cake, in which a pair of old school armed robbers are in prison for trying to steal a couple of grand. They sit amazed as a young man explains to them how he was making as much money selling drugs as robbing a bank, but the risks were minimal. The young man explained that the people wanting the drugs knew they were illegal, so they would never get the police involved. And as this was the seventies, the old Bill had no idea how much cash you made. Even if you got caught and did your time, any money hidden away would be waiting for you when you got out. The old criminals must have felt the game had changed. Who needed shotguns when drugs were involved?

The generation that now included the teenage Tony Tucker and Pat Tate were getting stoned listening to Bowie and John Holt on their record players. Everyone seemed to be smoking it. Sporting long hair and kipper ties, the criminals joined the hippies, and turned the drugs game into a business. An eighth of decent solid would sell quicker than the latest Bob Marley album. Soon it didn't matter what the music was; everyone just wanted to get high. Even the movie industry got involved. Making films about smoking the laughing gravy was almost as profitable as supplying it.

By now Tate had joined Steele to become another statistic in the Criminal records Bureau. Both had decided that if the world was going to give them fuck all, they wouldn't give a fuck, and take on the world instead.

When the eighties kicked in, things moved up a gear. Criminals went from importing cannabis to cocaine. The method of supply was the same, but the profit was ten times greater. Soon the nightclubs were filled with divvy Dave's in shiny suits and Tia Maria Tracey's in white stiletto's dancing to the latest Stock Aitken and Waterman. By now our players were all on the road. Steele had been arrested a couple of times, as well as Tate; both seemed more like chancers than proper wrong uns. Nicholls and Rolfe were finishing their education, mostly by smoking pot and drinking cheap cider in the local park. Only Tucker and Whomes were staying on the right side of the law. Tucker went into the health food and supplement business. Whomes, who could barely read or write, found he was good at fixing up motors. As more drugs came into the country, the price went down, which meant more people took it. Greed was good. You chilled on weed and got high on Charlie. The only bad one was heroin. Smack heads were the sort of people who could fuck up making a cup of tea, and were not trusted by anybody. Whenever the media wanted to scare the public, a picture of a heroin addict usually hit the spot. This was at the time when you could not only get addicted, but a big disease with a little name could kill you as well.

Then music in the late eighties changed. The News of the World reported about kids who were travelling to warehouses and fields for "Acid House parties," or "Raves." They then realised that five thousand people having a good time without alcohol must be bad. Why the fuck were all these kids gurning and waving their arms like demented frogs? It turned out the second summer of love was being fuelled by a new drug called Ecstasy. Soon you could buy a California Sunrise or a Rhubarb and Custard. Plus, it was easier for the seller to make some fake E's and disappear out of the nightclub toilets before anyone realised they had paid twenty pounds for a Pro-Plus pill. During these good times Pat Tate was now becoming well known amongst other villains. You couldn't miss him; he was built like a brick shit house.

In 88 he went into a Happy Eater with his girlfriend Sarah Saunders. Whether the tea was too hot, or the full English was too cold, he took umbrage, and decided to let the staff know by punching them; and then banging a couple of tenner's into his jeans. He was picked up and charged with robbery. Unfortunately, when he went to court for a bail application, he decided that prison wasn't part of his plans, and jumped over the dock. He escaped on the back of a motorbike driven by his brother Russell. Meanwhile Mick Steele had taught himself to fly and became the EasyJet of drug importation. It is not known who he worked for, but he must have been doing it for a while, because when he was caught the police took nearly a quarter of a million pounds of assets off him. Darren Nicholls had managed to get a job with a shady character, who offered him a bit or extra work. Someone he knew could get fake tenners. Nicholls went for broke. When trying to flog the counterfeit money, he told two people he could get hold of a quarter of a million pounds worth of dodgy notes. When they asked if he was scared of getting turned over, he told them he had a gun, and if anyone tried it, he'd blow their fucking heads off. They said they would buy the lot. Nicholls turned up at a motorway service station near Borehamwood in Hertfordshire , and was met by armed police.

Jack Whomes, along with his brother John, had been arrested for ringing cars. Even though it was their first offence, both got a couple of years.

As England hit the nineties, Craig Rolfe had become a low-level dealer and Tony Tucker set up a company of door staff who worked the clubs in Essex and London. He had always kept himself fit, and often went to the gym with his old friend Will Theobald. The pair would sometimes give each other lifts. Will owned a farm with his brother, which specialised in fishing and shooting. Next to it was an old track called Workhouse Lane.

Chapter 2.

The Usual Suspects.

"Dear hero imprisoned
With all the new crimes that you are perfecting
Oh, I can't help quoting you
Because everything that you said rings true
And now in my cell
(Well, I followed you)
And here's a list of who I slew
Reggie Kray - do you know my name ?"
The Last of the International Playboys

Most of the information in this book has come from the public domain; various books and the internet. Here is a breakdown of some of the people involved.

Pat Tate

This was a man whose life appeared to revolve around sex and violence, with a sprinkle of cocaine on his cornflakes. His childhood contained watching his dad beat the shit out of his mum on a regular basis. In and out of trouble from his teenage years, there is the story of him in the seventies finding a bag of cash on top of a motor, left there by a detective for the police stations Christmas party. Too young to drive, Tate got cabs for him and his mates to go into town and go on the piss. The police soon got word. Rather than see it as one lad being a chancer, they made Tate out to be like Billy the Kid, and he was sent to Borstal. From then on there was only one journey his life would take.

When he was released, he started buying and selling used cars. It was a nice little earner. For a start, you got traders insurance, which allowed you to drive any vehicle on the basis you were taking it somewhere to sell it. It also allowed you to have cars not registered in your name near your address, which made it difficult for police to get a search warrant for the vehicle. If they did find something in the boot you could argue that you didn't know it was there. Finally, selling cars was a good way for a bit of low-level money laundering. You bought a car for a thousand pounds, and then sold it a few weeks later for five thousand pounds, making it almost impossible for police to claim that the cash was actually drugs money even though the car was usually a shit heap. This got Tate through the eighties, and his first marriage; but it soon became clear to him that the real money was to be made by other means.

Everybody has their own special high; something that makes them feel good. And Tate really enjoyed being a criminal. He got a buzz from armed robberies, but this was dangerous, It was far better taking a dealer's supply by threat or force, knowing they would never go to the police. To some he was a lovable rascal, famous for jumping the dock and ending up in Spain. Whilst there he worked for the Blundell's, a crime family from Essex. Tate was a hit in Marbella at the start, but rumour has it he was already a bit of a space cadet. Why do three lines of Charlie when you can do six? If people were going on holiday to Tenerife, he wanted to go to Elevenerife. When he Looked around at the lifestyle these old east end gangsters were now living, he knew he could have the same if he was willing to take it. The problem was, he was also taking every drug he could lay his hands on. The start of the nineties saw Tate, a man in his thirties, beginning to miss the boat. He didn't want to be just another dealer; he wanted to be somebody. When he was asked to go over to Gibraltar to help bring back a friend, he forgot about the fact that half of it was English soil and didn't need an extradition treaty. He was promptly arrested and taken back home to finish his sentence.

They call drugs in prison a "Bird Killer." You ride out the days and weeks getting wasted until your time is up. The other option was spending all day in the gym. Tate did both. He was over six-foot, eighteen stone, dark hair, and muscular; not even the prison officers messed with him. To use the gym on a regular basis meant you had to be one of the wardens, which he got after promising to cause trouble if he didn't get it. And to be able to take drugs, you either had to run up a debt, which would be sorted by having to go on the rob as soon as you got out; or be a dealer, which in prison also meant you had to be an enforcer. Whilst he was inside he met Michael Steele again; both had been previously held at her majesty's pleasure in another establishment. They were soon joined the Whomes brothers, and Darren Nicholls. The open prison was so open they used to sneak in booze, drugs and take-aways on a regular basis. Tate must have listened to Steele tell stories of how he had been caught because he was using a plane; but now there was an even better way. These new mobile phones meant that transmitter masts were built in every country, and they also had GPS, Global Positioning Systems. If you bought one of these systems, and a small boat, you could cross the channel and land exactly where you want, even in the dark. To Tate, who always dreamed of the big time, it must have been like turning a light on.

Tony Tucker

There appeared to be nothing major in his youth that set him on a life of crime. Maybe it was his name. Here comes Tony Tucker, what a little fucker. But by the time he was sixteen he was big enough and ugly enough to handle himself. After school he done a stint in the army, then got into gyms and health supplements. He had never been convicted of any offence, if only because he seemed to be able to get others to do his dirty work. He was also a man who had the potential to rise head and shoulders above others in the drug world. He was clever. He would start up various small companies, which would often take all the tax and vat breaks, and then fold in the first trading year, owing debts that no one wanted to confront him over. Then he got into running a company which hired out doormen for various nightspots and events, such as boxing shows.

He soon realised that drug dealers would pay him to sell in the clubs he controlled rather than be kicked out. The new entrepreneur quickly turned into an old school bully. His legitimate companies and illegal drug dealing allowed him to live the luxury lifestyle without having to bother the taxman. This included being part of the boxer Nigel Benn's security team after Benn's manager Frank Warren was shot. His job meant he was out most nights, especially weekends, and everyone wanted to stay a bit lively. People would give him drugs as a way of saying "Hello." Soon he had a network of people, from major suppliers to low level dealers, all wanting to be a part of what he had; and some would do anything to join.

Craig Rolfe.

It's impossible to now see the real Craig Rolfe because of the various films that have been made since his death. Most of them portray him as a goofy fart knocker hanging on to the shirt tails of Tucker and Tate, waiting to see which way the wind blows. This comes from one of the first films, "Rise of the Footsoldier," which was based on the life of Tucker's friend Carlton Leach. His initial meeting with Rolfe didn't go too well when Rolfe took the piss out of him, and was only stopped from getting banged by the intervention of Tucker. It was almost as if he had a death wish. But chances are he was more ruthless than Tucker and Tate put together. His birth in prison made him infamous as a kid; and those with no future usually have nothing to fear. He took the route of bog-standard comprehensives, fags and fighting, before he was kicked out. The local estate offered nothing but stealing cars and drugs. No one liked him, and he didn't care. But self-employed criminals don't tend to earn much. His relationship with Donna Jaggers started off on their mutual appreciation of doing drugs. Jaggers calmed down a bit when they had a child, and Rolfe was smart enough to know that he needed a partner at home just as much as he needed a partner in crime.

He went from low level drug dealer to Tucker's right-hand man in a matter of moments. It is not known what he did to reach such heights, but his rise in the first few months of 1994 was a shot in the face to others who thought they were closer to Tucker. From around February 94 Rolfe overstepped O'Mahoney to become Tucker's main man. He became a director in one of Tucker's make-believe companies; but his main job was as an enforcer and a driver. Rolfe, just over six foot, was still young enough to have that curtain style haircut, which would go by 95.

Mick Steele.

By the eighties Mick Steele had more convictions than Ken Dodd had teeth. There was a big one in the sixties when he'd got caught in a fuel scam. Diesel used for agricultural purposes was dyed red because it wasn't taxed. Mick somehow managed to get hold of a lot, and did a deal with a local garage to sell it. Taxi drivers soon became aware, and drove across London to find him. The police, along with Customs and Excise, knew something was wrong when in one weekend a tiny pit stop in Bethnal

Green had sold enough fuel to fill up HMS Ark Royal. It would seem our Mick liked to get even with the government just as much as he liked to get one past the old bill.

At the start of the nitnies he was still a big guy, and although by this time his short dark hair was beginning to turn grey, you didn't want to mess with him. He was not known to use violence, but you felt that if you chatted shit to him you were going to get banged. When it came to drugs, he was happy just to be the courier. He didn't need all that palaver of going out and trying to sell it. Chances are, the last time Mick Steele had gone dancing in a nightclub the DJ was playing Chirpy Chirpy Cheep Cheep. He had been in the game long enough to never put everything on the line for the sake of that one big hit. He seemed to have been supplying drugs years before the Essex boys came on the scene. Which means he must have been trusted by the various people that he worked for. In prison he explained to Tate that he had been under surveillance by the police because they suspected he was flying drugs into the country using a plane he owned. So, he simply went out and bought a second plane and kept it in a different aerodrome. He would take out the first plane knowing he was being watched. Fly it over a couple of fields for a few hours, and then land. When the surveillance team had gone home, he drove to the next aerodrome and hop over to Holland to collect the drugs. When he was caught in 89, he never grassed as to who the drugs in the plane belonged to; even though it meant that the prosecution could argue that he was the main player. The judge sentenced him to nine years, and also took over a quarter of a million pounds worth of assets from him. Someone, somewhere, owed Mick Steele a massive favour for keeping his mouth shut to the police. It was the sort of favour that you could ask to return even a few years down the road.

Jack Whomes.
The ghost in our puzzle. Films and books portray him as the

silent killer. He had a lorry drivers' licence, and would often travel abroad to bring freight back. His main job was working as the mechanic for a haulage company based near Felixstowe in Ipswich. He was big boned and knew about engines. Apart from that, there is no mention of him being a major player in the drugs business, or a threat to anyone else's survival. His only conviction was from his involvement in a car ringing scam. An easy way of making money would be for someone to go around the local scrapyards and find a fairly new motor that had been written off. They would buy it and let the DVLA know they were going to repair it. Someone else then goes out and nicks the same make and model. Whomes would then change the plates and the chassis number from the car that had been written off onto the stolen model. It doesn't pay much; all the profit goes to the person selling the car. But for some reason the judge had a headache, and gave Jack and John Whomes a custodial sentence. It came as a shock to both of them, as they had no previous, and all prison was going to do was surround them with criminals.

Darren Nicholls.
A little sausage with a big chip on his shoulder. Another small-time car dealer, doing a bit of building work on the side. He met his partner had had a kid, then tried to set up various businesses. Originally in prison for fraud offences, he was just another pube lost in the wings until he got involved in a dispute over the canteen food. Mick Steele took a shine to him; anyone willing to make things a bit tougher for the establishment was alright in his book. And then Nicholls met Steele's mate Tate. His small stature and chubby build must have seemed slightly out of place between these two big men; but he appears to have the gift of the gab. In prison, making people laugh gave Nicholls protection. He was only about five foot seven and could have had it rough; but anyone that fucked with him soon found out they fucked with the beast three doors down.

II

When you look at the make-up of these men, there seems to be
a number of similarities. Nicholls shared traits with Rolfe. Both
appeared to be the minor players in the game, with one driving the victims into the lane, and the other driving the suspects
away. Both somehow just appear in the lives of others, and then
rise up to become the main confidants of the leading members
in each firm. One received that vital call which police believe
gave the time the men had been killed. The other was the only
one found in the Range Rover without a mobile phone. Both
were in long term relationships with the mother of their children, who both became vitally important after the murders.

Whomes was like Tucker, an unknown force. Both of them
were very good at their chosen profession, but outsiders said
they were difficult to know. Whomes never drank, not even tea
or coffee, but found a partner in Mick Steele. Tucker, who could
take enough drugs to knock out an elephant, found in Tate a
man willing to do more. Both men were seen as cold hearted;
but Whomes, who could barely read and write, once helped a
young girl who had collapsed, looking after her until an ambu-
lance arrived. Tucker saw a young boy crying at the boxing gym
because all his stuff had been stolen, so he went out and bought
him a whole new kit.

Researching this book, I noticed that after a while the two
people I was the most interested in were Pat Tate and Mick
Steele. Both had got into crime from an early age, almost for
a laugh, and a bit of a fuck you to authority. Both seemed to
be liked by everyone, especially the old school criminals from
the east end. And both relied on their word being their bond.
One had been accused of the main player in the killings, and
the other had been accused of causing the problem. One was
the only person who was meant to have spoken at the time the
murders took place. The other was the only one who went "No

Comment" throughout all the police interviews. It is a strange feeling to have almost a respect for one man who many felt had changed because of hard drugs; and another who had been accused over murder because of his involvement in a bad drug deal. But let's not forget there are others whose names appear throughout this book.

Bernard O'Mahoney

O'Mahoney seems to get a lot of stick on various media platforms, which range from him not being that involved, to being accused of the murders themselves. His life has certainly been colourful, filled with stints in the army, armed robbers and debt collections. When he came out of prison in the early nineties, he moved to Basildon to be with his partner, and soon got a job at Raquel's nightclub. As his reputation grew, he became the head doorman, and for a while Tucker's right-hand man. Whether you believe O'Mahoney is right or wrong, whether he talks fact or fiction, what he does do is give us a timeline from someone who was there. There seems to be a bit of friction between him and Rolfe from the very beginning, possibly because he has no idea why Tucker would suddenly make Rolfe his confidant. He was there as Tucker and Rolfe became more violent; bullying small time dealers when there was no need to. As for Pat, its Tate's downward spiral into drugs that seems to put an end to that friendship.

In those last few weeks O'Mahoney could see the writing on the wall. Not that they were going to be killed, but they had started making stupid mistakes. They should have slowed down after the death of Leah Betts; but they never. The Essex boys had started to believe their own hype. The problem was so did a few other people. O'Mahoney was there when Tucker and Tate went from running the doors to selling their own ecstasy in the club. And when Tucker threatened to kill him after he had spoken to the press about the death of Leah Betts, O'Mahoney took it so seriously he moved his family out and he stayed in a hotel until it was over.

Steve Nipper Ellis.

A man with balls as tough as walnuts. His dad was a bit of a face in the east end who did a stretch for armed robbery. When he was a boy Ellis was diagnosed with cancer. He said going through that gave him the courage to do anything. Unfortunately, that transpired into thieving and fucking around. He met Tate when they were in prison in the early nineties, with Tate promising to help Ellis get fit. Part of their training was doing steroids together. But Ellis took the Fred Flinstone philosophy when it came to drugs: a little dab'll do ya. He wanted to have a laugh rather than get wasted.

When Tate was released, he stayed with Ellis at his flat, and smashed the granny out of every drug going. He also introduced him to Tucker and Rolfe. Things started off OK, but soon got out of control. Ellis would introduce criminals from London, and the Essex boys would go out of their way to rob them. Then they started taking the piss out of Ellis. It wasn't the guns that Ellis minded, it was the prostitutes trying to nick his toaster that he was more upset about. There was a rule he learnt from doing time; you don't shit on your own doorstep. It turns out that later on in this story Tucker, Tate and Rolfe took this literally.

Billy Jasper

East end loon. Linked to various London Crime Cartels. He comes into play when he is arrested in January 96 for a separate offence. In order to get a reduction of his sentence he tells police that on the night of the murders he had taken someone to the scene.

Mickey Bowman

When asked by police if he was also an east end loon, he could confidently reply no; he lived in Kent. He also had numerous connections with various London Crime Cartels, and with corrupt police officers. He was arrested in February 1996 by Essex police, after Rolfe's partner Donna Jagger gave a statement about Bowman supplying Rolfe a machine gun in November. When he gave evidence in 1997, he was serving 16 years for armed robbery.

Sarah Saunders

Pat Tate's former partner. Had his child whilst he was in prison. When he came out the first time, he got a bungalow in her name, with him taking out an endowment policy on the life insurance; which meant that if he died the mortgage was paid off. When he was released from prison for the second time, he decided to kick her out instead.

Donna Jaggers.

Craig Rolfe's partner. Gave evidence at the trial that Rolfe had told her he was meeting "Micky the pilot" on the day of the murder.

Barry Dorman

Car trader that had helped Tate on numerous occasions. Part of that help included going abroad with Tate to collect drug money. He had a stint in the Metropolitan police for a few years, before leaving and going into the car industry. He sold the Range Rover and helped organise the finance payments. He was also one of the last people to see all of them alive.

Billy Blundell.

From the same generation as Mick Steele. Possible suspect at the time due to issues with the Essex boys. Although he was believed to have been involved in drug smuggling and various shootings for a number of years, he claimed he made his money selling ice creams. Fuck knows what he was putting in those choc ices, but it got him a villa in Marbella. Having been raised in the east end with his brother Eddie, they eventually moved out to Essex, where Billy bought a large area of farmland that included a lake, a couple of empty fields, and a couple of barns with which he wanted to set up specialist factories. This new employment opportunity was situated near the small village of Bulphan.

Along the way there are plenty of other people. Carlton Leach, whom Rise of the Foot soldier is based on, was a good friend of Tucker's and helped run the door firms. He seems to take a step back just as Rolfe and Tate appear on the scene. Possibly because he worked mainly in London, and Tucker was happy to take over the Essex clubs. Danny Woolard was another east end boy who worked with the Krays in the sixties. He also moved out to Essex. There is a story of him and a few others being at the Epping Forest Country club one night when words were spoken to Tate. Apparently, he had tried to rob a cannabis factory that was part owned by Woolard, and rather than apologise, got a bit lippy instead. He was given a few slaps and told to wind his neck in. Whether the story is true or not, it highlighted how in those last two years Tate had gone from wanting to be part of the old school to taking the piss out of them. From now on, all our players had become part of the criminal establishment.

Chapter 3.

Elephant Stone.

'There's nothing to tell! He's just some guy I work with!'
1st words spoken in 1st episode of Friends, which first aired in
UK in April 1995.

I

The second summer of love had finished with a recession and
Poll tax riots. The world wide web was born, and so was a new
name for the next generation – "millennials". If the eighties
had been the decade of buying your own home, the nineties
were the decade you moved to another one. "Upgrading" was
one way of calling it; "White flight" was another. The suburbs
got bigger: along with supermarkets and televisions. The cost
of everything went up, apart from drugs. There was also other
good news. In 1992 the first text message was sent. At the time
no one saw the point. We had fax machines. It would take another couple of years before all the transmitter masts were
changed from analogue to digital, just in time for something
even bigger to come along. But if you was the local postman you
still had plenty of work, and your route may have included a few
of these things.

Raquel's.
Anyone who lived through the eighties in a town with more
than just a train station and two sets of traffic lights may have

entered into a similar establishment. The club would be called anything from Cinderella's to Chevaliers. In daylight they had all the charm and class of a skid mark on a wedding dress. You could smell stale beer on the carpets, and even the chrome was sticky with cigarette smoke. But under the neon lights and a bit of Bananarama they were the best chance you had of pulling. Raquel's was purely a traditional nightclub; you not only expected a fight, there was something wrong if there wasn't one. But at the end of the eighties there was a change in music not seen since the start of the sixties. People just wanted to dance and have a good time. What the clubs lost on the alcohol the made up in bottles of water. But even after the town centre dives got late licences, the bouncers must have wondered how the fuck these gurning clowns in smiley face T shirts were ever going to get laid?

The Music.
If we start in 1987, the biggest star in England at that time was Rick Astley, and it seemed that the same old formula was still making money. Two pop songs, a ballad, an album, and then a tour. But in this year a song called "House Nation" made the charts. It had a fast beat, two words sampled over and over again, and was a shock to the Bon Jovi record buying public. It wasn't a classic by any means. The video was crap, and it was barely played on daytime radio; but someone was buying it from Woolworths. The music was part of an underground movement found mainly in the black clubs of America. The press labelled it "Acid House," as throwback to the hippies of yesteryear. Then similar songs began to sell, leaving the old media still unsure of what was happening. Surely people only go to clubs to try and pull, don't they?

The answer was, they weren't there to cop a feel. There wasn't much point. This was the first generation since the time of Jack the Ripper who new that sex could kill you. Teenagers had grown up surrounded by adverts about AIDS. As you watched a TV presenter put a condom over a banana, you didn't know whether to be scared about catching HIV, or that yours was only the size of a chilli pepper. Young men, all hornier than a scrap yard dog, knew that the next best thing to having a wank was getting wasted. Dropping an E, then floating in a field with a thousand others as the bass thumped inside mother earth was an experience that might not have been better than sex, but for most teenagers it certainly lasted longer.

The police
There were detectives in 1995 who could still remember the good old days when you could nick someone and leave them in the cells until they confessed. PACE, namely the Police and Criminal Evidence act, came into effect in 1984. Before that you had very little rights. PACE came about after the Brixton riots in 1981. Young black men, tired of being constantly stopped and searched, decided to fight back. This started a wave of riots across the country. Eventually, the Scarman report noted that there was evidence of institutional racism in the police. With PACE you could only be held in custody for twenty-four hours unless a superintendent or a magistrate granted extra time; everyone was allowed solicitor, all movements out of the cells and interviews had to be recorded, and you had to have evidence to be charged. But the past doesn't disappear overnight.

In 1993 Stephen Lawrence was killed in a racist attack. No one was charged, and there were accusations that the investigation failed because the police were still institutionally racist. This became the basis of another enquiry, this one by Lord Macpherson. What was often missed in this report was that just under the radar was also another accusation. It was noted that amongst the group of young men who had originally been arrested then later released without charge, some had family members linked to London Crime Cartels. And these people had connections with detectives who had access to the investigation. The police didn't think of itself as racist; it was just that the corrupt ones preferred working with white criminals.

Reefer madness

There was a massive rise in drug raids as we entered the nineties. Some of this was due in part to the change in the way goods were imported into the country. In 1968 large metal shipping containers were standardised worldwide to fit on ships and lorries. New ports were built, such as Felixstowe in Essex. These places could unload a container ship onto the waiting lorries with ten men in a day what used to take a hundred men a week. Giant ships were full of containers from China, India and Africa. The problem was, no one was actually looking at was what inside them. Maggie Thatcher wanted a consumer society. But consumerism is addictive. Those reading the News of the World or the Sunday Mirror might have seen the headlines and believed they were winning the war on drugs. They were wrong. Although politicians told everyone that they were being tough on crime, the reality was less than a tenth of drugs being imported were being seized. Some people could never grasp that the dealers didn't have to force drugs onto anyone. Council estates and wine bars were filled with people looking to score. Then towards the end of the decade two things changed the drug culture for ever. One was the mobile phone. What had been the symbol of stockbrokers was now used by dealers. Suddenly they were mobile, and could buy and sell gear in a matter of hours when it used to take days. The next was a new drug. Some gave it the official name of MDMA, but everyone knew them as E's, short for Ecstasy.

Class.

In the nineties the government had put drugs into three categories. Class A were considered the most dangerous. Not only because of the effects the drugs had, and how addictive they were, but also the public perception of the criminality involved. Cocaine was in this category. Cannabis was a class B drug. It was later reduced to a class C, then upgraded again when postcode wars broke out. But in those early nineties, when you were still allowed to smoke in pubs and clubs, most people saw it as "Whacky Baccy." Class C contained a lot of legal pills used by people to get high. In some ways Ecstasy was the perfect storm. Originally created in a laboratory to cure depression and PTSD, it chilled you to the point of wanting to hug everyone, and kept you dancing all night.

Another beauty was that it was already packaged. Dealers didn't have to fuck about weighing stuff up, mixing it and then go around trying to flog it. Most of the people at a rave needed one to keep going. You just turn up at a club, and everyone would come looking for you. It was the brave new world that Maggie Thatcher had always dreamed of. You had the foot runners, doing all the graft to get their tickle pickles for free. The suppliers, buying under a hundred at a time. Then the upper level, driving around in VW Golfs, and getting the stuff in bulk. The next up were the serious players. Here were your BMW or Mercedes driver. At the very top of the tree were the Crime Cartels. This is where the real money was made, but with it came the biggest risks. If customs caught the stuff coming in, you lost a lot of money. Getting ripped off was another danger. The only way to beat it was to have enough muscle to stop that sort of malarkey. You also had to be ruthless, and to know that everyone involved was loyal; because if one of them grassed to save their own skin, there was a worry that the police wouldn't nick you for the last job, but would watch you on the next one.

The other White House Farm

When you google the name, you may get another Whitehouse
Farm in Essex. This was the place where in 1985 Jeremy Bamber
is alleged to have shot his parents, his sister, and her twin boys.
The police, believing it was a murder suicide by his sister,
helped clear up the crime scene. One detective at the time
didn't think so. He thought it was strange that Bamber had
called the local police station after his father had called him to
say his sister had gone mad with a gun. Sometime later a cousin
claimed to have found a silencer in the house, possibly with
his sisters' blood in it. Bamber was charged with the murders,
and is currently on a whole life tariff, meaning he will never be
freed. He has always claimed his innocence.

London Crime Cartel.

To be more accurate, Crime Cartels. A cartel is when a firm
becomes big enough to run pretty much every aspect of its
empire. They organise the deal, bring the drugs in, sort out the
supply, give it to the dealers, and take the profits. Most cartels
expand their business to include gambling, prostitution, and
protection rackets. They have to turn all this money into semi
legitimate profit. You can't just pretend to buy and sell cars,
you have to buy the showroom, or anything that is a cash-based
business where you get a lot of money for little work. Open a
hairdresser salon that does hundred pound a time perms, as
long as you can justify the ten grand a week cash coming in, the
bank isn't going to complain.

And London is a big place; plenty of room for everybody
if they are looking for long term business. Only cowboys get
killed in shootouts. Some of these Cartels have been running
for years. From the Canning Town area of east London was
the Bowers family, who helped run the Peacocks Boxing gym,
and were said to be involved in drugs and armed robberies.
David Hunt was also from Canning Town. It was alleged that he

started off with a gang in the early seventies. He was arrested on seven occasions, but each time the case was dropped for various reasons. He later took over various clubs in Soho, including Freddie Mills old nightspot. His protection racket spread across London; and it was suspected that police corruption and witness intimidation had something to do with his ever-growing empire. Mr Hunt was later to move out to a nice house in Hertfordshire, just a stone's throw away from the border of Essex.

The Adams family were based in North London. They were linked to the Brinks Matt robbery, Kenneth Noye, and over twenty gangland killings. The Adams used to run a money laundering scheme where cash from drugs would be put back into legitimate cash business such as snooker halls and sunbed salons. Such was the amount of money rolling in, it is believed one of their snooker halls would have had to have been open twenty-four hours a day, seven days a week, and every table being used, to bring in the cash it did. If they were looking for an easier way of moving the money, they could have bought a nightclub. One of the people that used to work for the Adams was former doorman and bodybuilder Stephen Marshall from Borehamwood, Hertfordshire. He had previously been arrested for murder in 1996, but was released without charge. In 2009 he was dubbed "The Jigsaw Killer," after body parts started turning up all over the south east of England. Police were worried as the way the body had been dismembered showed some basic anatomical skill. Marshall and his girlfriend were arrested and charged. Marshall stated at his trial that he had worked for the Adams family in the nineties. He went on to say he had helped cut up other bodies which had been gangland hits, and they had been disposed of in Epping forest. Who these people were, and how they had been killed, we do not know, and Mr Marshall has so far refused to elaborate any further on the matter.

New Drugs syndicate.
It may seem strange that Tucker, who had paid cash for his

five-bedroom bungalow less than a year prior; and Rolfe, who had twenty-six had a three-bedroom house and no mortgage, needed to set up a little syndicate in 1995. The answer is: Don't put all your eggs in one basket, especially if those eggs are filled with drugs. The best thing to do would be to set up a little group, where everyone puts in a share of the money, takes a share of the risk, and gets a share of the profit. With cannabis you doubled your investment, but the risk was in the journey. You wanted to make sure the consignment was big enough to make a profit, but also, you didn't want to put everything down on a lucky brown. An easy way of spreading the risk was to do it threes. Three cars carried the drugs over. If one of them got stopped, you still made a profit. If two cars got caught, you came out even. Its only if all three cars were searched that you lost.

But a syndicate meant that you invited the attraction of bigger players. There were those who you could fob off if things went wrong, small time who didn't want to do prison time. But there were others who who were big enough to demand a profit no matter what. The boat sank, don't care. The courier got arrested, so what. The stuff turned about to be crap; I couldn't give a shit. If you promised a man with a gun to double his money, either come back with a bag of cash, or a bigger gun. And this was the world of the early nineties. People such as Tucker, Tate and Rolfe felt as though they could do anything; all they needed was to be in the right place at the right time. But like so many other pipe dreams, things could easily go up in smoke.

II

Timeline up to 1995

13th December 1942 - Mick Steele born.
17th November 1957 - Tony Tucker born.
7th August 1958 - Pat Tate born.
13th February 1961 - Jack Whomes born.

March 1964 – Steele gets his first conviction for theft.

1966 – Freddie Mills is found dead in his car with a gun next to him. At first it is listed as suicide. Police now believe he was murdered.

18th April 1968 – Darren Nicholls born

7th June 1969 - Craig Rolfe born

March 1972 – Steele sent to prison for theft.

September 1980 - Steele sent to prison for theft.

1988 – At Billericay court on trial for a robbery, Tate jumps over the dock, assaults police and escapes on a motorbike ridden by his brother Russell. He makes it to Spain, where he spends time with those linked to the Blundell family.

November 1989. Former light welterweight boxing champion Terry Marsh, from Essex, is accused of shooting his former manager Frank Warren. Although no one witnesses Marsh do it, and there were a lot of people who were listed as a suspect, Marsh was charged of the offence, based on the word of another prisoner who said he had overheard Marsh speaking about the shooting when he was on remand. The case went to trial. Marsh did not appear in the witness box to give evidence. He was sub-sequently found not guilty.

1990 – Tate goes to Gibraltar to pick up a friend, and is arrested. He is sent back to England, and prison, where he meets Kenneth Noye.

29th June 1990 – Steele convicted for the importation of canna-bis – sentenced to 9 years.

1992 – East London. Tony Tucker meets boxer Nigel Benn, who is managed by Frank Warren.

1993 – Pat Tate, Mick Steele, Darren Nicholls, Jack and John Whomes are all in prison together.

August 1993 – Nicholls and Steele begin to sell cannabis together.

September 1993 – Tucker takes over the door staff of Raquels'. Working with Bernard O'Mahoney, Tucker supplies the boun-cers, and decides who sells drugs in the club.

November – O'Mahoney meets Craig Rolfe. They take an instant dislike to each other, but Rolfe stays because he idolises Tucker.
January 1994 – Michael McCarthy is sitting wife his wife in Rebel's Café in Basildon Essex, when someone walks up behind him and shoots him twice in the back of the head. McCarthy survives, and the shooter is never caught.
February 1994 – Rolfe goes from being drug dealer to Tucker's business partner.
March 1994 – Kevin Jones dies at Club UK after taking ecstasy. Police are informed that dealers are paying a thousand pound a week in order to sell drugs inside the club to the man who controls the door staff, a Mr Tony Tucker.
May 1994 – Police carry out a series of raids. Suspicious of a vehicle, they check its details, and it turns out to be stolen, which gives them the power to search it. Inside are nearly two thousand ecstasy pills, but no one is arrested for them.
July 1994 – Pat Tate released from prison.
October/November 1994 – After making a comment to Tuckers mistress, Donna Garwood, Tucker and Rolfe assault Nipper Ellis and threaten to kill him. Ellis gets a gun and a shotgun from a contact in East London. He shoots Tate with the handgun, and later tries to shoot Tucker and Rolfe with the shotgun. Tucker, Tate and Rolfe all speak to the police and inform them that it was Ellis who did the shooting. Ellis is found with a different gun. The Essex boys retract their statements. Ellis is convicted for possession of a handgun and serves time. Whilst still in hospital a gun is found in Tate's bed. He is still on licence and receives a prison sentence.
17th November – Kevin Whitaker is killed by Tucker and Rolfe after they inject him with numerous drugs until he overdoses. Rolfe is questioned by police as he was the last person to phone him. Donna Jaggers gives Rolfe an alibi, saying he was with her all that night.
1st December 1994 – Rolfe gives a statement to police in relation to the last time he saw Kevin Whitaker.

Chapter 4.

Pardon me for Being Famous.

"There is no good and evil, there is only power and those too weak to seek it."
J.K Rowling.

Bigger than The Beatles, that was the promise. The Stone Roses were everywhere. With songs such as "I am the Resurrection," the group were on course to be the biggest in the world, as long as nothing went wrong. Perhaps the warning was there in one of their singles, "Fools Gold;" and that old working-class philosophy of "spend it like you stole it." When you go from council estate to country mansion in just a few short years there is always the problem of letting it go to your head. The group spent more time partying on their second album than actually playing on it. But at least the band paved the way for the last great guitar-based group in the country, Oasis. Britpop had arrived. But instead of the sale of ecstasy going down, it continued to go up. The old press didn't realise that people now looked at drugs the same way they did at alcohol. You drank white wine with fish, beer at a BBQ, cocaine at a social gathering, and took an E when you wanted to dance.

During this time Tony Tucker met Carlton Leach, part of west Ham's Inter-City firm in the eighties, who needed help organising the doors of clubs and raves around London and Essex. Tucker found out his skills turned being a bouncer into a big business. Having muscle not only stopped the dealers getting in, there were those who would even pay him to make sure they were the only ones selling. He started making serious money. His contacts allowed him to meet the boxer Nigel Benn, whose promoter, Frank Warren, having been shot, agreed that it would be nice if security staff help protect the future middleweight champion of the world. Tucker should have stepped up a few weights in the business world, but for some reason kept sparring with idiots. Leach gives the story of a load of them going to see a show, and caught Rolfe and Jaggers injecting at the back of the bus. At that point the ball should have dropped for Tucker, but he kept Rolfe on.

The national lottery allowed the poor to become millionaires by chance, rather than having to rely on sport, music or drug dealing to get rich. Sunday trading was introduced. The channel tunnel was opened, and the people were told there would never be any chance of illegal immigrants flooding the country. Prime Minister John Major was publicly promoting a "Back to Basics" style of politics, with Victorian values at the centre of society. He forgot to say that he had been secretly smashing the back doors out of Edwina Curry, the junior health minister, as she was bent over the desk of number ten. With Major having all the personality of dust, and Curry with a face like a slapped fish, I don't know who I feel more sorry for; the cleaner probably.

On the other side of Westminster, the new labour leader, Tony Blair, realised the public would vote for anyone who would let them buy more stuff. Of course, that did not include drugs. No political party wanted to lose elderly voters by legalising the stuff. But Blair was a man of many faces, all of them smarmy. He told the press that he had not smoked it, but had been in the room with others when they had, thinking that it made him sound cool, rather than a twat. Blair also hinted that cannabis could be downgraded to a Class C drug, the same as most tranquilisers. He knew it was used by all classes, from black kids on a council estate, white students desperate to go back to Ibiza before university, all the way up to BBC executives in the drama department who still thought they were deep and edgy. That little taster might be enough to push Tony into Downing Street without losing the solid working class votes the Labour party relied on. As for the other drugs, cocaine was the marching powder for wannabe gangsters; and heroin the nosh bag for shoplifters and prostitutes. They would always be a political no no. Tony would be tough on crime, tough on the causes of crime (but not the businessmen and politicians who made money out of it). To help appease everyone, he mentioned supermarkets being allowed to sell more alcohol, the end of fox hunting (at the same time letting the rich pay less taxes), and a smoking ban in public places (but not on formula one racing cars, as some of the companies had donated to the Labour Party). As for ecstasy, many believed its close link to dance music meant it would disappear once the trend for raving died down. This was a future prime minister who played guitar. Rock and roll was coming home.

Steele, Nicholls and Whomes were released from prison during a fundamental transformation to British justice, when the Government quietly changed the law in relation to the right to remain silent during police interviews. For the last three hundred years, not answering police questions was not to be seen as an admission of guilt. This was the cornerstone of "Innocent until proven guilty." But from 1994, even after taking legal advice, any police questions answered with "No comment," or by remaining silent, could now be inferred that you were hiding something. If the case reached court, a prosecution barrister could tell the jury that you said nothing to the police because you hadn't had time to make up a story. Anything you say now could be seen to "Harm your defence."

But it was a different part of Police and Criminal Justice Act that was being blared out by the press and radio at the time. The police would now be able to close down any event if there was an illegal gathering of twenty or more people. So, an organised elderly swinger's festival was fine as long as no loud music was played to blot out the sound of saggy balls banging. The general public were so happy that a small minority of young people could be prosecuted for dancing that they missed the fact the establishment had fucked them all up the arse.

The move to stop illegal raves allowed nightclubs to change tactics, and apply for a licence to stay open later. Councillors believed their children were more safe dancing under plastic palm trees and neon lights rather than standing in a field of cow shit trying to get sorted for E's and whizz, so they readily agreed. Clubs such as Raquel's began to have customers again.

Mick Steele got straight back into a bit of low-level cannabis importation with Nicholls. He knew he wouldn't be allowed to get near a plane again, so he decided to use a boat. He might have got the idea from Whomes, who had a small boat with his brother, and kept it at his yard in Ipswich. When Tate was released from prison, he did a bit of robbing off drug dealers whilst he was living with his old mate Steve "Nipper" Ellis. Then he met Tucker, and became even more involved in drugs, taking them as much as selling them. Tate was the ideal man for Tucker, as he had a reputation of resolving all problems with violence. In some ways Tate was becoming like the hero he had met in prison, Kenneth Noye.

Noye, a violent career criminal, a police informant, and a Freemason, was the father figure that Tate never had. He was involved in the Brinks Mat robbery in the early eighties. Believing some of the gold bars were hidden in his back garden, undercover police went over the fence one night to find them. Thinking he was being robbed, Noye caught one officer and killed him. At the Old Bailey he told the jury he was acting in self-defence, and was found not guilty. A few years later he was back in relation to the gold bars found in his garden, and was sentenced to fourteen years. When he was released in 1994, he promised to keep in touch with Tate. But Noye was fabled to become famous for so much more.

When I was growing up in what was considered a small town in the suburbs in the seventies, eighties and nineties, you heard stories about the people and families who had a reputation in the sixties. They had usually been moved out of the city after the war, and continued to keep the same mentality even when the streets sometimes looked out onto fields. One or two often went on to be legends in their own lunchtime, One example is when a lorry load of trainers was stolen from a motorway service station. Within two weeks every kid at my school was walking around in the same make of footwear.

In the film Goodfellas, the narrator tells of how when he started working for the mafia in the fifties, word soon got around the town. He got the thing he always wanted...respect. So much so that when his mum went shopping the local kids offered to bring it home for her. But this is England in the nineties. The stories about Tucker, Tate and Rolfe hurting people probably all have an element of truth. They had reached the point where they needed to move up the ranks to get the respect they believed they deserved. But that would mean stepping away from beating up people in pub car parks. This was the moment the Essex boys should have taken a look at how the mafia worked, and how it dealt with other criminals. Those that want respect, give respect. Either treat it as a business, or keep thinking its a game.

So, what do you reckon? We've got great drugs, great music, pubs and shops open all hours, and technology that allows us to speak to someone on the other side of the world; do our working-class heroes fuck it up? Or course they do. Its chapter twelve on how to fuck up at life. At least in the old days when you had to go knocking on a dodgy door to get your supply, the person opening it may have been a gormless idiot but they would be an adult. Market forces and technology dictated that a sixteen-year-old dealer with a mobile phone could set up base opposite the Chicken Cottage, and pretty soon fourteen-year olds were walking around the skate park as if they were from the hood. People who used to have an E once a month were now taking a couple every weekend. With so many drugs around you lost the quality control. Tucker and Tate were dishing them out like smarties. Suppliers, frightened of getting robbed, employed criminals to help them, and then the criminals realised there was more money in robbing suppliers than protecting them. The police kept up with the drug raids. Months of work, ten officers, doors smashed, and one person arrested for half a joint in the ashtray was somehow deemed a good result. Everybody believed they had won, Tucker, Tate, the police, the Government, and Mick Steele, must have thought things could only get better. The truth was, everyone was getting high, but had no idea what the comedown was going to be. All of them were waiting for something to go bang. Welcome to 1994.

Chapter 5.

Ellis and Whitaker.

Barry the Baptist: "Hello my son. Do you want a lolly?"
Little Chris: "Piss off, you nonce."
Lock Stock and two smoking barrels.

I

Michael Caine said that Get Carter was actually based on a true story. Not a lot of people know that. In 1967, Angus Sibbert, a London criminal, had gone up north for various reasons, and worked for a well-known crime boss. He met Dennis Stafford and Michael Luvaglio. They were into a lot of things, such as protection in the clubs and running the pub jackpot machines. Someone thought that Sibbert was creaming off the takings. One-night he was found in his mark ten Jaguar with a couple of bullet holes in him. The police arrested Stafford and Luvaglio, even though there was no evidence, and they had said they were both somewhere else at the time. But the Government had recently been made a laughing stock by the Krays getting away with murder and wanted a result. It was difficult for the two men to get their witnesses to talk, as they were all criminals. The police did helpfully suggest to Luvaglio that if he gave them a statement to say that Stafford had left the club they were in for a short while, as in the time they believed Sibbert was shot, they would let Luvaglio go. Luvaglio refused. Both men were found guilty of conspiracy to murder and did a lot of time. But even now still insist they were innocent.

The story of the feud between Steve 'Nipper' Ellis with Tucker, Rolfe and Tate is well documented in the book "Last man standing." Ellis and Tate had been good friends in prison, and when Tate was released in 93, he stayed with Ellis after another row with Sarah Saunders. Both men were very likable and funny; the typical cockney charmers into a bit of ducking and diving. When Tate met Tucker and Rolfe in a Southend bar, Ellis became friends with them as well. But Tucker and Rolfe brought out the worst in Tate. They robbed an east end dealer friend of Ellis of over twenty thousand pounds worth of drugs; Ellis kept quiet rather than tell his old mates who it was. Then Ellis told Tucker and Tate about another friend wanting to get rid of two hundred grands worth of traveller's checks. Tucker arranged the meet, and Tate tried to rob him. Ellis again hoped no one thought that he was part of the rip off. The Essex boys were becoming a liability.

In March 94 Kevin Jones died in Club UK after taking ecstasy. The police made enquiries around Southend, and it transpired that there were a couple of regular dealers in the club, the same dealers' week after week. The police now moved on from the young man's death to look a bit more closely at what was clearly a professional operation. They found out that dealers were paying the door firm to be allowed in the club to sell. The managing director of the firm was a Mr Tony Tucker. His associate, Mr Craig Rolfe. They watched as numerous raids were carried out. Thousands of pounds worth of drugs was seized, but no one was willing to talk. Some say this was all part of the game. You could have a wad of notes in your pocket one night, and the next day have nothing but a cup of custody coffee for breakfast. The best you could do is laugh it off and move on to the next caper. But criminals, like police officers, tend to lose their sense of humour as they go up the ranks. The more power Tucker got, the more short tempered he became. He wasn't happy about losing so much business, almost forgetting that someone had died because of it.

And now he had Tate, who kept telling him that the real

money was in supplying the drugs rather than just protecting the dealers. Fuck the kid who died. If they were ruthless and violent enough no one was ever going to grass on them. Tate believed the criminals who had been big in the sixties and seventies were now too old to fight back if the Essex boys started getting heavy. In an increasingly drugged up state of mind, Tate told them that the world was their oyster; and then things began to suck.

Nipper received a phone call in October 1994 from Donna Garwood, Tucker's young mistress, who wanted to know where Tucker was. Ellis, the eloquent bon viveur, casually replied that Tucker was probably at home fucking his wife up the arse. Donna passed the message on to the affronted Tony, who took umbrage that his sixteen-year-old girlfriend had been given the verbal finger. Whether Tuckers fury was over the fact his teenage mistress had been given a bit of a tongue lashing from Ellis; or the idea that he was having anal sex with his long-term partner, we shall never know. Tucker went to the flat and threatened Ellis by putting a gun to his head. He then got a large knife and asked Ellis if he wanted his foot or his hand cut off. Ellis told him to take the hand in the belief that he would still be able to run after Tucker and shoot him with his other hand. It was only the intervention of Rolfe, who pointed out that it was the middle of the afternoon in a suburban street, and people might be surprised of seeing a naked limbless man running down the road, that probably saved Ellis from never being able to pick his nose and wank at the same time. Tucker threatened to come back to finish the job, and they left. But not before Rolfe took a shit and rubbed it over the wallpaper. Even though Tate, Tucker and Rolfe were all big men; Nipper, who at 5ft 7 stood slightly shorter than an elephant's penis, wasn't going to forget the threat.

But before he could do anything, the Essex boys stepped up the pressure. They weren't going to be mugged of by some little balding tosspot. Rather than Tucker realising he'd been a bit out of order, he wound Tate up tighter than a Scottish watch.

Tucker rang Elliss and told him he was going to put him on his knees, make him beg for forgiveness, and then blow his head off (it's worth remembering that line for a bit later). Ellis replied that Tucker could blow something else, and hung up. A few days later the Essex boys came round looking for Ellis and smashed up his flat, then demanded Ellis come and meet them. If not, they were going to kidnap Nipper's young sister, and give a running description to Ellis as they tortured her until he gave himself up. Tucker, Tate and Rolfe had broken the second rule; don't get civilians involved, especially kids.

Nipper, a hairless Mickey Flannigan, went back to the old east end haunts he knew when he still used a comb. As he stood by the bar and told of his situation to an audience that you would not want to upset, they wondered if this was the same Tucker involved in various shenanigans that had fucked over quite a few people. Nipper got a shotgun and a bullet proof vest. Then the Canvey Island cowboy went back to sort out the problem like a man. On 20th November 1994 Ellis found Pat Tate in his bungalow getting ready for Tucker's birthday party. He had the perfect shot, but then Sarah Saunders came into the room carrying her baby. Ellis didn't want to do anything in front of them, so he waited until Tate went into another room. That bit of emotion, and almost falling arse over tit on a sandpit in the back garden, meant that Tate saw Ellis coming as he went into the bathroom, and only got shot in the arm. Ellis went on the run, still looking for the other two chumps. When car dealing friend, Barry Dorman visited Tate in hospital, he sat and waited as Tate spoke to a police officer, and named Ellis as the man who shot him. Many were surprised at Tate doing this. No matter how bad things were, you didn't break the first rule and grass to the police.

A few days later the tooled-up Tucker and Rolfe went out looking for Ellis. When Ellis produced his shotgun and fired, they ran away. In another blow to their reputations, Tucker and Rolfe also went to the police. They would now go into the book of criminals willing to become informants if the deal was right.

If a corrupt copper knew the Essex boys were willing to speak to the police, how easy would it be to pass on that information to serious criminals? And if Nipper Ellis had made them look like a pair of wankers, who would trust them with bigger stuff? Don't forget, this mess had all started over a joke about someone taking it up the Gary Glitter.

A few weeks after the shooting Nipper was eventually arrested for attempt murder. On him was a handgun, but not the one used on Tate. When they found out that he would get a conviction just on the gun alone, Tucker, Tate and Rolfe all retracted their statements. Ellis was only given a year. Inside, he heard about a ten-grand mark on his head, to be paid out by Tucker if Ellis slipped in the showers and didn't get up. But Ellis knew people, and gave his side of the story. No one in prison likes it when someone threatens to hurt a kid. Lags from Essex and east London who knew or had heard of Ellis and his dad said they would protect him. He was old school. He didn't grass to the police; he just went out and got the job done. In a bizarre twist, one of the men he met was a bloke called Micky Bowman, who told Ellis a story about how he and another mate had been set up by Tucker and Tate over a cocaine deal. They had gone to sell some of it to Tucker, but were instead met by firearms police. It would seem quite a few people had their own tales to tell about the Essex boys.

II

Kevin Whitaker was similar to Craig Rolfe. Both grew up on council estates with no chance of going anywhere in life. Both enjoyed taking drugs as much as selling them. Whitaker knew a few people, and was soon selling cocaine on a regular basis. Then he got a girlfriend, who fell pregnant, and Whitaker gave up the lifestyle. When they separated a few years later, he went back to what he knew best, and ran into Rolfe. Soon he was back in the game. He got turned over when he acted as a courier and collected some gear from up north. He didn't count what was in the bag, and when he came back Tucker told him that a bar was missing. This was going to come out of Whitakers end, and he had to run around to pay the money back. He should have stopped there, but instead focused on the friends he knew in London to sort out deals. Around November 94 Tucker wanted to buy a load of drugs. Whitaker knew someone who knew someone. He travelled down to London with sixty grand of Tucker's money. The dealer took it, and then fucked off, leaving Whitaker with nothing. Whether this was a bit of reprisal for Tucker we don't know.

On the night of the 17th November 1994 Tucker and Rolfe kidnapped him. Tucker blamed Whitaker, who swore on his life that the supplier had stitched him up. If he was telling the truth it would mean the supplier didn't think Tucker was big enough not to rip off. If Whitaker was lying, it meant he didn't think Tucker was that important. They decided to drive back to the supplier in London to sort it out. Along the journey Whitaker kept saying he was innocent. But that wouldn't wash with the steroid induced Tucker. He probably liked it when Whitaker was begging for mercy, it added a bit of spice. In order to teach him a lesson Tucker and Rolfe injected Whitaker with copious quantities of drugs until he went into a coma. Then they injected him with some more. At some point in that car he died. The car drove down a country lane with three men in it. The car stoped. Kevin Whitaker was thrown down a roadside ditch. He was found a few days later. Even though the needle marks were on the right arm of the right-handed Whitaker, and the level of drugs showed that it would have been physically impossible for him to have injected himself with the last three shots; the coroner declared it as a death by accidental overdose.

Tate heard Tucker and Rolfe tell the story whilst he was in hospital recovering from the shooting. The NHS must have been good in those days, because he was getting his nob noshed by prostitutes and doing more drugs than all of the Happy Mondays put together. But there was still the problem with Ellis, who at the time was still on the run. Mick Steele visited, as well as Bernard O'Mahoney, and Darren Nicholls. He spoke to Tate about working with him. But Tate decided on taking the piss out of Nicholls instead, and tried to get him to have a fight with another man who was there. Nicholls declined and left. If he spoke to anyone about the matter we do not know; but the next day police found a gun under Tate's bed. As he was still on licence, he was sent back to prison for a year.

As Rolfe was believed to have been the last person to have spoken to Whitaker (he called Whitaker at his home when his father was in the room at the time), the police wanted to know what the chat was about. Both men had links to drugs, and Whitaker clearly had been dumped down a country road; so, someone must have taken him there. Rolfe stated that Whitaker was an acquaintance he had lost touch with over the years, and then about a week before he died, he had seen him at a phone box, and they spoke about the old times. On the day he died he had phoned Whittaker at his parent's address, and again it was just a general chat. Rolfe then went out with his partner Donna Jaggers that evening, not getting home till late. Jaggers confirmed this by giving a statement that Rolfe was with her at all times.

Rolfe was required to attend the inquest. This is when a coroner holds a public enquiry in order to determine how someone died. Rolfe gave the same evidence that was in his statement. The police knew at least two people must have been involved from the start to threaten and force him to take drugs, or hold him down whilst he was injected, and then at the end to carry the body out of the car. There were no eyewitnesses, no forensic evidence, the main suspect had his long-term partner as an alibi, and trying to pin a murder on someone based on a phone call was never going to be enough. The coroner had no choice but to let Rolfe go. If he had looked across at the people in court that day he might have noticed that watching the proceedings at the back was Tony Tucker. Perhaps Tate had been right, the

Essex boys really were going to be unstoppable.

As we stepped into 1995, with Tate back in prison, Rolfe seems to step up, almost replacing Tate in the process. He didn't have the muscle, but he was willing to do whatever Tucker wanted. There are a lot of stories around this time of the two men waiting until someone was alone and then giving them a good kicking. This seems strange, as Tucker had a firm of very big men working for him who could all handle themselves. One could only assume that Tucker got a certain amount of pleasure from bullying and playing power games. Both he and Rolfe now knew what it meant to see someone die, both now had a bond that couldn't be broken.

And as for Tate, I can only say from personal experience that becoming addicted to something, whether its illegal drugs, gambling, alcohol, or even power, takes time; and it's so much easier if you have an excuse to use. Tate had the bullet hole in his arm. The painkillers he said he needed were boosted by heroin. And here's the thing; addiction is a mental trap way before you show any physical signs. I have no doubt that when he came out of prison he probably still looked as big and a strong as before; but he was thinking like an addict. From now on reality would take a back seat. No addict is ever going to deal with the problem when they think they are winning; or when they believe the next drink, snort, or gamble is going to solve all their problems.

Mick Steele had gone back to importing cannabis, but it was small scale. He was now in his fifties and didn't need the shit of flying to stuff over. He had a bungalow he shared with his partner Jackie Street, and another bungalow which he was renovating. An often-overlooked factor is that Steele was a free agent who could have also worked for other people. On his conviction in 1990 for importation he never disclosed who he was working for; but it wasn't Tucker. I don't know why Steele returned to importing drugs at his stage in his life; perhaps he had promised Jackie just a few more trips to get the bungalow done and then he would retire from the crap and they could live off the profits from selling one of their homes. But for both him and Tate, the

47

problem with pipe dreams is that they always need one last hit for them to come true.

III

In September 95 half a million pounds of cannabis was found in Hanningfield reservoir near Rettendon. Police believed a plane must have missed its marker and dropped its consignment into the water. It was rumoured the drugs were meant to be going to a London Crime Cartel based in Canning Town. It may seem strange that this particular Essex spot was used by the Cartel; but a light plane could cross the channel and fly into the Crouch estuary. Then they could use the river for guidance (these were the days before terrorist knew how to fly). At the end of the river was Rettendon, a load of old fields, three fishponds, and then the Hanningfield reservoir. Next to that was the A13 road, which went straight into the east end. The plan was good, if you were aiming for the three ponds near Workhouse Lane; but chances are the pilot had overshot the target. There is no suggestion that Steele was linked to this; but someone had clearly fucked up. If the Cartel were going to do another run, they would need a new pilot, someone they could trust. And if Tucker knew the perfect man for the job.

IV

Timeline – 1995
February 1995 – Tucker helps Nigel Benn walk out to the ring for his fight with Gerald McClellan.
17th March. Ronnie Kray dies. Bernard O'Mahoney is asked by Reggie Kray to help, but he declines. Various underworld figures are involved in his funeral.
June – Gangland boss Jason Vella, from Essex, was sentenced to

17 years for conspiracy to supply ecstasy and cannabis, GBH and ABH. Operation Max was launched when Reg Nunn was brutally attacked by Vella, and an accomplice and had to jump through a closed first floor window to escape being killed. Another victim, Mark Skeets, was invited out for a drink by Vella and then tied up and beaten. Prosecutor Andrew Munday said: "Mr Vella began chopping at his hair, his eyebrows were shaved and photographs were taken. He was jabbed with knives, burned with cigarettes, the soles of his feet were burned and he was forced to lick LSD coated paper and snort cocaine.

3rd October – jury in the criminal trial of OJ Simpson find shim not guilty of double murder.

October – Tucker applies for a shotgun licence.

31st October. Tate released from prison.

O'Mahoney signs the contract for his house.

Steele asks Nicholls to get him two shotguns (this date changes depending on which account Nicholls is describing).

3rd November – large haul of cannabis is found in West Hanningfield reservoir after possibly being dumped from an airplane.

November – Tucker, Tate and O'Mahoney travel to Rettendon to see if they can find any of the dropped cannabis. They talk about meeting with the Cartel involved, finding out when the next drop is coming so they can help, and robbing them of the next consignment. Tate goes to various people to try and raise more money for a cannabis deal. Sarah Saunders leaves the bungalow to go on holiday with her sister.

5th November – Tucker, Tate and Rolfe give Steele the cash to buy the cannabis.

6th November – Steele gives Nicholls the cash and asks Nicholls to get him two shotguns.

7th November – Nicholls buys the bad cannabis in Amsterdam.

8th November – Steele brings back the bad cannabis. Steele and Whomes are stopped on the beach. They are arrested on suspicion of importation after a very tiny trace of cannabis is found on the boat. Steele is bailed back to the police station for 20th

December (he received a letter after the murders had happened to tell him his bail had been cancelled and that no charges would be pressed. Technically, the police are meant to have new evidence in order to charge someone with an offence they have been arrested and released for. That new evidence was Nicholls confession, which should not have been enough to be able to charge someone with).

Tate crashes Tucker's Porsche, arrested for drink driving, no insurance. If he is still on licence, he could be remanded and receive a prison sentence if found guilty. He was released later that day, but it is not known if he was charged or bailed.

November – The cannabis turns out to be duff (although a third of it is believed to be good). People start returning it and asking for their money back.

Saunders returns from her holiday. Tate decides to throw her out. She is offered a hostel, but goes to stay at her mums instead. Tucker, Tate and Rolfe then take umbrage at a male friend who helps Saunders move some of her stuff. They kidnap him, force him to take drugs, strip him naked and burn cigarettes on him, before finally dropping him home. He spends three days in a psychiatric ward before deciding he does not wish to give a statement.

11th November – Leah Betts collapses after taking Apple ecstasy pill.

15th November. Nicholls goes back to Amsterdam to collect money from the Dutch firm. Nicholls states that Steele is told that a third of the cannabis was good, but the Dutch firm still give all of the cash back.

Peter Cuthbert signs the payment contract for a blue Range Rover, reg F424NPE, to be used by Tucker, Tate and Rolfe. Tucker will pay off the loan on the car, telling Barry Doorman that at some point it will be paid off in one lump sum.

16th November – Leah Betts dies after taking ecstasy bought from Raquels. Her parents agree that the photo of her in the hospital bed can be used. It appears on the front page of the News of the World with the headline "So this is Ecstasy?" The prime minister will later make a statement in parliament that he intends to crack down od the pedlars of this killer drug.

Steele books a hotel Ostend. He tells the jury that it was for Tate. He claims he was there to help sort out a problem Tate had with Nicholls.

16th/17th November – Steele, Nicholls, Tate, Rolfe and others stay at a hotel in Ostend. Donna Jagger and Darren Nicholls state that it is here Steele tells Tate about a plan to rob a London Crime Cartel of a plane load of cocaine.

17th November. Tucker goes out for a birthday meal with Donna Whitehead to the Global Café. Other people also attend, including Mickey Bowman.

November - O'Mahoney's last night working at Raquels. He walks out without telling Tucker he has resigned, and ends up in Ad Lib nightclub in Southend. Outside, he meets Tucker and Tate in the blue Range Rover, where he says he puts his hands on the vehicle. Friends of the murdered men are adamant Tucker and Tate were not in that vehicle that night.

19th November – Mark Murray is named in the News of the World as being one of the men involved in selling the drug that killed Leah Betts. Also mentioned is Raquels nightclub.

20th November – Tucker threatens O'Mahoney, saying he was responsible for Murray being in the newspaper, and that he will deal with him. O'Mahoney takes the threat seriously enough to move his wife and child away from the area.

November – Some point in the last week of November Nicholls states that Steele asks him to get him two shotguns. The only Thing Nicholls can recall is that the request came before the murders took place, but he cannot remember if Steele asked him before the trip back to Ostend, or even before the bad cannabis deal happened.

O'Mahoney appears in The News of the World, which reports he knows where the pill that killed Leah Betts was bought; implicating Mark Murray and Tony Tucker.

Mickey Bowman supplies Tucker, Tate and Rolfe with a machine gun (Jaggers not sure of the date, but states Rolfe was driving the Range Rover at the time).

24th November. Bowman returns to Essex and hands over the machine gun to Craig Rolfe. He also sells a VW Corrado to Barry Doorman.

Steele helps Tate's former partner Sarah Saunders move out of their home. It is possible that Nicholls is there. Bowman is also there. He states he gets a lift back to Essex from someone he doesn't know.

O'Mahoney goes to Raquels to confront Tucker. With Tucker that night is a bit of back up, including Mickey Bowman.

25th November – A VW Passat appears in Barry Dorman's car showroom.

Tate and Rolfe go out looking for O'Mahoney.

28th November – Rolfe is stopped by the police whilst driving the Range Rover. He gives his brothers details. The police later return after identifying him as Craig and summons him for the offence of driving whilst disqualified and no insurance.

30th November – O'Mahoney is informed by police that Tucker is intending to shoot him, and the threat should be taken seriously.

End of November – Drug raids across Essex and London in the belief that a bad batch of pills could end up causing more deaths over Christmas and the new year. The press report on December 1st that the raids had been a success, with thousands of pounds worth of drugs seized, including cannabis, cocaine and ecstasy, and also various weapons. In Basildon alone there had been five arrests. The press also complains that as yet no one has been charged for selling the pill to Leah Betts. Essex Police hope that the public would continue to give them information on drug dealers in the area, and assure them that there would be a lot more arrests in the coming weeks.

Chapter 6.

Leah Betts.

"I read the news today, oh boy
About a lucky man who made the grade
And though the news was rather sad
Well, I just had to laugh
I saw the photograph."
The Beatles.

I

By the mid-nineties Britpop had well and truly arrived. Parents at home watching Top of the Pops suck the life out of anyone with a personality must have wished their children would listen to wholesome musicians such as George Michael and Whitney Houston. There were also two deaths in 95 that made the national headlines. Everybody wanted to be part of the first one; no one wanted to be linked to the second.

When Ronnie Kray died in Broadmoor, his twin brother Reggie wanted a big east end send off. Various criminals said they would help. Bernard O'Mahoney, who was working for Tucker at the time, was also a friend of Reggie's, and was asked if he could organise it. For whatever reason he declined to be part of the security. It was a wise decision. People such as South London gangster Dave Courtney took over. He ran a door firm similar to Tuckers. The funeral became a publicity event, whether those in charge wanted it to or not.

As the horse drawn carriage went through the crowded east

end, many voiced an opinion that times were better when the boys were in charge. You could leave your doors open (to be fair, the Krays only robbed people who had money), and old women could walk the streets safely at night (again, I think all women were safe around these two). Some blamed immigration; whilst others said it was due to drugs now being everywhere. This may be true; the Krays were the last real gangsters not to have their empire built on drug money. But the press was not going to glorify criminals. There were pictures of men doing lines of Charlie (not their brother) off the coffin lid; and there were stories that the Krays had been involved in more murders than they had actually been convicted of. The Government had always hated the fact that the Krays had been the stars of their own life, and not the coppers that caught them.

As we headed towards the millennium, it seemed the past became even more important. One of the big films of 95 was Casino, in which Robert De Niro ended up losing everything because his partner and his business associate could not keep their nose out of the sniff. Other films such as The Godfather and Goodfellas pointed to how drugs had ruined things. But the new breed of criminals were only taking their cue from modern politicians. Making money was a drug, even if it was at the expense of community and culture. That summer that pubs were allowed to be open all day. Larger supermarkets were built on the outskirts of towns, which signalled the beginning of the end for the high street. And Britain sent a peacekeeping force to a far-off place in Eastern Europe called Bosnia, setting up sign posts for a mass of immigrants, legal and illegal, to start making their way to England.

Everyone was on the move. When Tate was in Whitemoor prison, Reggie Krays boyfriend Bradley Allardyce was also moved there. Reggie asked O'Mahoney to ask Tate to look after him. Bradley turned out to be a pain in the arse, and not in the way Reggie liked it; to the point where Tate told O'Mahoney to get someone else to protect the idiot, as Allardyce kept saying he was going to kill people for the way they had taken the piss out of Reg. Truth was Allardyce was a plank who would run to Tate every time he got scared. This led to friction between Tate and O'Mahoney, which would continue when Tate got out.

In the meantime, Tucker and Rolfe seemed to have moved on from the death of Kevin Whitaker. Although I am reminded of a scene from The Sopranos. where Tony Soprano's therapist tells him that sharks have to keep swimming otherwise they will die. Some criminals, to avoid taking responisbility for their actions, will seek endless thrills to try and block out what they have done. Too often we focus on Tate being the addict, but chances are Tucker and Rolfe were not too far behind.

After the imprisonment of large scale drug dealer Jason Vella comes the rumour of Tucker talking to the police. We are not talking about the Witness Protection Programme or being a registered informant. This was more where an individual built up a relationship with a detective. It was as secretive as the Freemasons, and a two-way street. The police got information, who was selling what, who was making threats, where the drugs were hidden. And the other side also got information; who was being watched, when and where the next raid would take place. For a man like Tucker, it would be easy to tell a detective, even a corrupt one, who else in Vella's firm had the drugs. The warrant would be sworn out, the address searched, and if you found the bag of pills and put them in your pocket, the person at the address isn't going to complain if he lives to sell another day. The pills are sold to Tucker, and so it goes on.

The Vella empire was up for grabs. Far easier for Tucker to get his rivals nicked than try to fight them, especially with Tate in prison. Steele did a few cannabis jobs for Tucker, but clearly there was more going on. Tucker was able to pay two hundred and fifty grand in cash for a brand new five bedroomed bungalow. Rolfe paid a cash deposit for a three-bed semi, and Tucker would give him the mortgage in cash every month. As other people associated with Vella were rounded up, many suspected someone had been passing on information. At the same time, Tucker applied for a shotgun licence.

In October 95 the police again raided Club UK in Southend, after reports that drugs were being sold openly. This was the same club where someone had died the year before. Tucker, who had been linked to the death by way of running the door staff, had still managed to keep his licence. But this time his main dealer Mark Murray lost hundreds of pills. As the lights went up, his dealers let the pills fall down. More raids continued. More drugs were seized, people went into hiding. Murray now owed Tucker around twenty thousand pounds. If you include other dealers, Tucker lost somewhere in the region of sixty thousand pounds in the course of a few weeks. He knew that Tate, who was going to come out after serving less than a year in prison, expected to take over the drugs business that Vella had left behind. To do that they would need some quick cash.

II

Tate hadn't spent all his time in prison taking drugs. There was an issue with Tucker that has never really been explained. At some point he asked Steele to collect the twenty thousand in cash that he had left with Tucker, and take over giving Sarah Saunders money every month for his kid. It may have been that he had heard about Tuckers new home, the rounding up of Vella's associates, or the big drug raids. What we do know is that when he came out of prison on Halloween 1995, he had left the old Tate behind. His addiction had reached the point of no return, and although he didn't know it, he didn't have that much longer to go. The issue with Nipper Ellis seems to have been resolved when a London Crime Cartel informed Tucker that if Ellis stayed away from Essex, then he, Tate and Rolfe wouldn't have to worry about getting a shot in the back of their heads. The deal would be that the rest of the Ellis family would be safe. Whether this happened whilst Tate was still in prison, and whether Tate was happy with the decision, we don't know. Tucker had agreed for all of them.

And on his release, Tate realised his home life had broken down. Within days Sarah Saunders had booked a trip away with her sister. One of those make or break holidays, but Tate wasnt even invited. He couldn't give a shiny shit if she returned or not. She had already become aware that he was a heroin addict, even if he didn't want to accept it. Maybe she hoped he would either sort himself out or do something stupid whilst she was away. In typical Tate fashion he tried to do both. He found a place for one of his prostitutes that he decided to keep as a mistress. The escort company which his mother helped to run was beginning to lose its way, always a problem when the boss keeps boning the staff. You would think that with a job description that included sucking cock and shagging, it would be fairly easy to maintain morale. But addicts tend not to be reliable employees even in that game; and being an addict himself, Tate was becoming incapable of making rational decisions. Shouting and making threats may work for Gordon Ramsey, but we all know Tate was not that good around food establishments. It reached the point that Tate's own mother kept a note in her purse that if anything was to happen to her, then her son Pat was to blame. Tate now spoke a lot about shafting other dealers, and this time they wouldn't be expecting a happy ending.

One of the first things that happened when Tate was released was that he took a trip to Rettendon with Tucker and Bernard O'Mahoney. They were looking for any of the cannabis blocks that had been found a few weeks ago after it had been dropped from a plane, most of which landed in the local reservoir just up the road. The drugs were found in video cassette sized blocks by a fisherman who saw some by the water's edge. The carp must have been absolutely mashed, but the cartel who had put up the money couldn't have been happy. They certainly would have been asking questions from the moment the drugs disappeared; and one those who might have been spoken to would have been Tucker. It is not known why the Essex boys thought they would find anything in Rettendon; but Whitehouse farm would seem the ideal choice. The land had been subsidised to be left free from any sort of farming for a couple of years; and because it was fairly flat, it was ideal for pheasant and clay pigeon shooting. There was really only one way in. Workhouse Lane was a track road, not suitable for the average police car. And for those in a four by four, you could cross the fields and get on to Rectory Lane. For that they must have had a bit of inside information from someone who knew about the original delivery. It could also mean that they would know something about the next consignment.

But the Essex boys still needed money. Tucker had lost alot of pills, and Tate wanted to take over Vella's empire. A cannabis run was agreed, and a syndicate would help even out the risk. Within a couple of days of being out, Tate was asking around and getting up the cash. Who he borrowed the money from has never been clarified, but somebody was able to hand over forty thousand pounds on the basis they would be getting double back, no matter what. Steele and Nicholls were called in to get the stuff, and the deal was made by the 5th November. Steele and Nicholls took the cash to Amsterdam and came back with the drugs. Everything was going to plan, But here destiny took a wrong turn, and even though the boys didn't know it, they were already driving towards a dead end.

At the same time a young seventeen-year-old girl was asking her mates to score some pills for a birthday party she was going to have that weekend. She was just another kid from the streets of ex council houses that lined the country. Leah's life was ordinary. She was no different from the millions of young women who had just left school. She was never going to be a supermodel, she was never going to cure cancer; but she loved, and was loved, by her family and friends. Whatever hopes and fears she had; they were hidden away behind a smile. She wished what everyone else her age wished; to be popular, and to be happy. Her world was similar to so many in the suburbs. She lived few miles away from the town centre; a few miles away from the country, and her home was only four miles away from Workhouse Lane. She had her whole future in front of her. She had already been to Raquel's nightclub even though she was underage. She had already tried an ecstasy pill even though she knew it was illegal; her father was a retired police officer. For her eighteenth birthday he had agreed to a small party. His only worry was drunken boys, he didn't want anyone to do anything stupid.

Leah handed over the money. Someone who knew someone who knew someone was going to go to Raquel's nightclub to sort out the stuff for the party. The dealer was easy to spot; he stood in the same place every week his trainer marks were embedded into the carpet. Cash changed hands, pills were put into a pocket, and the deal was done. Once outside you might have looked under the street lamps to see that these pills had been stamped with an image that your grandparents may have linked to Adam and Eve, or your parents might have remembered as being part of The Beatles. But for Leah and her generation they probably thought of a computer company. For when you looked closely, embossed in each tablet was the image of an apple.

Chapter 7.

Three trees on the Low Sky.

"Every man has his breaking point."
The Shawshank Redemption.

Six weeks of chaos, where the only thing that didn't get topped
was a pizza.

I

Pat Tate was out, and he wanted it all. Tucker and Rolfe had
got away with the murder of Kevin Whitaker, and chances are it
must have given them a great sense of power. From now on, Tate
talking about armed robberies was not going to get the same respect it used to. Instead, it quickly became a competition to see
who could take the most drugs. Rolfe, trying to curb his enthusi-
asm for the sake of his partner Donna, didn't go the full-on with
the coke, E, crack and heroin that the other two now seemed to
dare each other to take on a daily basis. Tucker felt invincible,
Tate felt left behind. They also were both partial to cannabis,
steroids and Ketamine, a horse tranquiliser. What all this was
doing to their brains and bodies we don't know, but it's doubtful if any decision they made was going to be rational, so let's
look at how the bad cannabis deal was played out.

Tate seemed to have put the bulk of the money into the deal. If Rolfe felt a bit like a third wheel in that first week, he made up for it by getting seven thousand pounds and adding it to the syndicate. Things get a bit hazy as to who else was involved. Tucker put some in. Barry Doorman apparently put money in; but there are also stories of Kenneth Noye and the Blundell brothers adding to the pot. Everything was going well, until Tate caused an issue at another club. Head doorman at Raquels, Bernard O'Mahoney, must have felt he had been played by the way Tucker had pushed him aside for Rolfe the year before, and now lavished all his attention on Tate. When he heard that his friend Chris Wheatley, who ran a different club, had been sacked on the say so of Tate because he wanted a bigger share of the drugs coming in, O'Mahoney knew his working relationship with Tucker was over. He didn't want to end up like Rolfe, driving around like an errand boy sent to collect a bill.

We can assume the drugs being talked about are ecstasy pills. How and where Tate got these from, we don't know. Nor do we know if these pills had an apple symbol on them. O'Mahoney says he had already declined to be the back-up driver in the robbery they were planning, although does not give a date. But this must be before the 11th November. There was talk about money being put into a cocaine deal, and here the name Kenneth Noye appears again. O'Mahoney tells the story of going to meet him with Tate. On the drive down to Kent, Tate keeps telling O'Mahoney how close he is with Noye after they became friends in prison. They wait in a pub; to which about an hour later, Noye enters, hands over the cash in a bag, and then leaves. Marvin Gaye and his dad probably had a better reunion. Either way, when Kenneth Noye asks you whats going on, its best not to to start dancing.

Darren Nicholls now appears. It is not known how and why he gets involved, as from previous occasions he can't seem to be able to tell his arse from his elbow. But then Nicholls has spent the rest of his life claiming to not being the main player in the drug runs. As such, he doesn't explain why he is the one to go to

Holland with the money to get the drugs from John Stone. He is the one who waits an extra day, as Stone cannot get hold of enough herbal cannabis, and eventually they settle on blocks of cannabis resin. He is the one to pass the message back to England, and changes everyone else's plans.

On the 8th November Steele comes back on the boat and meets Whomes at the agreed meeting point. Whomes is just about to hitch up the boat to the Range Rover when he is surprised by the police. He tells them he's just been out doing a bit of diving. The police are naturally surprised. Its three o'clock in the fucking morning. Steele then appears. The police continue to ask questions. Steele tells them he took the boat out for testing but ran into engine trouble. He asks to wash the salt deposits from the boat to stop it rusting. The police agree, and he is able to swipe the memory from his GPS tracker, and any bits of cannabis from inside the boat. He finishes just as Customs and Excise officers turn up, and go absolutely bolo. Steele and Whomes are arrested even though there were no actual proof they had done anything wrong. They clearly know of Steele from old, and a search of the area was carried out, but no drugs were found.

Whilst in custody, Steele might have wondered how the police knew where to find them. Nicholls knew where the landing was going to be, but so did Tucker and Tate when they had been told the trip was going to be an extra day. But what no one else knew was that Steele had already parked another car further down the coast to unload the cannabis there. What Steele wasn't aware of at the time was that Tate was in another police station after crashing Tucker's Porsche and being arrested for drink driving and no insurance. As he had been out of prison for less than a month and would still be on licence, he would have to say something very good to be released. It may have been that Tate had decided on taking a blood test. As such he would have been bailed to come back when the results were ready. This can take up to 28 days, which would have made it the 6th December.

Rolfe and his partner Donna Jaggers were summoned by

Tucker to go and get Tate. Rather than show any concern for one of his girlfriend's, Lizzie Fletcher, who had been in the car at the time; or even how Tucker felt about writing off his Porsche, Tate demanded to go and see a drug dealer to score. He wanted to celebrate. He had called Steele's partner Jackie Street and had been told the delivery was safe; they still had the cannabis. Steele was later released from police custody. His boat had been seized, and he had been bailed back to the police station for 20th December. It meant that he wouldn't be doing any more trips for a while. The cannabis was quickly distributed over the 9th and 10th November. Then word began to come back that the stuff is basically dog shit. The only way you were going to get wasted was if you threw a nine bar up in the air and headbutted it. This may be when the story starts of Tate speaking to certain people and telling them Steele is the one who has stitched them up; but that doesn't make sense.

And here another rumour starts about a third of the consignment that was actually good. But again, this story comes from Nicholls, who says that Tate somehow gets it all; and then smashes up the blocks of crap cannabis so that Steele wouldn't know how much he returns. But Tates financial input would have been about a third; so what drugs is he smashing up? This story is corroborated by Donna Jaggers statement, written before Nicholls is arrested, who said that Tate smashed the blocks in anger. Steele, a man who would double count the money, would have at least weighed what he was carrying.

Tate has only been out less than two weeks, and already he's got rid of the door staff at one club so he can sell his own pills, kicked out his long term partner and the mother of his child from the home that's in her name, picked up for driving offences after smashing a Porsche, fucked up a cannabis deal, and now he's up to his balls with a lot of heavy hitters', trying to fob them off. It was like he was walking around saying "throw it into the fuck it bucket and let me know when its full." Worse, he is about to be the only drug dealer in Essex about to have to smuggle drugs out of England just to prove to the Dutch firm the gear was crap. The criminal underworld must have been pissing themselves; but if the story about a third of the cannabis being good was true, he now had sixty thousand pounds in cash at his disposal.

11th November 1995 was a Saturday night. Tucker, Tate and Rolfe were doing their usual rounds in all the clubs. Steele and Nicholls were booking tickets to go back to Amsterdam to try and get the money back; and Leah Betts took an ecstasy pill. We can argue that it wasn't the actual pill that killed her. She thought she was burning up. So she swallowed nearly ten pints of water in just under ninety minutes, and the shock put her into a coma. We can argue that she was an adult; she made the decision, and it turned out badly. No matter what; it was a shit thing to happen for the price of wanting to have a good time, and the police were going to make sure someone paid.

II

On the morning of the 12th November a rumour started firing around Basildon like a bullet. A young girl was in a coma after being supplied with an apple ecstasy pill someone had bought from Raquel's. Worse, her dad was a retired police officer, and the old Bill were running all over the shop. No one knew if the next knock was going to be carol singers or ten coppers and a dog. Tate was now stuck with a load of pills he couldn't sell. Even if he rubbed off the apple symbol; if another kid fell ill and died, he would be going back to prison for a long time. The best thing to do would be to get rid of them. The bullet wound in his arm added pain killers to the list of all the other drugs he was taking. Now he was hitting the crack pipe. A drug that felt like someone had shoved a rocket up his arse when what he really needed to do was get a few hours' sleep and start thinking straight. He owed money for the bad cannabis, and if he had got the apple pills on tick, even if he threw them away, he was still going to have to pay his supplier. And it still wasn't over.

Working at Raquels was doorman and part time delivery driver Mark Hall. Now some people can be a bit light fingered, but this guy took the piss. In November he had helped himself to a van load of Head holdalls. These were expensive good quality large bags, up to three-foot-long (enough to carry a shotgun), good enough for the gym, or taking on holiday, and Mark was selling them at the club. They were very popular, to the point that if you didn't get one as a Christmas present it was only because you were Jewish. He was later arrested in January 96, when the police and Parcel Force did a joint raid on his home. There were rooms filled with hundreds of parcels, and large quantities of drugs. He must have been a combination of Pablo Escobar and Postman Pat. How many Head bags the Essex boys took and gave away to their friends we don't know, but they started to turn up everywhere.

For a big bag you needed a big car. Tucker went to Barry Doorman's showroom and picked up the blue Range Rover on the 15th. He had a green Range Rover in Spetember of that year, but for whatever reason, it had to go. For this one he had to get his mate Peter Cuthbert to cover the finance agreement, but told Doorman that he would soon have enough to pay the money in one hit. This can't be money from the bad cannabis deal, as thats already gone wrong. And the story of Steele telling Tate about robbing a plane load of cocaine doesn't come until two days later. But let's assume that they were the ones sorting out the cocaine deal, and they needed a four-wheel drive was because it would be the only thing to get across the fields in a hurry, and they were smart enough not to put the car in their name; so perhaps they really were thinking ahead to when the good times would roll.

On the 16th November Leah Betts life support machine was turned off. The News of the World put her face in every living room. A young girl who would never wake up. The public wanted more than answers, they wanted justice. The prime Minister John Major demanded that something must be done. The police went looking for someone to blame. But it took journalists to tell everyone the pill had been bought at Raquels. One name that kept cropping up was Mark Murray. Reporters were surprised about how could he be so open about selling in the club? The answer was with the people running the doors, and the person who ran them was Tony Tucker. Reporters who had no idea of how deep Tucker's criminality went, now swarmed over Basildon asking questions.

A lot of people must have known it wouldn't take the police long to start asking questions as well. A task force was set up to deal with all the information that was coming in. Usually, when police go to obtain a search warrant, they have to stand in front of a magistrate and explain all the reasons why they believe they would be likely to find drugs in the premises. If a magistrate was unsure, they could refuse the warrant until further information came to light. In November 1995 it was doubtful if any drugs warrant got turned down in Essex and London. No magistrate wanted the press to find out they had possibly helped kill another child because they didn't want a door being boshed in. After all the resources, intelligence, perseverance, courage and hard work, the police finally got a result.

Two teenage boys who had been at Leah's party were arrested and questioned. They were not really criminals, not really drug dealers, certainly not killers. They had admitted they had bought the pill because Leah had asked them to get one, and they wanted to go to a party. They were desperately sorry, desperately wanted to help, and they were the only people charged in relation to the death of Leah Betts. If the public thought that justice had been done, they were being sorely mislead. Murray had been spoken to, but with no evidence the police were stuck. Bernard O'Mahoney then appeared in a newspaper after trying to get another apple ecstasy pill so that it could be given to the reporter and tested. Tucker gave him a bollocking for going public, but the damage was done.

Steele and Nicholls were in Amsterdam having their picture taken with a waxwork of Tina Turner, with Nicholls wearing a light fawn coloured top. The initial arrangement was to take all the cannabis back and change it; but the supplier John Stone was told some very heavy people in Essex were involved in this syndicate, and were not going to waste their time getting caught bringing drugs in Amsterdam. From Nicholls account, Stone tells Steele that it was all a mistake, Nicholls had picked up the wrong delivery; but a third of the cannabis was of good quality. And in one of the most bizarre busines transaction the drug world has ever known, Stone agrees to give all the money back. Why? Stone is on home ground. He could easily tell Steele that he thinks he's bluffing, and good luck getting out of town. He could say Steele was only getting two thirds of the cash back, and then tell him to go fuck himself. Also, it's not clear why no one thinks about getting more cannabis? You are in Amsterdam speaking to a drug supplier. He only makes a profit selling cannabis; why doesn't he just give them a couple more kilos of cannabis to help weigh off his own loss? Instead, the men get their deposit back.

Steele does not want him and Nicholls to bring so much cash through customs; he is already on bail for smuggling offences, and it might look a bit dodgy if he was caught with a holdall full of money. Tate agrees to meet them in Ostend. He, Rolfe, Barry Dorman, and a couple of girlfriends, go out on the 16th November to get the money. Records show he stays in the same hotel as Steele. Nicholls using his credit card, helps back up his claim that they were all involved in a conspiracy to supply drugs.

Whatever is said in the hotel room, it is not known if anyone speaks about the death of Leah Betts, if Steele mentions anything about a third of the gear being good, or if Tate says anything about some people in the syndicate not being happy. The truth is they were lucky to get any money back at all. If Steele had not dropped off the drugs further down the coast, they would have lost everything and he could have been facing another long spell in prison. The fact that some people were getting their investment back was a pretty good result. Barry Dorman says that he sees Tate give Steele a couple of grand "Drink money" for getting the cash back, but we still need to clear up the story of the plan to rob a plane load of cocaine.

One of the basis of the murders is that Steele sets up a trap so he can kill the Essex boys. He is going to fly back a plane load of coacinae destined for a crime cartel, and the Essex boys will rob him. Rolfe's partner Donna Jaggers, states that Steele told Tate that he had been offered the job of flying back with a million pounds worth of cocaine to Clacton with only one member of a crime cartel on board. He would be given fifty thousand pounds to buy the drugs, then the plan was to land in Clacton, but he would land in a different location where the Essex boys would be waiting. They would carry out the robbery, and split the drugs between them.

From the start, the plan seems so ridiculous that no decent criminal would believe it. No one is going to give you a million pounds worth of cocaine on the back of a fifty-grand deposit. Thirty kilos of cocaine isn't that big, you could fit it into one of the many Head holdalls that were now being used by everyone. Why take the risk of landing a plane (in the dark?) in a field that you could easily crash because you have no idea of what is actually in the ground, you could easily be seen by a member of the public, who, thinking you're going to crash, would probably call the police. Then, if you did land, you had no way of taking back off, and could be caught before you got to the end of the field; all for something you could fly in low and just throw out of the plane? Let's not forget it pretty much includes the certain death of either the member of the crime cartel in the plane, or Steele later on when the cartel gets hold of him. I think the only reason the story is written this way is because it's the only story that matches why the Essex boys were in Workhouse Lane that night.

There is also the issue that the idea for the robbery is based on Steele believing that Tate was going to kill him. Again, it is not clear where this comes from. How did Steele know that Tate was blaming him for the fuck up? And Steele may have been threatened by Tate over the phone to get the money back, but then Tate thanks him at the hotel for getting the cash back? So why should Steele make up a story after that means getting Tate, possibly Tucker, and possibly Rolfe, perhaps even others, down a country lane, and let's be clear about this, to kill them?

But we cannot dismiss Nicholls account (which must have come from being told about it by Steele), and Jaggers account (which must have come from Rolfe being told by Tate, who had been told about it by Steele). So, let's say that there is an element of truth in there somewhere, but they got the story the wrong way around. What if it was Tate talking about the robbery, and Mickey (the pilot) Steele being just the man they needed?

You see, Steele had been in Holland for the last two days. It certainly wouldn't have been John Stone asking him to smuggle the cocaine over. It's not his drugs, and it's not his money, so it can't be his plan. So whose paln was it? Tucker said he couldn't make the journey because his partner had booked a night out in London for his birthday. For a man who would push over a tramp to pick up a penny it seems strange he wouldn't want to be there to get his cut in person. But then we get a statement from the owner of The Global Café, who says that tucker, his partner, and eight others turn up for a meal on the night of 17th November. Amongst the group was Mickey Bowman.

If we look at Tucker over the next few weeks, he clearly seems to be very worried about something. He threatens Mark Murray, Bernard O'Mahoney, and Steele; but perhaps his biggest threat had just been released from prison? Tate had told Barry Doorman that when a car he had left with Barry was sold, not to give any of the money to Tucker. Doorman would later state that when he did put a 'sold' sign on the car, Tucker appeared and asked for the money.

And what about Tate's meeting with Billy Blundell a few days before he was shot? Blundell warned him that if he stayed with

Tucker he might end up with a bullet to the back of the head. This has often been believed to be that it was Tuckers life that was in danger, but let's take it literally. What if it is Tucker who is setting up the fake cocaine robbery in order to eliminate the biggest headache in his business empire, namely Pat Tate? Tucker knew Workhouse lane took you up to a set of woods and a couple of small fishing lakes. It would be easy to get Tate psyched up about the job, take him past the gate, into a field, and leave the body under water. The police would probably be looking for Nipper Ellis when it was all over. Tucker could have easily approached a London Crime Cartel to get a hitman. Steele would have known something was wrong as soon as he heard the story about landing the plane. He could have been told Tate needed to be spoken to, without being armed. So, Steele agrees to go along with the plan; but knowing that something is going to happen he decides to have Whomes and Nicholls along for backup.

But if you were a London crime cartel, why not take out Tucker as well? They had both ripped off other criminals, they had not only threatened to kill their friend Nipper Ellis and his young sister, they had the fucking effrontery to grass him to the police when he stood up to them. And now they were linked to a drugs death that not only the police were all over, but the prime minister as well. If Tucker was arrested, the only way out would be for him to tell a lot of secrets that some people might want to keep in the ground. Far better if he was taken care of as well.

III

Question: you've got a couple of crack heads who are also doing coke, steroids, ketamine, threatening people, kicking girlfriends out their home then beating the shit out of their friends, messing up a cannabis deal, and now the police have got their beady eye on you because someone has died from taking one of your pills. What's the most fucked up thing they could do right now to really show the world they are absolutely crackers? That's right; you get yourself a machine gun. Not only that, let's get it from someone called "Mad Mickey Bowman." Those with a certain level of intelligence might have thought it wise not to deal with any man whose moniker starts with the word "Mad," especially if you're planning on buying a semi-automatic weapon.

We know that the machine gun was obtained after the 17th, as both Jaggers and Bowman say that Rolfe was driving the Range Rover. We don't know if it was originally asked for before then (Bowman was with Tucker on the 17th), or why they wanted that particular weapon. Perhaps if you were hiding in the trees and your opponent was standing in an open field, you would certainly have the upper hand. But we know the Essex boys, and there is no way Tate wouldn't have told anyone about it. Since leaving prison he must have thought he was always getting the last curly egg sandwich at the drugs buffet. The machine gun makes him the King of sausage rolls. He didn't even have to use it for the cocaine robbery, he just had to let people know he had it.

But what the police would need for an arrest is the actual gun itself. Even if they heard about it, they could be happy to wait, perhaps expecting the boys to take out Nipper Ellis, or other drug dealers trying to fill the gap left by Jason Vella?

Tuckers main dealer in the clubs, Mark Murray, knew a lot of high-level suppliers. But after a series of raids and the death of Leah Betts he couldn't get someone to supply him with laxative chocolate. The police and the press were after him, and he owed Tucker over twenty thousand pounds. Both men knew that problem would be gone if the other one was in prison, or dead. Bernard O'Mahoney was also within firing range. Things had gone south between him and Tucker after he had spoken to the News of the World about drug dealing inside the club. O'Mahoney had run Raquel's for a number of years, and had also worked for Tucker and Tate in collecting debts. He had recently been arrested for possession of a firearm, and knew his door licence would be revoked if he was convicted. Helping the police could resolve that issue; and if Tucker was no longer the managing director of the door firm, he was quite capable of taking his place.

Around this time, he spoke to an old friend about fronting a company to run the doors for him. It looked promising until O'Mahoney mentioned that someone who had upset Tucker had moved out of Essex and was hiding in the West Country. Killing him would give them a financial boost of ten grand. At this point the old friend decided to look for another line of work. A man in the West country would later appear when a woman goes missing after the murders.

At this point Darren Nicholls claims that just a week after Ostend, Steele asks him if he can get hold of a gun (although Nicholls gives about three different dates for when Steele possibly asked him).

This now puts us bang on the 24th November. The is the day day Sarah Saunders moves her belongings out of the bungalow, helped by Steele and his partner Jackie Street. It is also the day that Mickey Bowman turns up at the bungalow, on the basis he is selling his white VW Corrado to Barry Doorman, which Doorman is required to buy on the advice of Tate. Bowman later gives an account that he is only there as he is a good friend of Tate, and to sell his car; but then mentions going out for Tucker's birthday meal a week before, and meeting them on another occasion in order to sell his car, but he doesn't get the asking price, so he goes home.

Was this for the machine gun, and was he going to be part of the robbery? When he is at Tate's bungalow on the day Sarah is moving out, he says he gets a lift back from a friend of Tate's. But he comes back that night to be with Tucker at Raquels after Tucker hears that O'Mahoney is looking for him. Although it is Tucker who has made the threat, its O'Mahoney who turns up for the fight. Realising he is outnumbered, O'Mahoney wisely walks away.

Bowman would later tell police he sold his car around the 24th November, telling them it was a VW Corrado. What is interesting is that a VW Passat appears on Barry Doorman's' fore-court from the 25th November.

In this last week of November, the name John McCarthy now appears. He agrees to buy the whole consignment of cocaine for one million pounds. This is a good deal for both sides. The thirty kilos were probably worth a street value of nearly one and a half million; but it allowed the Essex boys to get rid of the stuff in one hit. McCarthy seems to want to deal with Tate rather than Tucker or Rolfe, which gives Tate the edge. The problem was Tate was hardly thinking straight by now. He had been made to look a mug by Nipper Ellis. He had been made to look a chump in front of the old school criminals who had given him money for a drug deal, He had crashed Tuckers Porsche whilst off his head and must have felt that people were beginning to laugh at him rather than with him. Worse, some even wondered how he managed not to be sent back to prison after getting arrested. They already knew he was willing to talk to the police when he had got shot. Perhaps he had become a liability? For a man who never cared about the future, it was beginning to look as if he didn't have one.

On the night of the 28th November Rolfe was seen driving the Range Rover by the police. He gave the two coppers a bit of verbal, and his brothers details. It surprising he was not arrested anyway. The car was still registered to its original owner, and Rolfe had no idea who that was. He was being abusive, and had quickly failed the attitude test. Instead, the officers went back to the station and did some digging. They realised who it was and returned in the middle of the night. A crafty copper stood on the driveway and called out "Craig?" Rolfe opened a bedroom window and replied "yes." He was then summoned for the offence of driving whilst disqualified, and not having any insurance or tax on the vehicle. That would mean a date for him to attend the local magistrates' court; and as he had been convicted of driving whilst disqualified before, it could possibly be a custodial sentence. It is not known if Rolfe told the other two of his predicaments, but perhaps these sorts of things seem to gain a momentum of their own.

What is missing during the month of November are the police themselves. Tuckers name must have come up during the investigation into Leah Betts. Tate's name must have come up after smashing Tucker's Porsche. He was still down as having a problem with Ellis, who would soon be out of jail as well. And Rolfe, linked to another drug death last year, whose CV had him down as a director in one of Tucker's door firms, was now driving around without a licence. The only reason the police wouldnt be watching them was if someone was giving them a running commentary from the inside.

And what about Nicholls? Now that Tate is out of prison, we have Nicholls saying Steele wanted a shotgun before the drug deal went wrong. We have him fucking up the first part of the trip to Amsterdam to collect the drugs, meaning everyone has to wait a day. We have the trip back where nearly everyone but him is arrested. He tells us that a third of the cannabis was good quality, but never explains how Tate gets all of it. We have Nicholls saying from then on there was a problem between Tate and Steele. We have Nicholls saying that at some point (possibly even before Tate is released from prison) Steele buys an old VW Passat from him; but cannot remember when, where, how much and what condition the car was in. And also, Nicholls saying about Steele going to the bungalow where Tate, Tucker and Mickey Bowman are, in order to help Sarah Saunders move her and her child's belongings. The only thing missing is Steele telling Nicholls about the cocaine robbery. Does any of this sound like a man planning to commit what would at least be a double murder? Tate could blow hot and cold like an Eskimo hooker, but Steele was a safe bet, and you knew he would never grass if he got caught. But if Nicholls was the one who decided Tate had to go, who better to get involved than Mick Steele, a man who had fallen into the trap without even realising it.

On a side note, the news that month had also been filled with the trial of Rosemary West. She and her husband Fred had been arrested for a series of murders, including on her own children. Fred had hung himself whilst on remand. The appropriate adult who had been assigned to Fred because he couldn't read or write, was ordered to attend court by the defence, as they believed Fred had formed a sexual attraction to her, and would have agreed to say anything. When the appropriate adult went into the witness box she was asked if she had spoken to a journalist or television company with a view to writing a book or making a programme about what had happened with Fred prior to giving evidence. She lied and said "No."

But the defence team had found out she had been in contact with a journalist about giving her story. The breach of protocol was serious enough that it could have caused the trial to collapse. Luckily, she had only been the appropriate adult for Fred, and had never been officially part of the investigation into Rose. As such, whatever information she gave was only hearsay. On the 22nd November Rose West was found guilty of ten murders. The judge sentenced her to life. Fred's appropriate adult was not prosecuted in relation to speaking about a book deal before the trial. But the judge said that the jury must not have any evidence tainted by the lure of a witness gaining financially even before they had given evidence.

Chapter 8.

Shall we take a trip?

"Nothing really matters, anyone can see,
Nothing really matters, to me."
Queen.

I

December 1st 1995 was the day of Leah Betts funeral. As the procession made its way through the streets of Essex, many were asking why no one had been brought to justice? Two young men had been arrested, but they were not the real criminals. The police did. knew the real killers were still out there; but how much they had on Tucker, Tate and Rolfe, is still subject to secrecy. Darren Nicholls claims he officially became a police informant just after Christmas. His account is that a detective was drinking in the same pub when they bumped into each other and the detective offered to help him out by not getting his home raided. Nicholls then becomes an official registered informant in February, when he tells the copper where the bad cannabis had been dumped. The problem was that the detective he was speaking to was later arrested for corruption. Also, a lot of the paperwork regarding Nicholls status was either lost or placed under the Official Secrets Act; and could remain out of public view for at least fifty years. But even at this stage it would be ridiculous to believe that the police were not keeping an eye on

Tucker, Tate, and Rolfe; but which police force are we talking about?

During the last months of 95, the Metropolitan police were still being accused of failing to do anything about the murder of Stephen Lawrence. There had been ongoing investigations into police corruption; including officers who were linked to Mickey Bowman. Other operations highlighted the fact that a lot of London Crime Cartels had infiltrated the police by paying/threatening numerous police officers. If there was a cartel out there that had lost half a million pounds worth of cannabis, and were now involved in a million pounds worth of cocaine, the chances are they had at least one copper on the payroll.

It is around this time that Billy Blundell, the man who had helped Tate when he was in Marbella all those years ago, is on record to say that he was approached by a drug dealer (possibly Mark Murray) who told him all the problems Tucker and Tate were causing. This time Tucker seemed to be the main issue. Blundell got straight to the point and told the dealer he should shoot Tucker in the clackers. Probably not a kill shot, but it would be enough to remove him from the Essex underworld for at least six months, and never ride a horse again. A man on a motorbike appeared, with a gun. The official story is that the drug dealer declined to do it himself; but how much that dealer knew of all Tucker's activities and future plans, such as the machine gun and the cocaine robbery, and if he told Blundell, we don't know.

On the 2nd December Barry Dorman, the used car salesman who knew Tate and Tucker, and had been to Ostend to help bring some of the cash back, was visited by Blundell. Dorman was not a criminal in the strictest sense; even though he had put money into the cannabis syndicate, and had failed to change the owner details on the Range Rover. So it must have come as a bit of a shock when he had Blundell in his office. Why he went to visit Dorman has never been fully disclosed. We must remember that it didn't matter if Dorman had heard something about a third of the cannabis being good; when Blundell turned up with what we might call "associates," I have no doubt Doorman would have told Blundell that Tate had got all the money back, and even gave Steele some drink money for doing it. Which meant that Billy Blundell was now aware that Steele wasn't the one who ripped him off. But what is interesting is how Blundell got Dorman's name in the first place? Someone had clearly said something to make the man go down in person and find out what was going on.

On the 3rd December, just three days before their deaths, Tate and Tucker were called to a meeting with Blundell at his farm in Bulphan. How far away it is from Jack Whomes uncles house we don't know. Only Tate went. We do not know if this was the moment Tate blamed Steele. The story goes that if needed, he would bring Steele here, put him on his knees, make him beg for forgiveness, and then blow his fucking head off. This was the same threat Tucker had made to Ellis. It would seem strange that if this was when the threat was made, as its already been two weeks since the cocaine robbery idea in Ostend. But when you look at it, if Blundell went to see Dorman, he could have also gone to go see Steele and front him out.

Both men came from the same generation. Both had a code they were willing to stick to. It is quite probable that Blundell saw Steele first, who told him about Dorman, who confirmed Steeles' account. And Blundell, who in his heart of hearts wanted to give Tate a pass, offered to meet the boys to discuss getting his money back, plus the profit. When only Tate turned up, the decision was made. You have to nip this sort of shit in the bud, overwise everyone is going to walk all over you. He tells it that he says to Tate that he needs to stop associating himself with Tucker, otherwise he's going to get a bullet to the back of the head. Most sensible people would have agreed and promised to take the advice seriously. But Tate gave the most stupid answer that anyone could think of, and replied that "What will be will be," like the Doris Day of Debden. Billy let him finish, but knew Tate's days were numbered. He must have felt like someone had put rabbit shit in his rum and raisin ice cream. He had called a meeting, and only one of them bothered turned up; and he looked like he was off his tits. The other one was no better, the fuckwit Tucker who couldn't give a shit about the girl dying from a pill brought in his club. He was always with his benny mate, Rolfe, like the Harris, another plank who was always out of it. People like them are going to start causing problems. What if one of them got nicked and told the police everything they knew to get a lighter sentence? Like those dribblers in the stained trousers you see wandering the streets, perhaps it would be better to put them all out of their misery?

Is the decision to kill that easy? Perhaps. My view is that the conversation between Blundell and Tate went slightly differently; because on this date Tate goes away and tells Sarah Saunders about Steele taking a trip up north. And from what I have read, he never actually says that he is going to carry out the job, only that its going to happen. Which sounds to me that it is Blundell telling him he is going to sort out Steele.

As for Steele himself, if he now decides to murder Tate, it only gives him two days to plan it getting a shotgun and a getaway car. Forty-eight hours to get other people involved, and chose the location.

II

Before the trip to Ostend, Sarah Saunders was kicked out of the bungalow that was in her name. She made the mistake of calling a female friend, who's boyfriend came over to collect Saunders and some of her belongings. When Tate found out he had been into his home, he lost the plot. He, Tucker and Rolfe almost killed him with drugs and cigarette burns. And this is because he gave your ex-girlfriend a lift? When the man recovered and left the hospital, he refused to press charges. Just like the shooting in the Blind Beggar pub all those years ago, the boys thought they had got away with it again. But there could be little doubt that word of what happened reached a lot of people. The police and thieves of Essex must have thought that Tate was living on borrowed time.

When Sarah Saunder does find somewhere else to live, surprisingly enough, no one would help her move, apart from Mick Steele and his partner Jackie Street. Steele had contacted Tate to make sure it was OK; and when it came to moving day on 24th November it would appear that everyone was there, including Mickey Bowman, and possibly Darren Nicholls, which seems strange if he was scared of Tate giving him a good kicking.

By this time Saunders has also started a relationship with an old friend. She says nothing to Tate about it, which is not surprising. She now has her own place, and a car which was given to her by Tate so she could take their son to wherever he needed to be. But it would be true to say that their relationship was pretty much over. So, it is not clear why over a week later on the 3rd December they have a conversation in which Tate says to her that Mick was going to take a trip up north, and wasn't coming back. He may have been doing it to frighten her, but why he is telling her at all? If Steele had been killed, did Tate not think that it might come back and bite him?

On the 4th December Saunders meets Steele in a McDonalds to tell him that his life is in danger. She later tells police that he seemed very calm about the whole thing. Steele believed it was just Tate trying to get a reaction from her, and appeared not to take it seriously. He may have been right. At no point does Nicholls ever say that Steele asked for two shotguns and a VW Passat a few days before the murders; and if we go back to the cocaine robbery being a lie; he has already had two weeks to plan the job.

The phone records that would be shown to the court start on the 5th, and list Saunders calling Steele's mobile that day; but again, we do not know what that conversation was about. The only thing you can predict with the Essex boys is that they often have a tendency to go bat shit crazy for the most stupid reasons.

Bernard O'Mahoney would know. The issue with Tucker had

WHO KILLED THE ESSEX BOYS?

reached King size proportions. On the 3rd December he had moved into a hotel to avoid running into the Essex boys. If Steele was taking a trip up north, it would seem this magical mystery tour had a few other people on the coach. On the 4th he disappeared for the day, then told friends he had gone to Birmingham. On the 5th December the police contacted Bernard O'Mahoney and said they wished to speak with him in person. The doorman had walked away from Raquels only a week before, and wanted to know what the problem was? They asked if he could come to the station, he said he was busy. Eventually they told him that word had got back that his former boss was threatening to kill him, and the threat should be taken very seriously. This could only mean there had been talk of a weapon involved. Perhaps he would come in and have a chat with them. O'Mahoney said he had been aware of the threat for a while, and even though he didn't mention that he had moved his family out of their home, he said he wasn't particularly bothered. When they asked to speak to his partner as well, it changed the game completely, and he told detectives exactly when and where he wished to have that conversation. It would be at South Woodham Ferrers police station, between two and four in the afternoon of the 6th December. What he didn't tell the police was where he had been spending the last few days. It was a small hotel, somewhere quiet, away from the crowd, near a village called Rettendon.

And what were Steele and Whomes doing on the day before the murders? By the time the case got to court, a lot of the evidence relied on mobile phones. Steele rings Nicholls on three occasions, but only rings Whomes once. Nicholls rings Steele on two occasions, which he thinks are about doing work on his second home. As the day ended, Steele made one more phone call at 10.34pm. I don't know how long the call lasted, nor what it was about, but it must have been important for him to ring Sarah Saunders at that time of night.

Perhaps he was worried about Tate not eating well? The man mountain clearly had a problem with cuisine. Earlier that evening was involved in another fracas over food. One of his girlfriends, Liz Fletcher, was at the bungalow with him, and had called a local pizza restaurant for a takeaway. Rather than half and half, she asked for a large pizza with a different topping on each quarter. The manager told her to order two small pizzas with different toppings on each half instead. This might have been too difficult for Liz to understand. She couldn't eat two small pizzas, only a single large one. She asked again for her original order. No joy. Tate took hold of the phone. In cyberspace no one can see your size. He argued that the customer was always right. The young manager thought he must have been talking to another bumder from Basildon, and explained that the chef could only make what was on the menu. Half and half, or no pizza at all. It didn't matter what sort of topping you wanted. Tate replied with the legendary "We're talking about cheese, you cunt." He told the manager if they didn't get what they wanted, he would come down and sort the problem out himself. The manager told him to read the menu, learn some manners, and terminated the call. Tate, off his nut on coke topped with steroids, drove to the pizza parlour, and explained his predicament by dough balling the managers head against the salad counter until he blacked out.

The police were called. They had a description of the suspect and the landline number. It wouldn't take long for an arrest to be made. Assault and criminal damage. It seemed like an easy arrest. But then someone in the police explained to the manager that getting a man like Tate nicked might not be a good idea. It seems crazy to think that the police wouldn't want a person still on licence, recently arrested for crashing a drug dealers Porsche, and a known psychopath, locked up over Christmas? But within an hour the manager decided to retract his statement.

No one in the police has yet come forward and explained why this was so. Even more strangely, most criminals would have done a runner that night rather than having to spend Christmas inside, on the basis the old bill might kick his door in at any minute. Tate had just left a civilian covered in blood, knowing the police have his description and his phone number; and at no point does he know that the manager will not press charges. So, what does he do? Fuck all is the answer. Not even lie low on a different sofa for a few days until he knows whats happening. Nothing. The only reason this could be is because at some point that night he is told not to worry about it; which must have come from someone in the police. Whether this was an official order, they wanted him for something really big, or a single copper being very helpful, we don't know. All we can say is that the night before he was killed, Pat was just a cunt hair away from spending Christmas inside. On the morning of the 6th December 1995, Tate must have felt he had blown out all his birthday candles at once.

Chapter 9.

We see things they cannot see.

"Tomorrow, and tomorrow, and tomorrow,
Creeps in this petty pace from day to day,
To the last syllable of recorded time;
And all our yesterdays have lighted fools
The way to dusty death. Out, out, brief candle!
Life's but a walking shadow, a poor player,
That struts and frets his hour upon the stage,
And then is heard no more."
Macbeth.

I

The 6th December 1995. People woke up listening to Gangsta's Paradise on radio One, and were looking forward to going to see Seven at the cinema. They'd heard it was a bit gruesome; but before the days of social media, no one knew how it would all end. The big news was about the weather. Snow had covered the country on the 4th, and was expected to fall again later that evening. Mrs Theobald, who lived with her husband and son at Whitehouse Farm, had already been up for a few hours getting the farm shop ready. They usually did a good trade in Christmas trees, and some were lined up on the parking lot out the front. The shop was just a few hundred yards from Workhouse Lane. When she looked out of the window at around 8am she saw a Range Rover on the forecourt with three large men in it, and a white car. Around the same time another witness was driving along when they see a Range Rover in Workhouse Lane at the junction of the main road, with three men standing near it. A Range Rover could have been a common sight along the country lanes of Essex; but to have the same type of car, with the same amount of men in it found dead exactly twenty-four hours later seems more than just a coincidence.

Workhouse Lane was less than thirty minutes away from the Essex boys' homes. Had they gone there because they expected to find someone, or something, waiting for them. Or had they gone before anyone else was up to look in daylight at the place where the robbery was going to be carried out?

Later that morning Tate and Liz Fletcher attend Basildon Tyre Services. Tate is driving a black Mercedes, Fletcher leaves a VW Polo, saying they will pick it up later. Tate drives away in a Vauxhall Vitara, and Fletcher drives the Mercedes. Tucker and Tate have a conversation on their mobiles at 11.30am. At the same time a neighbour sees a Range Rover outside Rolfe's house with two men in it. At 11.46am Tate's home phone calls Tuckers mobile. The boys then head down to Barry Doorman's car showroom where they meet Peter Cuthbert and arrange the finance payments on the Range Rover. The payments will be in Cuthbert's name, but Tucker is paying the bill. To celebrate they go to TGI Friday's at Lakeside shopping centre. Tate also wants to go there because he is dating one of the waitresses, and has invited her out for a meal at the Global Café that evening. At no point so far has there been any known contact with Mick Steele.

But he hasn't been sitting on his arse. He gets four phone calls from Nicholls that morning. At first glance it looks as if it is actually Nicholls who seems to be dictating events. After the last call, Steele then contacts Whomes for the first time. On the other side of Essex, Tucker, Tate and Rolfe finish their meal, and drive up to L.T. Carpets along Timberlog Lane, as Tucker wants to pay for some work done at an address in Mill Green. This could be the same address in Mill Green where Donna Jaggers later hides the machine gun. A witness believes Tucker pays the bill between 1.30 and 2pm.

A payphone in Sorrell Horse Lane, Ipswich, then calls Tuckers mobile at 2.29pm. The same payphone then calls a payphone at Timberlog Lane at 2.32pm. This is the nearest payphone to Tate's home address just around the corner in Gordon Road. A minute later the payphone in Ipswich calls Tuckers mobile again. Twenty minutes later the same payphone calls Nicholls mobile. It is not clear why the payphone in Ipswich called Tucker that afternoon, as Tate seemed to be the one running things. But it must be Tucker that uses the payphone in Timberlog lane to make the return call. Which raises the question of why didn't Tucker want Tate or Rolfe to hear what he was saying? Perhaps the next talking point is that Steele lived a few miles away from the Sorrell Horse Inn, but Whomes worked less than ten minutes away from it. Both have denied it was them using the payphone. Steele argued why would he call Nicholls from a payphone, and then ten minutes later call Nicholls using his mobile?

At the same time, the Essex boys have turned up at Sarah Saunders mums' house. Sarah had called Tate earlier in the day to say that the car had broken down. When Tate turned up, he turned the ignition on, and the car worked. He then turned on Saunders, to the point Tucker and Rolfe had to restrain him. Tate throws everything out of Saunders VW Golf and drives it away. Within the hour Rolfe must drop Tucker off, and then goes and picks his daughter up from her nans. He then gets a phone call at home from Tate at 3.50pm.

Rolfe is seen driving the Range Rover by detectives outside Grays police station at 4.30pm. Although a disqualified driver, he is not arrested. A detective speaks to Rolfe, and then believes he goes into the police station. Tate picks up his third car of the day; a VW Passat, between five and five-thirty from Barry Dorman's car showroom. Dorman states that Tate had originally spoke about getting the car for Saunders, then changed his mind, but as he had said he would buy it he would still keep his promise.

Doorman doesn't actually see Tate, he has already left, and

this is the showroom calling his mobile; but he does speak to Tate. For whatever reason, Tate wants to take the VW Passat that evening, and said that he would pay Dorman the next day, as he had a lump of money coming. We do not know who was with Tate at around 5pm to either take him to the showroom, or take away the VW Passat. If Tate knows he is going out, why does he need to pick up the VW Passat that night? So now we have Tate leaving a VW Polo at Basildon Tyre services and driving away in a Vitara. Taking Saunders VW Golf from her mum's. And in the early evening he goes to Barry Doorman's car showroom and takes away the VW Passat.

Before this, Bernard O'Mahoney and his partner had been speaking to detectives about threats from Tucker at South Woodham Ferrers police station. They left at around 4pm. O'Mahoney then drove to the mother in laws, which takes a while because it has started to snow again. He drops off his family (I'm not sure if that includes his partner), and then claims he reaches his hotel in Rettendon at about 6.30pm, unaware of the shit storm that is happening up the road.

Now time slips backwards and forwards as we try to follow each person. Donna Jaggers states that Rolfe has driven her to Lakeside shopping centre at around 5.45pm. She is there to get a new dress because they are all going out for a meal to celebrate that night. We know a table for four was booked two days prior, and that some point Tucker calls the restaurant between 6 and 7pm tonight to add another two guests (another call that is not on the edited phone list). The table is booked for 8.30pm.

Rolfe then picks up Tucker from his bungalow in Fobbing at around 6pm. We know this because Tuckers partner, Anna Whitehead, states that he waves goodbye from the front passenger seat as the car drives away. But where is Tate? His bungalow would be about twenty minutes away at this time of night. A witness who works for Basildon Tyre Services states that he closes up the garage at 6pm, leaving the VW Polo on the forecourt for Tate to collect. He then drives out of the garage in his white escort van until he gets to East Maine Road less than five minutes around the corner. He sees the Range Rover with all three men in it driving towards the garage. The same witness also states that when he drove back past the garage sometime after nine, the VW Polo had gone. But how can this be? It's going to take at least fifteen minutes to get from Fobbing to the garage in Cranes Close, and that's without picking Tate up? Now let's include picking this VW Polo up and driving it to...where? And even if they were on their way to the Halfway House pub to meet Steele, they wouldn't be driving along this particular road. Is it possible that Liz Fletcher had arranged to collect it; or that at least one of these three witnesses has made a mistake?

At 5.30pm Tate's next-door neighbour hears a car sounding its horn. He looks out to see a Range Rover turning around. A short time later he hears Tate's front door close, and the Range Rover drive away. But Rolfe should be driving Jaggers to Lakeside.

Workhouse Lane is fifteen minutes from Tate's door. An independent witness driving through Rettendon sees the Range Rover at 5.45pm and identifies two of the men in it as Tucker and Tate. She also goes on to say the Range Rover appeared to be following a white Sierra Cosworth, which possibly had three men in it. Two of them she described as "Large build."

With both of these statements we have witnesses who have no other motive than just telling the police what they saw and heard. This witness goes on to say that the Cosworth and the Range Rover pull into the forecourt of Whitehouse Farm shop. What are the chances of two similar vehicles carrying out exactly the same manoeuvre at exactly the same location in the morning and in the evening and not being linked? This is the last independent confirmed sighting of Tucker and Tate. Even Nicholls, whose account we will get to later, is at pains to point out that when he is waiting with Whomes near the Halfway House pub in Horndon, he sees what he thinks is a Range Rover in his rear-view mirror, but never sees who is actually in the car.

But if we agree that the last confirmed sighting of Tate at 5.45pm is at Whitehouse farm, where does the Range Rover go for the next hour? Where is the VW Passat? They could still get the VW Polo from Basildon Tyre services, but it would be impossible to drive it home and then be at the Halfway House pub (if we go by Nicholls account) in time to meet Steele.

Let us now go to the last time that someone hears Tate's voice. We know that Tate receives a phone call at 6.44pm from Saunders, who has only just got off the phone from speaking to her new boyfriend. For a woman who has been kicked out of the home she owns, and only a few hours ago was almost attacked by an eighteen stone body builder, she spends the next four minutes speaking with him, until at 6.47pm he tells her he has to go as he "is with people." After that, the three men effectively disappear.

Nicholls states that the Range Rover is in Workhouse lane at this point, with Steele sitting next to Tate in the back of the car. The drive from Workhouse Lane to the gate is only a matter of a few hundred yards. The car stops. Rolfe leaves it in drive, handbrake off, with his foot on the brake. The rear door behind him opens. A shotgun cartridge can fire out of the barrel at around 400 miles per second. To reload a pump action shotgun takes under two seconds. As the magazine pulls back, it will eject the empty cartridge through a hole in the side. The empty cartridge can land up to three feet away. The sound of each shot can travel up to a mile. Jack Whomes calls Nicholls at exactly 6.59pm. The call only lasts four seconds. From then on, we will spend the next twenty-five years discussing what happened, and who did it.

II

Timeline. December 1995

1st December – funeral of Leah Betts.

2nd – Billy Blundell visits Barry Doorman at his car showroom. It is not known if they knew each other; nor is it known if the conversation mentions Tate getting the all the drugs money back from Steele at the hotel.

3rd - O'Mahoney moves out of Basildon to the hotel near Rettendon after Tucker threatens him again. He hires a vehicle from "Tavern Hire" in Maldon Essex, despite the fact that he owns at least 3 vehicles of his own.

Billy Blundell calls the Essex boys for a meeting. Only Tate turns up. He is warned that Tucker is upsetting a lot of people, and there may be a hit on him. With Tate being so close, he may also become a target.

Tate calls an associate called Mike on two occasions, thinking he was calling "Mad" Mickey Bowman.

4th - O'Mahoney disappears. He tells friends he spent the day in Birmingham.

Saunders calls Steele and arranges to meet in a nearby McDonalds. She tells him about Tate and the story of Steele taking a trip up north, but he doesn't appear to be too concerned.

5th - Tate assaults the manager in a pizza restaurant in a dispute over the topping. The manager is seriously injured. The police have the suspects address and a description. Initial enquiries quickly show who it is. Someone in the police tells the manager the offender is an extremely dangerous individual, and the manager declines to press charges.

O'Mahoney receives a call from the police. There is a threat to kill him, and could be carried out very soon. He is invited in to the police station for a chat.

One of the last calls Steele makes that night is to Sarah Saunders.

6th December – Day of the Murders.

Approx. 8am. A witness sees a Range Rover at the junction of workhouse Lane with three men standing next to it.

8am. Mrs Theobald is working in the farm shop near Workhouse Lane. She sees a Range Rover with three large men in it, and a white car as they turn into the farm shop car park.

10 – 11am – Tate attends Basildon Tyre Services, leaving a VW

Polo, which he says will pick up later.

11.30am. A neighbour sees the Range Rover outside Rolfe's house. In it are two men.

Morning. Tucker, Tate, Rolfe and Cuthbert attend Barry Dorman's car showroom to sort out the finance for the Range Rover.

1pm – The Essex boys have lunch at TGI Fridays Lakeside shopping centre. Tate asks one of the waitresses to get Clair, another waitress, to call him, as they are going out that night to celebrate.

1.30 – 2pm – Tucker, Tate and Rolfe attend L.T Carpets in Basildon to pay for a carpet that had been laid at an address in Mill Green.

2.29pm – Tucker receives a call from a payphone.

3pm. Tate arrives at Sarah Saunders mums house with Tucker and Rolfe to collect the VW Golf.

3 – 4pm – Rolfe picks up his daughter from his mums' address.

O'Mahoney and wife attend South Woodham Ferrers police station in relation to the threats. They leave at around 4pm. They go to her mothers, leave children there, and head back, passing Rettendon at about 6.30pm.

4.30pm. Detectives in an unmarked car see Rolfe in the Range Rover as drives along Brooke Road and then parks outside Grays police station. They stop behind him. One detective speaks to Rolfe about getting a statement from Donna Jaggers. Rolfe then goes into the station. The detective notes Rolfe is wearing tracksuit bottoms and a puffa jacket.

5 – 5.30pm – Tate collects a VW Passat from Dorman's car showroom.

5.01pm. Receipt signed by Mick Steele for petrol from garage about twenty minutes away from Marks tey. Meaning Steele could not have met Nicholls at 5pm, nor could he have been driving the diesel run Toyota Hilux

5.30pm. Tate's next-door neighbour hears a car horn, looks out to see a Range Rover turning. A short time later he hears Tate's front door close and the Range Rover drives away.

5.45pm – Donna Jaggers states that Rolfe drops her off at Lakeside shopping centre.

5.45pm– Witness sees the Range Rover and three occupants at the Rettendon turnpike. She later identifies Rolfe and Tate.

6pm – Anna Whitehead states that Rolfe picks up Tucker from his bungalow, who gets into the passenger seat and waves goodbye as the Range Rover drives away.

6.05pm – Tucker, Tate and Rolfe are seen in the Range Rover driving towards Basildon Tyre Services.

G. Jackets states that sometime before 7pm on the 6th, Tucker called him to increase the booking from 4 to 6 people at the Global Café. This call is not on the phone list.

6.44pm – Sarah calls Tate on his mobile. He tells her he has to go as he is "with people." The call ends at 6.47pm

6.59pm – Whomes calls Nicholls.

7-7.30pm – Mrs Theobald at Whitehouse farm hears the sound of a shotgun.

10pm. Mr Wilkin sees an estate type vehicle come out of the back of Pound Farm (the other side of workhouse Lane) and drive away. Nicholls thinks his VW Passat may have been an estate, but then again, he cannot recall what car he was driving that day.

7th December –

6.30am – Superintendent Bright of Essex police is informed by a detective in the drugs squad that three men had been shot in a Range Rover in Rettendon.

8am. Two farmers drive up Workhouse Lane to feed the pheasants. One of them walks up to the car and sees the bodies. Police are called. It is not known if this mobile phone call ever subjected to cell site.

8.15am – Police arrive. Crime scene started.

Early morning - O'Mahoney calls his friend Gavin, who worked at Raquel's, and Sue Woods. O'Mahoney tells them that Tucker, Tate and Rolfe are dead. This is before 10am.

9.15am – Police doctor arrives to confirm victims are dead, but does not give a time of death in order to preserve crime scene.

12.15pm – Dr Lannas arrives. Checks bodies, but does not examine for time of death in order to preserve any forensic evidence. In the Range Rover is an empty Head sports bag, and among the three dead men is a total of two thousand pounds in cash.

12.20pm. Acting upon information received, armed police arrest Barry Dorman and two others on suspicion of murder, after stopping a car in Essex.

Afternoon – the bodies are kept in the Range Rover and taken back to a police station. Although an autopsy is carried out, there is still no record of a time of death.

Afternoon/evening – After all three bodies have been identified, the family of each victim are told. On hearing the news, Tucker's father has a heart attack and dies.

8th December

From information received to the police, they are quoted as saying "it was a brilliantly executed assassination. The victims were lured to the lane to discuss having someone else hit, but the tables were turned on them. We had excellent information that Rolfe and Tate had been trying to hire a killer to rub out a rival drug dealer, but it seems the intended victim got his shot in first. Their intended victim pushed ecstasy in Raquels Nightclub in Basildon."

Police get information that it was someone from Hertfordshire who carried out the killing over a cocaine deal.

12th December. A new set of door staff take over Raquel's nightclub. O'Mahoney attends and threatens them. They decide not to take the job, and O'Mahoney and his team are reinstated. A week later O'Mahoney loses his doorman licence.

Chapter 10.

I read the News today oh boy.

JAN. 26, 1998—"I did not have sexual relations with that woman, Miss Lewinsky."
President Bill Clinton.

AUG 17, 1998 - After being told there was evidence to the contrary. "Indeed, I did have a relationship with Ms Lewinsky that was not appropriate."
President Bill Clinton.

I

7th December 1995, the anniversary of Pearl harbour, and now new information as to whether or not the English Government was secretly aware the attack was going to take place. Then you get a phone call. A triple murder. Three men found dead in a car down a country lane. You are going to be the person in charge. You have dealt with a couple of murders already this year, so there isn't much that can shock you. You make your way there as scene of crime officers do their work. Rettendon is a small village near the A130. Most of the surrounding fields are used for pheasant shooting and fishing. There is a farmhouse shop nearby. Workhouse Lane is off a road that leads up to the Rettendon turnpike. The traffic is already slowing down to try and see what's going on. A line has been set out to avoid contaminating possible tyre and footmarks. You walk up the cleared route. On the left is another track. This leads past White House farm and all the way down to the Wheatsheaf pub. You walk up and around a bend. There is snow and ice on the ground, but no frost on the Range Rover. A rear window has been smashed and the sunroof is slightly open; any heat from the three bodies would have dissipated fairly quickly. The farmers say the lane leads to some woods and a small fishing lake. In front of the car is a locked gate, and blood on the tracks.

The engine is turned off, but the key is in the ignition and the car is set in drive with the handbrake down as if it was about to move towards the gate (you make a note to ask if the lights come on when the engine is started again). As you move closer you get told the car was stopped yesterday outside Grays police station. The driver was Craig Rolfe, a young man linked to the death of a drug dealer last year. He was in the same vehicle a few weeks ago, and was summoned for driving whilst disqualified. His description matches the man in the driver's seat. He's been shot in the back of the head at close range. The headrest has damage to it. Rolfe is also linked to drug dealing in Essex. You think this is probably a gangland hit. It looks like he has been shot twice.

Another officer tells you that the front passenger matches the description of Tony Tucker. Strangely enough, his name was also mentioned yesterday during a conversation with Bernard O'Mahoney, the former head doorman of Raquels nightclub; the place where the ecstasy pill that killed Leah Betts was obtained. Tucker had threatened to kill O'Mahoney after he spoke to the press. Tucker has also been shot into the back of the head at least twice.

You wonder if the shots were fired when the double boot on the Range Rover was opened up. In the boot is an empty hold-all. There are shotgun cartridges around the car. were there two killers? But no one seems to have tried to defend themselves. Perhaps the killer was in the car, got out using the door behind the driver, opened the boot, then fired. But where were the victims going?

You look at the third man in the back. Somebody mentions Tucker's other associate, Pat Tate. Again, his name came up yesterday for an assault of the manager in a pizza parlour. Tate had been released from prison for a firearms offence about a month ago, after he had been found with a gun in hospital. Apparently, he had threatened to kill someone, and they shot him in the arm. It is not known why he wasn't arrested last night. Fuck me, you've got one man making a threat to kill, another who got away with murder, and the third who was trying to shoot someone just before he went back to prison. Why weren't any of them arrested yesterday? No one answers. Seriously, why was not one of them arrested after all being suspected of committing a criminal offence?

You notice that Tate has been shot into the right side of the stomach, and then two into the left side of his head. Why would someone fire from one side of the car, and then walk around and fire from the other side. Eight shots from a double barrel would take a bit of time to complete. Again you wonder if there had been two killers?

The blue shotgun cartridges were dropped when there was snow on the ground (get a full weather report for last night). They all look the same. There is one footprint near the front passenger side of the vehicle. Looking back down the lane, you notice there are other tyre tracks, quite a few of them, which must have happened in the last couple of hours.

Now you are thinking the killer was in another car, which has driven up behind the Range Rover (possibly to go into the field). But the killer wouldn't have been driving. He would have been sitting in the back with the shotgun ready, hidden in a holdall (and possibly a backup gun). Someone in the Range Rover gets out, leaves the rear door open, the interior light on. The killer drops the holdall, and fires. You take another step back. This must be at least a three-man job, possibly four. Tate is holding a mobile phone. Did he call his killer? Was this a drugs meeting?

You assume it must have been for a meeting with someone they knew, otherwise you might have picked somewhere a bit more public. You remember that a large consignment of cannabis had been found dumped in the nearby reservoir. They must have been waiting for a while, as there is a small trace of black powder on the ground just under the exhaust pipe. You look again at the bodies, and think that another car turned up with the lights on full beam, forcing the men to look away. Someone gets out of the Range Rover to say they are getting something out of the boot, possibly drugs. The killer walks up, unseen. The first shots are fired before anyone in the Range Rover can react, especially if it's a pump action. Between the moment the man got out of the Ranger Rover and to when all three are dead, it could have taken less than three minutes.

You look across the fields. Did anyone hear the gunshots (another question about the time of death)? The decoy and the killer then get into the getaway car. It reverses until it can turn around in the track road, and then it's gone. Three men dead. Possibly three men involved in the killing. You make the decision to lift the car with the bodies still inside. Hopefully the forensics or phone calls will give a result for the time of death.

II

This was a rough idea of what may have happened based on the scene that morning. It's easy to see how you could come up with the two killer's and a gangland hit theory. When I look at photographs of the Range Rover by the gate, I find it extremely difficult to believe that someone was hiding behind a clump of bushes ready to sneak up unannounced. From Darren Nicholls account we are expected to believe that the Range Rover parks in the exact spot that allows Jack Whomes, who is hiding behind a thin strip of bushes, to get up, walk around until he is able to walk through the gap that just happened to be in the right spot by the fact the Range Rover has stopped just in front of it, down the embankment at least fifteen feet away from the car in his wellies and overalls carrying two shotguns, puts one down God knows where, realises he had been lucky enough to have picked the side of the road that matched the same side of the car where Steele was sitting, and gets ready to fire from just inside the rear door, all without being seen or heard by the three men in the car?

Forensic evidence shows the Range Rover had been stationary for a number of minutes. I am not sure when the police officially come up with the theory that there was someone hiding behind the bush, but the only reason they stick with it is because there is mention of some of the earth behind the clump of bushes having been disturbed, and it fits Nicholls account.

There was mud on Tuckers boots, which if they came from Workhouse Lane meant he had got out of the car at some point. A leaf was also stuck to the blood underneath Rolfe's seat. The Range Rover had stopped far enough away from the gate to allow it to open; but how did Rolfe know which way the gate went? The window next to Tate had been smashed (possibly by Tate as there are fragments outside). But some of the glass is on the seat behind Tate, which indicated someone had fired from the offside, and then taken the time to come around to the other side and shoot him again at very close range. In front of the vehicle between the tyre ruts was a trainer print, size seven or eight. Not something you'd be wearing walking around a field in the winter. In 1995 DNA was still a new science. Photographs showed various items in the back; and empty crisp packet, a sweet wrapper, a plastic lid from bottle. They might be worth a go. The only problem was that they were all movable objects. Anyone whose fingerprints or DNA were found on them could claim they had been dropped ages ago. Two mobile phones had been seized. One on Tucker, one on Tate. Strangely, all three men have address books on them. What happened to Rolfe's phone?

But now other information about the killings is coming in; some of it before even the police knew it had happened. There is the mysterious report logged at 6am that morning by the Essex drugs unit of three men that had been killed in a Range Rover. This seems to disappear by the time the trial comes around; then resurfaces a few years later, but nothing seems to come of it. What we do know is that the vehicle and its occupants would no doubt be on the drugs units' radar. They would have already had the car linked to Rolfe, Tucker, and Tate, and so would no doubt pass any information on to the enquiry team dealing with the death of Leah Betts. They, having only recently spoken to Bernard O'Mahoney about the threat to his life from Tucker, probably contacted the surveillance unit for them to discretely check on his address, just in case there are more bodies yet to be discovered. The vice unit had an interest in Tate and the prostitution business he was running with the help of his mother. They might have also contacted the probation office in relation to the release of Nipper Ellis, who had shot Tate last year. At the same time, it would have been a good idea to contact the registered informants' unit to see if anyone knew anything about the killings; perhaps that job was given to DC Wolfgang Bird. You might have also asked the officers who stopped Rolfe yesterday, the officers, who went to the pizza parlour on that that as well; and those who spoke to O'Mahoney.

It gets better. The murder unit is being set up next door to the unit dealing with the death of Leah Betts. Already, reports were coming in of television crews and reporters turning up at the scene that the two were linked. Police had only just confirmed who the dead bodies were. Then the police became aware that Tucker had a mistress when the sixteen-year-old Donna Garwood kept calling to say she was his partner, and so did Anna Whitehead. Believing it would be easier if they told Tucker's parents, his father subsequently had a heart attack and died when informed of the news.

Tate was just as eventful. He had been married and divorced in the early eighties, then had a child with Sarah Saunders, but was now in a relationship with at least three different women. He was running a brothel with his mum, who was scared that her own son was trying to kill her. Sarah Saunders, who had spent the night going out for a drink with her new partner, and then staying at his address for the first time, said she heard something about it when someone called her partner and told him three men had been shot in a Range Rover. They looked on Teletext, the pre millennial version of the internet, but couldn't see any names. Only Rolfe seemed to be the one with the most stable home life. His partners details were on file, as she had given a statement to confirm Rolfe's alibi after he had been suspected of being involved in the death of Kevin Whitaker.

Ivan Dibley had joined the police in 1974. He was there when the first investigation into police corruption took out a lot of officers; and again when PACE was introduced in the eighties. In 1995 he had already solved ten murders that year, and the only difference with this one is the amount of bodies. He was to later say it was Donna Jaggers who told him the story of how the Essex boys were going to meet "Mickey the Pilot;" although I think it was someone else who told the police that information. The only bit of luck Dibley had at that time was when he was told about cell site analysis – finding the location of a mobile through its strength against three transmitter masts, and how it may be the clue to solve this case. If you had the list of who they spoke to that day, you could also do cell site on those phones as well. Not only does it give you an idea of who they were speaking to; it would also give you an idea of when the time for talking was over.

III

Perhaps even more surprising was the number of possible suspects that Dibley had from the very start. Most murders have three things in common: Means, Motive, Opportunity. A shotgun is a serious piece of kit. If it was a professional job you would want to get the right man in. They would be carrying two weapons (you don't want to take one gun only to find out it doesn't work). And a shotgun, because of its adaptability and its anonymity, could be got illegally if you knew the right people. A swan off was easier to turn, especially if you point the it inside a car. As for motive, if this is a gangland hit, then where do you start? There are those who may have been robbed by them, and those who were out to take over them. There are also other motives. Fear, jealousy, revenge. Leah Betts father would later be arrested for the murders; but how would he arrnage to meet them; and why were there no weapons in the Ranger Rover?

The day after the murders the police search Tate's bungalow and find a handgun in the garden. Rumour had it that he never went anywhere without a gun. So what was he doing at the end of Workhouse Lane? Whoever did this would have links with the Essex boys, which probably makes them a criminal as well. Ok, not a good start, but we can be more specific and say the killer had close links with the three men killed. Let's be even more specific. Tate has only been out six weeks. He was the one somebody took the time to come around to his side of the car and shoot him at point blank range. Lets say the killer had targeted him specifically. That narrows it down to someone who had dealings with them since November.

Tucker ran the doors of a lot of clubs, including the one where the pill that killed Leah Betts was bought. If he had been arrested and decided to tell police everything it would certainly be a big problem for a lot of people.

Rolfe was the only dark horse. He had been linked to one death, but was there anything in his past that would make him the target? It was possible that he had done something, and someone waited long enough to get the proof. It was also possible that he was just a man in the wrong place at the wrong time.

What about opportunity? The killer, or at least someone able to get them to the lane, must have known the victims well. But was this a spur of the moment thing, or had it taken a couple of weeks to plan? You are aware that drug dealers often have a burner phone, one they use solely for criminal purposes and cannot be traced back to them. Was this Rolfe? Had the killer contacted him on that phone, and that was the only one they needed to take after the killings. The killer had organised the meeting, choosing the location and time. This means they know the area and would have been up a few times to check. The farmer says he closed the gate around four when it got dark. That gives you a starting time. Hopefully the pathologist will give the time of death within a few hours. All threevictims planned to go out for a meal at 8.30pm. If it wasn't for the empty holdall in the boot, you would think they had taken a wrong turn.

So how far have we got in trying to build up a picture of the killer, or at the very least someone who knew what was going to happen. A fellow criminal, probably previous convictions for drug offences, and was able to get hold of a shotgun. He must have known at least two of them, and certainly seemed to have an issue with Tate. But they were able to lure all of them down a country lane in the dark without any of them concerned that something bad was going to happen. So, what does that mean; something good was going to happen? Even without any names, that jigsaw puzzle is beginning to piece together of a fellow criminal who knew them well enough to be able to,lure them to their deaths.

As the police looked into the lives of their three men, they were surprised they had not been killed earlier. Tate would regularly take what would be called a "heroic" quantity of drugs; enough to make the daily schedule of Hunter S. Thompson seem tame in comparison. Some of the reporters at the scene had also covered the death of Leah Betts, and when they had heard the names of Tucker, Tate and Rolfe, they quickly linked it to the death of Leah Betts. In another article, it was reported that a crime lord had offered the father of Leah to kill the men because of it. No doubt Dibley thought it was bollocks, unfortunately, he was only half wrong.

The story of the leader of a crime cartel offering to take out the Essex boys had an element of truth. The Metropolitan police had been running their own secret investigation into corrupt officers; and just after the death of Leah Betts there was a meeting between one detective and a major criminal. Knowing that business was going to be severely hampered by an upsurge in police raids; the crime boss offered to kill the people involved and put it down to a gangland hit. How the press got hold of it was unknown. There had long been a link with detectives, criminals, and reporters all drinking in the same pub, or going to the same lodge. The problem grew worse when the Metropolitan police and Essex police said they never made deals with criminals. Only for them to have to make a deal with a criminal in order to solve this investigation.

Chapter 11.

Pot shots.

The aftermath, and the pauses in-between.

"I watched a snail crawl along the edge of a straight razor. That's my dream. That's my nightmare: crawling, slithering, along the edge of a straight razor and surviving."
Apocalypse Now

I

Supt Dibley has always claimed that within forty-eight hours he had someone called "Mickey the pilot," as a person of interest. Whether this information came from Donna Jaggers, after having been told her partner of eight years had just been killed, or someone else, remains to be seen. Dibley then says he has another stroke of luck, when he asks an intelligence officer if they know who "Mickey the Pilot" is, and he is given a name straight away. Mick Steele, a man who was last arrested whilst washing down his boat.

There were other bits of information about the murders coming in. "The Adams family from London are heavily involved in drugs. There was meant to be a fourth person in the car with the three deceased. This person is supposed to have been killed and burnt in a car." But Dibley barely had time to read anything.

On the 7th three men were stopped by armed police and arrested on suspicion of the murders. One of them was Barry Dorman, the used car salesman. How and why police decided

Dorman was a suspect is still not known. All three were interviewed, and afterwards Doorman gave a statement. In it he spoke about selling the Range Rover and the Passat; but nothing about Billy Blundell coming to see him just a few days before the murders, or his trip to Ostend to help bring back drug money. This would have been significant due to who else was in that hotel at the time; but we have to remember that not everything people tell the police goes into the statement.

Doorman mentioned that he had seen all of them that morning, along with Peter Cuthbert, to sort out the finance for the Range Rover. The last time he heard from Pat Tate was sometime after 5pm. Doorman had left the office when he got a call from the showroom to say that Tate had come back to pick up a VW Passat. He told Doorman that he would pay for the car the next morning as he had a "lump of money coming". Doorman never saw Tate, and possibly the car, ever again. It is unclear why Tate suddenly needed the VW Passat that late in the day, when he was in the middle of what he believed to be a million-pound cocaine deal.

On 8th December the police received information that Tucker and Tate had been looking for someone to carry out a hit for them on a rival dealer who had been trying to take over Raquel's. They had gone to workhouse Lane for a meeting, and to pay the hitman and his associate. The rival dealer had heard about it, and double crossed them instead. But surely this would have been old news, as we knew at the start of december that Tucker was making threats to kill someone.

Now we can say that this points to O'Mahoney, but his argument seemed to be about controlling the doors rather than being directly involved with the drugs. What this bit of information shows us is how early the theory of the double cross starts. None of the Essex boys were believed to be carrying weapons at the time; which adds to the story of them meeting someone they trusted. We also have the Essex boys waiting for two people to turn up.

We are now 48hrs into the investigation. The two phones

were being checked. Information as to who the killer might be went as far as London, Kent and Hertfordshire. Dibley was old enough to remember the Krays, with Ronnie being able to kill someone in a packed pub and seemingly get away with it. Some people didn't grass because they thought the twins were great; others wouldn't speak because they were scared of them. Now police were facing a similar thing with the Essex boys. Everyone had an opinion, but that doesn't mean they would be willing to attend court. Dibley remembered the Krays were caught after one of their gang turned Queens evidence and decided to work for the prosecution. Perhaps that would be the way of solving these murders? There was no forensics, no eyewitnesses, and not much else happening as they went into the new year.

In January 1996 the police got a surprise. East end criminal Billy Jasper had been arrested for a different offence; but in custody he started to speak about what happened in Rettendon. He said he was with Jesse Gale and a man named Paul in a pub one night a few weeks prior to the murders. Jasper was told that Tucker and Tate were going to rob the Canning Town Cartel of a consignment of drugs, but it was going to be a double cross, and they were going to be set up. Paul asked Jasper if he wanted to drive him when he organised the meet before the robbery happened. On the night of the 6th Jasper drove into east London in a stolen car to pick up Paul, wearing a tracksuit and trainers, and carrying a Head sports bag. Jasper thought it was going to be some sort of cocaine deal., but then saw what looked like a sawn-off shotgun in the holdall. Paul told Jasper where to go, and got out somewhere in Rettendon. Jasper parked up and waited for about forty minutes. He believed it might have been around midnight, but couldn't be sure. Paul returned with the holdall, and they go back to London. It is not known if the car Jasper was in had false registration plates, and if any part of the shotgun was thrown away.

Jasper told police he did not know Paul was going to shoot them until after it had happened. On two occasions he directed police to Rettendon. His account fitted with some of the witness's statements; such as one person hearing a "fusillade" of shots at around midnight coming from the direction of Workhouse Lane. Both Jasper and Jesse Gale were well known in the criminal underworld. The man known as Paul could have been the "Mr D" that police wished to speak to in relation to other killings. He was believed to be a former soldier, and professional hitman. The Met must have thought they had solved the case for Essex themselves when they made the call. But for whatever reason Essex police decided not to investigate Jaspers account. Perhaps they were aware that the London Crime Cartel that Jasper was linked to was also being investigated due to its links with corrupt police officers. This would have caused problems, as Essex had only just started their own internal investigation into the same thing.

Operation Apache was set up at the start of 1996 to investigate police corruption in Essex. For it to have been approved by the Home Office, there must have been some evidence of serious police corruption. The time it would take to authorise such an event would take a few weeks. That means Essex police may have had very good information about police corruption linked to the death of Leah Betts, or even the murders themselves. As for why a detective may wish to get involved with such things, the reason was simple: money.

Felixstowe and Harwich ports were known to be bringing in millions of pounds worth of drugs every years. Planes were dropping it from the sky, and we knew that it was coming over in small boats. It would be easy for one copper to look the other way, pass on sensitive information, alter evidence so that no one would be charged, or make sure the wrong people were, all for the right price. But this was a dangerous game. Sometimes the line between detective and criminal became so blurred it was impossible to tell who was who.

Donna Jaggers first statement, dated 8th Feb 1996, is about the machine gun hidden at the Mill Green address. She named Mickey Bowman as the man Rolfe got it from, and believed it was in the middle of November 1995. Bowman was driving a white car when they meet, and the exchange took place just a few miles away from Workhouse Lane. Strangely, Jaggers gave the gun to the police on 11th Jan 1996, but there is no explanation as to why it took nearly a month to get the statement about it.

It's not until the 15th February that the police arrested Bowman on suspicion of the murders, and possession of a firearm. In interview he spoke about the various meetings he had with Tucker, Tate and Rolfe, essentially to sell a motor car. Now it is worth pointing out that Bowman had been nicked more times that Stevie Wonder having a shave, so he knew the ropes. He puts himself at Tate's bungalow on the day when Sarah Saunders is moving out. He mentions that someone gives him a lift back to south east London in a cream coloured car. This driver may have been called "Tommy," who was short, and aged around 27-28 (Darren Nicholls was 27 at the time of the murders). Bowman never admits to handing over the machine gun, but can remember being in the Range Rover (just in case his fingerprints had been found in it). On one occasion he mentions going out on Tuckers birthday (the time of the deal). This would mean he is at the Global café with everyone else, apart from Tate and Rolfe. Which is strange, as he goes out of his way to tell police that he was mainly friends with Tate. He makes a passing reference about meeting Bernard O'Mahoney at a club just before December. This is possibly when O'Mahoney confronts Tucker about the threats to him. He tells police that Tate called him the day before he was murdered, just for a chat, but he knows nothing about a machine gun, nor who could have wanted them dead.

We've had a couple of arrests now, and still the list of suspects keeps growing. There are those, such as Mark Bates, a bodybuilder and cocaine dealer from Hertfordshire with links with the Adams family, who comes up a few times as being involved. Luckily, Dave Courtney, who owns a doorman company similar to Tuckers, and helped organise the funeral of Ronnie Kray, gives a statement to say that around 6pm he saw Bates in a pub in east London that night.

It would be fair to say the police needed a breakthrough, no matter what the cost. And it was costing a lot of money. The Government was losing control of law and order. The drug dealer Mark Murray was still hiding somewhere in Spain. There was a worry that the killer may have done as well after being tipped off by someone in the force. In one of life's strange ironies; even though the investigation was costing millions, if anyone was looking for one of the main suspects, they could have gone to the staff canteen and asked some of the detectives having their bacon sandwich which one of them knew Darren Nicholls.

II

In his book Bloggs 19, it is just three weeks after the murders that Nicholls is approached in a pub by a detective who knew he was a drug dealer. It's unclear where that information had come from, as Nicholls had been fortunate enough never have been arrested for any drug offences. That is the official version. Unfortunately, the detective was one of those cops being investigated by other cops. For all involved it would certainly be better for all if the official meeting took place in January. Any suspicion that Nicholls was speaking to police before the murders would raise some very serious concerns. Nicholls writes that over the coming weeks and months he grew very concerned for his own safety regarding Steele and Whomes.

When he takes the shotgun to Steele's place after the murders, he says that Steele took the rifle out of the case…and waved it around in front of him. That was when it dawned on him, he was in trouble. And does he tell DC Bird? Of course not. Instead he tells the detective where he dumped the fake cannabis in order to get a financial reward; and to become a registered police informant. This is a strange relationship, as Nicholls and DC Bird discuss who to grass on, including former friends, and arresting the people who had previously bought cannabis off Nicholls.

There is also mention of stealing the drugs money when it is in the boot of a car on its way to Amsterdam. They talk about setting up a drug factory with the profits. None of these things seem to be the work of a man concerned for his own safety. If anything, the only man in danger was Steele. For he was not only about to be stitched up by Nicholls, DC Bird, and DS Stimpson, the Government were also looking to set him up.

Operation Edzell was the investigation into the murder of Rachel Nickell on Wimbledon Common in 1992. Part of the investigation involved a female officer going undercover to be a "honeytrap," a term first used during the Profumo scandal in the belief that men are more willing to talk if sex is on the cards. In Op Edzell, the police arranged a female officer to become friendly with the prime suspect Colin Stagg, a man into light bondage and black magic. As there was no evidence to arrest Stagg, the police decided to make some up. The female officer began to call and write to Stagg saying that she got turned on by the thought of being abused and strangled. Colin, an unemployed single man in his thirties with teeth like tombstones, readily agreed that he would be willing to do all of that, on the basis that he thought he was going to have sex.

During a recorded interview the officer asked Stagg about the murder on Wimbledon common and how it turned her on; to which he replied that he knew nothing about it. He may have lived in the area, he may have even seen her out walking on previous occasions, but he didn't do it. The police decided that even though there was no forensic evidence linking him to the murder and no eyewitnesses that saw him anywhere near the scene, they had enough to arrest him. On the advice of his solicitor he went "No comment" in interview. He was charged in August 1993 and was remanded in prison until the trial got to the Old Bailey a year later in September 1994. At the preliminary hearing the judge declared the police had shown "excessive zeal" and had tried to incriminate a suspect by "deceptive conduct of the grossest kind." Stagg was released to a world where a lot of people thought he had done it. The police couldn't have been wrong on this one, surely?

It was not until November 2007 that police arrested Robert Napier for the murder, who by then was in Broadmoor after being convicted of a similar killing. He subsequently pleaded guilty to the manslaughter of Rachel Nickell on December 2008. After fourteen years of having to wait to clear his name, Colin Stagg was given a formal apology by the Metropolitan police, and awarded damages of over seven hundred thousand pounds.

Rather than a honey trap, Essex police decided to go for an Irish one. In February 96 Dibley authorised Operation Century. This was a series of phone calls to Steele and Sarah Saunders in which police pretended to be two brothers working for the IRA. They were demanding money back that they had given to Pat Tate for a drugs deal. Clearly this was to get them to talk about the murders, with each call becoming more and more sinister. One can only assume that this conduct was authorised because either Steele or Saunders phones had been bugged, and it was hoped that they would talk about the murders after being threatened. But the whole notion of who sanctioned this investigation is very dubious. For a start, there appears to be no written policy in what the two "Mullock" brothers could say. Secondly, you may think it part of the course to go after Mick Steele; but to threaten a young single mum at home alone with a baby after her partner had been murdered seems beyond the realms of what the police are actually allowed to do in the name of the British Government. Thirdly, this secret operation may not have seen the light of day if Steele had not recorded some of the phone calls after the threats took a more serious turn. Saunders later went to the police because she was terrified, only to be told that the phone number used by the brothers did come from a well-known IRA pub in Ireland, and that the people involved may already be in England.

It was only when Steele put the recorded phone call in as part of his defence because he believed that the IRA could have been the killers that the truth finally emerged. When the defence asked for an answer, the police declared that some of the people involved were still subject of the Official Secrets Act, and so not one officer attended court to account for their actions. The police also claimed that they were not going to show the policy document for the operation, and that they themselves had not actually recorded all the conversations.

It would seem by February the police had the choice of investigating Jasper or Steele, and went for the easier target. But before we move on, let's look at someone else who was still just outside the frame.

You may wonder why the police didn't bring in the man they had spoken to on the day of the murders about a threat to his life from Tony Tucker. Bernard O'Mahoney writes in his books that he left the police station around four that afternoon and drove to his mother in laws house. He then went back to the hotel at around 6pm, a hotel that was less than a mile away from the murder scene. He does not say what he did for the rest of the evening. On the early morning of the 7th, O'Mahoney writes he's in London. When he checks his voice mail, there is a message that a detective wants to speak to him. He may know already what this is for, as Sue Woods, who used to work at Raquel's and knew both O'Mahoney and Tucker, later says that O'Mahoney had called her at 10am to speak about the murders.

When O'Mahoney returned to Essex to meet his wife, police officers were also waiting. He handed over the large holdall he was carrying for officers to search, but they didn't even arrest him. This would have given the police due cause to check phone records and get O'Mahoney to go into more details about his actions the night before. Could it be because he was also the star witness in the Leah Betts enquiry? If he walked away from that, the case would collapse, and chances are the police would be criticised more about a member of the public killed by drugs, than three criminals who were killed because of them.

Instead, they drove him home. As they drive, O'Mahoney tells them he remembers meeting Tucker and Tate outside a night club in Southend a few days before the killings, and definitely remembers putting his hands on the Range Rover as they chatted. When they reach his house, for some reason the door is open. O'Mahoney and armed police go in; but luckily his wife must have just not closed the door properly when she left earlier. One strange thing about this is at what point did O'Mahoney feel it was safe enough for him and his wife to book out of the hotel, leave her mum's house, and go back to the home they had left because of the ongoing threats by the Essex boys? They were not named until a lot later in the day.

On the 25th January O'Mahoney met DI Storey, possibly to speak about the Leah Betts enquiry, but there is no record of the conversation. He makes a statement on 30th Jan in relation to drugs at Raquel's nightclub; and in it he claimed to know nothing about how the system worked and who were the dealers. Things change on February 13th after a report appeared in the Sun newspaper, when reporter Ian Hepburn stated that police believed the weapons and ammunition might have been hidden at the scene beforehand by the assassin, who had travelled with the ill-fated trio and had picked up the murder weapon after pretending to open a farm gate. This article appeared at the same time police were speaking to Donna Jaggers about the machine gun, and pretending to be the IRA when they speak to Mick Steele and Sarah Saunders.

On 15th Feb Mad Mickey Bowman was arrested for the murders. It possibly means another search of the area. O'Mahoney calls Ian Hepburn and tells him just a few days prior to Bowman being arrested, he had been to see where his friends had died, and whilst standing at the gate he had disturbed the undergrowth and found a live shotgun cartridge that was possibly a few weeks old. He picked it up, then lobbed it into a field. It is not until he got home that he realised if a new search was carried out and the police found the cartridge on which he had only just put his fingerprints on, he would be in a right pickle. He told Hepburn to report it to the police, saying the cartridge may have been there for a month or so. I am not sure if the fact that the men had been shot eight times but only seven cartridges were found had been made public at this stage; but it certainly seems a bizzare coincidence.

A few days later O'Mahoney was invited in for another conversation by the police. He said he had finally gone to see where his friends had died, and couldn't believe it when he found the shotgun cartridge. He only realised what a palaver it would cause after he had thrown it away. He then had to admit he had been to the scene before when police informed him that his car had been spotted at Workhouse Lane on six separate occasions since the murders. It was also strange that he could not identify where he had thrown the blue shotgun cartridge. He was a big man, but he was getting out of shape. For the police search team, this was a full-time job. But they did not find the cartridge.

O'Mahoney was questioned again on May 1st by detectives from Leicestershire police, this time about the murder of Danny Marlow. He was a low-level criminal who owed money to various people, and the year before O'Mahoney was asked to recover the debt by a friend of Tate, a car dealer by the name of John Marshall. O'Mahoney was never arrested for being involved in the murder of Marlow; but within weeks there would be more arrests in relation to the Essex boys, and two men would eventually be charged with the murders of Tucker, Tate and Rolfe.

III

Donna Jaggers made six statements in total. In the one dated 8th February when the machine gun was obtained, she stated Rolfe was in the blue Range Rover, Bowman was in a white V.W. Corrado, and another male was in a Vauxhall Cavalier. Jaggers described the driver of the Cavalier as a small man about 5'6 tall, aged early thirties, with short cropped hair and wore glasses. She mentions that Craig used his mobile phone, so we know he had one. She also says that her and Craig went back to Tate's bungalow on the day Saunders was moving out of it. We know that Bowman said he also goes there, which seems inconsistent with her account. She says that Tucker is there with his partner, but she does not mention Steele or his partner. And if we remember Bowman's account, there was a male waiting outside in a cream coloured car, possibly a Saab 900 or a Fiat. The driver might be called Tommy, short, aged about 28. He drives Bowman back to the car showroom to collect his cheque, and then back to South east London.

What is remarkable about this mystery driver is how similar he is to the man Jaggers saw; and the description could match that of Darren Nicholls. And it is surprising Jaggers cannot recall Steele being there, as her statement from 14th March, three months after the murders, seems to show Jagger's amazing memory skills, and is worth going through in detail.

"I am the common law wife of Craig Rolfe whom had been my partner for seven years. I have been asked about Craig's association with Tony Tucker and Pat Tate and their involvement with drug dealing, and the circumstances surround their deaths. Craig had been involved with Tucker for approximately three or four years and was registered as a director of Tucker's security company running nightclub doors. This was in name only and I know that Craig never had any involvement in running the business. His association started as a result of Tucker buying drugs from Craig. They then became more involved as time went on and they started doing drugs deals together. In early 95 Craig was not being very active and was not completing many deals therefore he did not have much money.

He was being promised that a large deal was due which would provide him with plenty of money, in the mean time we were scraping to get by. I later learnt from Craig that a person called Mickey 'The Pilot' who I now know to be called Michael Steele, was a friend of Pat Tate, who in turn was a friend of Tony Tucker. Steele, I understood to be a pilot who brought drugs into the country, and I understood that he had been in prison for it. Craig told me that Steele was a ruthless person who really didn't think very much of other people. In early 95 I was aware that Tate was in prison and I recall Tucker and one other person, whose details I do not know, running around getting Tate's money together for him to finance the deal. I am fairly sure that John McCarthy had some of Tate's money. Craig told me that this was happening and stated that Steele was happy to continue bringing it in until they were all millionaires. I cannot say when the deal took place but I can say that at that time I witnessed the changeover of the drugs. Mickey Steele drove to Longwood Stables in Basildon, where Tucker had two horses. I arrived there with Craig and met Tony who was with his horses.

We waited for Mick to arrive, which he did in a blue Toyota RAV4. Although I had remained in our car and I had my back to where Mickey Steele had parked, I was able to look over my left shoulder towards the rear of his car. I saw Steele take a large dark coloured kit bag, measuring approximately three feet in length by about twelve to fifteen inches in diameter, from the boot of his car. By the way he was holding the bag it appeared to be very heavy. He handed it to Tucker who put it in the boot of our car which was a Vauxhall Senator. Craig then got back into our car and drove to another location. Craig took the holdall out of the boot and took it to a "safe house' where all the drugs were stored. I went into the house with Craig who then placed the bag on the table.

He opened the bag up and I saw that it contained bars of brown cannabis resin which were all individually wrapped in a clear film. I was present when he checked that it was good quality by burning and smelling a sample and then counting the bars. I am unable to say how many bars there were. I have only met Mickey Steele on a couple of occasions and that was only in passing. I have not actually spoken to Steele. On each occasion when I have seen him, he has always made me very aware that he does not want me to look at him. The last deal which Steele carried out for them was approximately two weeks after Tate was released from prison. Craig told me that Steele was arranging to bring in sixty thousand pounds worth of cannabis from abroad. Craig put in seven thousand pounds, Tucker put in twenty, Tate and a fourth person called Barry Doorman were putting in the remainder of the money. A couple of days before the cannabis was collected, I went with Craig to Tucker's home address in Fobbing, Essex, to hand him the seven thousand pounds which was in a Tesco's carrier bag. The money was handed to Tucker who was in turn going to hand it to Steele.

We were only at the house for about five minutes and as Craig and I were leaving and walking down the driveway towards our car, I saw Mickey Steele walking up the driveway towards the house. He passed by us and nodded to Craig. He did not speak or acknowledge myself. Steele had come from a white car which I believe he had been driving. I cannot say what the car was but it was clean and had the appearance of an average family saloon. There was a second male in the car who had short dark hair and appeared to be a little bit younger than Steele. He appeared clean shaven but I did not take any further notice. We got into our vehicle which I believe was a Vauxhall Frontera which had been loaned to Tate by Barry Doorman, and left. A couple of days later Craig told me that Steele had been arrested by Customs Officers whilst he was taking his boat from the water.

This was following him dropping the cannabis off at a safe point on the coastline about three miles away. That same day Tate was arrested during the early afternoon having crashed Tucker's Porsche car in Southend. I was at work and would have finished at 1500hrs that day. Craig picked me up from work and told me what had happened to Steele. About 1600hrs Tucker phoned Craig on his mobile phone and told him about his car and what Tate had done to it. About 1800hrs that day Craig and I drove to Southend Police Station to collect Tate. Once in the vehicle I became aware that Tate already knew about Steele being arrested. He then used Craig's mobile phone to ring Jackie Steele. He asked her if everything was 'safe'. I took it that it was as a result of Tate's manner and subsequently what he said to Craig. He said that it was all 'safe', I took this to mean that the drugs had not been found. On this occasion I did not know where the meeting between Steele and the others was to take place but after a couple of days Craig brought his share of the cannabis round to our house in Chafford Hundred. Because the cannabis had already been sold on, the same day Craig and I took it up to the Golders Green area of North London where Craig handed it onto a coloured male called Gary.

No money was exchanged because the cannabis was what's known as 'laid on' Gary for him to sell and then pay Craig. The agreed amount per kilo worked out to be approximately ten thousand pounds for the lot. Already the others had placed their own share with other dealers but very quickly they started receiving phone calls telling them that the cannabis was very poor quality. I learnt through Craig that Tate and Tucker were very agitated because Steele during this time was trying to push the price that he wanted up. In affect this was eating into their personal profit from the deal. They contacted Steele and told him that they wanted their money back because the cannabis was rubbish. Steele didn't want to take it back. Tate and Tucker then started putting real pressure on Steele to recover the money. By pressure I mean through intimidation. I cannot say exactly what they did, because I do not know, but I recall hearing conversations they had with Steele on the phone where they were renting and raving at one another and pacing up and down. I understand that Steele finally agreed to return the cannabis and get their money back for them. Tate in a fit of temper about the whole affair smashed each slab before it was returned.

Steele had told them that a parcel the same size had been picked up by mistake and that's how the problem had come about. I am not certain but I think that on this occasion Steele had to collect the cannabis from Tucker's home address in order to return it. Steele arranged to hand the money back to them on the continent. He was going to return the goods to his suppliers and then take the money to a pre-arranged location where he was to meet Craig, Tucker and Tate. The day they were going to meet coincided with Tony Tucker's birthday which was the

17th November. His girlfriend, Anna, had pre-booked a surprise night in a London hotel prior the trip to collect the money being made. Therefore, Tony was not going to go. They wanted a group of people to go over in order that the money could be divided up to bring it back into this country.

Craig asked me to go but I refused because I was not happy about getting involved and didn't want to go. The eventual party consisted of Barry Doorman and his wife who went in their own car. Pat Tate and Craig with three girls. Donna Garwood, Liz Fletcher and Gaynor Hayzer. They travelled in the Range Rover and left via Harwich. Craig did tell me where they went to but I cannot remember the location or where they stayed. I know that they stayed overnight in a hotel and were met by Mickey Steele. I was told that he met Tate and they went into a separate room. They returned the next day with the money. Whilst all this was going on, I was told that Steele was promising Tate that he had a 'big job' lined up for him. Craig told me that Steele had approached Tate and asked him to nick someone else's gear from them. I understood that Steele had been asked by a London based drugs firm to import 30 kilos of Charlie (Cocaine) and I believe that he was going to bring it in by plane from Holland. He had told Pat Tate that he was going to be given fifty thousand pounds as an up-front payment to take to Holland and he was going to bring the Charlie back in company with a member of the London firm.

The idea was that Pat Tate and Tony Tucker would rob the firm of the Charlie when it arrived over here. Steele had stated that he wanted to share it between them and had told the firm that he was going to land near to Clacton. Craig told me that Steele was planning to actually land in South Essex but I never knew exactly where this was likely to be. Craig, Tony and Pat had previously obtained a machine gun from a man called Mad Mick Bowman and the details of this are subject of a previous statement. Tate and Tucker were going to use the gun on the man from the firm in order to take the Charlie. I knew that they had made sure the gun worked but I did not know how far they were planning to go when they robbed the firm. Steele was going to land the plane and Tate and Tucker were then going to take the complete load. It was going to be split, eventually, ten kilos each, and was going to be taken to John McCarthy. Craig told me that McCarthy was going to pay them nearly one million pounds for the load which was for Tate or Tucker to divide. Not long after Craig had told me about this, he told me that Tate and Tucker had decided that he was going to drive the load away once it had been taken and go to McCarthy's with it. They had told Craig that they intended to rip Steele off by cutting 3 kilos of the Cocaine into ten kilos of impure.

This would have resulted in Tate and Tucker having twenty-seven kilos between them. The remaining three kilos was going to be taken to Mick Bowman and he was going to cut it for them. I do not know what the arrangements were to get the three kilos to Bowman or to get the ten kilos of impure back to Steele. By this time, I was getting very worried by Craig's involvement and told him that I didn't want him have any part in it. He told me that Steele didn't know that he was going to be driving and he convinced me that he wasn't as heavily involved as the other two in what was going to happen. He also talked about the money which was likely to be coming their way and how that would enable us to go ahead with whatever plans we wanted. I realised that I wasn't going to be able to talk him out of it and, albeit I really didn't want him to go through with it, I gave up in the end.

I believed that by this he was in too deep. Craig told me that the money had been paid to Mickey Steele who had taken it to Holland. The weather had changed and there was now snow on the ground. Craig told me this was causing them delay and they were waiting for it to clear. On the day of the murder I was working as normal and was due to finish at 1500hrs. That evening Tony Tucker and his girlfriend Anna, Craig and I and Pat Tate and a girlfriend named Clare, were all going to the Global Net Cafe restaurant in Romford. We were going out because they believed they were coming into money and they were going to have a pre-celebration. Craig phoned me at work in the after-noon and told me that Mickey Steele had contacted Pat Tate and said that he wanted to meet with Tate and Tucker to go and look at somewhere they could land a light aircraft. Craig mentioned to me that they had been to or were going to, I can't remember which, to the T.G.I. Friday's restaurant at Lakeside. I later found out that this had been Tate, Tucker, and Craig and a person named Peter Cuthbert.

I do not know why they met or what was discussed. I left work at 1500hrs that day and went home. The meal at Romford was booked for 2000hrs. I was busy wrapping Christmas pre-sents when Craig returned home with our daughter Georgie. We were at home together for about an hour and a half. Craig told me that I was to be ready for 1900hrs to go out. He was going with the others to look at the air strip and then would come to collect me. Craig wanted me to have something new to wear for the evening and took me to the Lakeside shopping centre at 1745hrs. He was driving the Range Rover and left me to go and pick Tony Tucker up. Craig told me that he was going because he didn't want Tony to be in a position to say that he hadn't had any part in the arranging. I also understood that Craig was going to collect Tony Tucker from his home and they were going to meet Tate and Steele later. I did not have contact from Craig, Tate or Tucker after this point."

So, it starts with her relationship with Craig Rolfe, and how he knew Tucker and Tate. She then goes on to state that Rolfe men-tioned that a large deal was coming their way, and that it would include another person. "I later learnt from Craig that a person called Mickey 'The Pilot' who I now know to be called Michael Steele was a friend of Pat Tate who in turn was a friend of Tony Tucker." She believes that "Steele was a ruthless person who really didn't think very much of other people." (This seems a bit harsh when Rolfe and Tucker had murdered Kevin Whittaker, and Tate had tried to kill Nipper Ellis). Jagger also mentions John McCarthy, but this seems to be about a deal taking place at the start of 95 rather than the end of it.

It reads as if Steele is bringing over drugs even when Tate is in prison, and there is another man involved who is helping to get the money together. Who this mystery person is we don't know; it could be Nicholls, Whomes, Blundell, or even Kenneth Noye? Jaggers talks about the bad cannabis deal. "Steele had come from a white car (white cars seem prominent in this investigation) which I believe he had been driving. Is this a VW Passat (although Nicholls was insistent that it was cream coloured)? There was a second male in the car who had short dark hair and appeared to be a little bit younger than Steele." Is this Whomes, or Nicholls? When Jaggers mentions the drug deal she puts it two weeks after Tate has come out. This is nearly a week over, and it seems strange that she would get it so wrong, as she then talks about Steele getting arrested, and states that he dropped "the cannabis off at a safe point on the coastline about three miles away." Who speaks like this apart from the police? And has she accidentally let slip that this drug deal two weeks after Tate had come out not the bad cannabis, but a new deal?

When Rolfe and Jaggers pick Tate up. "Once in the vehicle I became aware that Tate already knew about Steele being arrested. He then used Craig's mobile phone to ring Jackie Steele." (How did Tate know about the arrest if he had been in a police cell all day; and whatever happened to Rolfe's phone?) When the cannabis turns out to be crap, the Essex Boys want their money back. We then have a lot of information, almost as if Jaggers is with them when they are speaking to Steele. At no point does she mention anything about Nicholls; even though Steele must have explained to the Essex boys that he did not collect the drugs personally from Amsterdam. Are we to believe that during all these phone calls where she watches Tucker and Tate pace up and down, that they did not think the rip off might have been when the drugs were bought? Surely Steele would have told them he just brought the stuff over by boat?

After the threats everyone is off on a jolly boys outing. In another bizarre moment, Rolfe mentions to her that Tate and

Steele go into another room to talk. I am not exactly sure what we are meant to gain from this, and how Rolfe, in any context, would tell his partner when he got back that two men went into another room to have a chat. When Rolfe returned, he now talks about the big job. "He had told Pat Tate that he was going to be given fifty thousand pounds as an up-front payment to take to Holland and he was going to bring the Charlie back in company with a member of the London firm." In what world does any crime cartel believe that you can hand over fifty thousand pounds and get over a million pounds worth of cocaine? Fifty thousand pounds would probably be able to get you four kilos from abroad, which you could triple your money when you sold it over her.

She continues, "Craig told me that Steele was planning to actually land in South Essex but I never knew exactly where this was likely to be. Craig, Tony and Pat had previously obtained a machine gun from a man called Mad Mick Bowman." It seems strange that Rolfe mentions Bowman, but never names this London based firm? "Tate and Tucker were going to use the gun on the man from the firm in order to take the Charlie...Steele was going to land the plane and Tate and Tucker were then going to take the complete load. It was going to be split, eventually, ten kilos each, and was going to be taken to John Mccarthy." Wouldn't the man from the firm also be armed, and put the gun to Steele's head the moment he misses the real landing site? And when they landed, wouldn't the man from the firm shot back as soon as he realised it was a robbery?

The super talkative Rolfe continued to give his partner a full and detailed explanation of what he and his cohorts were planning to do once they have pointed a machine gun at people and left an airplane in the middle of a field. Rather than kill Steele (which would be the obvious choice), they are going to get Bowman to cut Steeles share, and keep the rest. Rolfe keeps Jaggers regularly updated, telling her that Steele had been to Holland and handed over the money (again, who hands over the money to a stranger and walks away with nothing?); but the weather had changed and there was now snow on the ground. (It started snowing on the 4th December). We now move to the day of the murders.

"Craig phoned me at work in the afternoon and told me that Steele had contacted Tate and said that he wanted to meet with Tate and Tucker to go and look at somewhere they could land a light aircraft." (Again, whatever happened to Rolfe's phone?). And if they are looking at the landing site at night, does that mean Steele is going to try and land a light aircraft in a field he does not know, in the dark, with snow on the ground, oblivious to tree lines and electricity pylons, knowing that a machine gun is waiting in the woods? 30 kilos is about four stone. Small enough to be able to be put into a large (Head) holdall, and drop it from the plane to a couple of guys in the field holding up torches.

Jaggers ends the statement saying that Rolfe comes back with their daughter and stays for an hour and a half, but this clearly cannot be right, as he is seen outside Grays police station at 1630hrs. She continues, "Craig wanted me to have something new to wear for the evening and took me to the Lakeside shopping centre at 1745hrs." This idea that the night was going to be a celebration seems to come from a lot of people. "I also understood that Craig was going to collect Tucker from his home and they were going to meet Tate and Steele later. I did not have contact from Craig, Tate or Tucker after this point." The first thing we should say about the last part is that the time does not corroborate with any of the other witness statements, but this will be explained more when it comes to the trial. Secondly, Jaggers level of recall is pretty fucking extraordinary. Not only is Rolfe telling his partner all this in the run up to the day he died, much of it third hand from Tate or Tucker; she is able to remember it in detail.

At least now detective superintendent Dibley has a statement that puts Steele in the picture. He has a motive of Tate threatening Steele that unless he got his money back (although something more serious, such as threatening to put Steele on his knees and make him beg for forgiveness and shoot him, just like Tucker said to Ellis, would sound better). And the opportunity of arranging to meet up in a country lane to look at a possible landing site in the middle of nowhere. The problem is Dibley also knows that if Steele was interviewed, a "no comment" to all questions would mean he would have to be bailed. The IRA ploy hasn't worked, the surveillance operation with Customs and Excise has so far found nothing. What he needed was a break.

In another room the name Mick Steele cropped up during the investigation into corrupt police officers. Dibley must have shat his pants when he heard that. Had Steele got inside information about what was going on? was a police officer involved in the killings? Luckily, it transpired that Steele was mentioned by an informant speaking to a bent copper about a drug run Steele and Whomes were going to bring in. The plan is to nick the cash whilst it's in the boot of a car as the ferry travels over the water. The corrupt police officers agree. Dibley asks for the name of this police informant. Then he probably does shit himself. The informant is called Darren Nicholls. Another surprise. The police had carried out checks on Tucker and Tate's phones on the day of the murders (let's call it Tucker's luck); and in the afternoon Tucker he was called from a payphone in Ipswich. Checks with British Telecom show that the payphone called Tucker's mobile; and shortly after another payphone called back. This one was in Timberlog Lane in Essex, near Tate's home. Anything else? Yes, the payphone in Ipswich is used pretty much less than a minute after the call from Timberlog Lane. This time it's to another mobile. No, not Pat Tate, not even to Mick Steele, but to a phone registered to someone in the name of Darren Nicholls. This would be the same Nicholls who got a call on the same mobile on the night of the murders from Jack Whomes, who earlier that night had got a call himself, from a Mick Steele. The triangle was complete.

At this point Nicholls does not know that DC Bird and DS Stimpson are also being investigated by the anti-corruption squad. Their conversations are being monitored, including Nicholls telling them another big cannabis shipment is going to be bought over at the end of April. Dibley must have thought he had enough to bring Steele, Whomes and Nicholls in; but the police force is a strange beast. Even though you are halfway through a murder enquiry, the law states that when your time is up, it's really up. Dibley had done his thirty years; the ten thousand days service required to get your pension. He retired on 20th April and handed over the investigation to superintendent Storey, who had just finished investigating the death of Leah Betts.

The first thing on the list must have been Operation Apache. Any officer believed to be involved with Steele, Whomes and Nicholls would also have to be arrested. Next was the surveillance operation that was being carried out alongside Customs and Excise on Steele. They had missed the boat in November, and weren't going to make the same mistake again. It may have come as a shock to Supt Storey to find out the main murder suspect had been seen in conversation a couple of times about cospiring to smuggle cannabis with Russell Tate, Pat's brother, this time from Portugal. Now you had Customs and Excise, the Murder squad, the drug squad, the covert unit, the Operation Apache investigation unit, Interpol, and corrupt police officers themselves, all watching Steele, Whomes and Nicholls. Any hint of a trap, and Steele could have been in Spain before police had even got their feet wet on the beach. But as April turned into May the tide was about to turn in their favour.

Chapter 12.

Arrests.

"We're the middle children of history, man. No purpose or place. We have no Great War. No Great Depression. Our Great War's a spiritual war... our Great Depression is our lives. We've all been raised on television to believe that one day we'd all be millionaires, and movie gods, and rock stars. But we won't. And we're slowly learning that fact."
Fight Club.

I

At 2pm on the 13th May 1996 police stopped the Jaguar that Nicholls was driving. When Nicholls realised that there was another police car in front of his van, driven by his friend Kevin Bridges, another police car behind, and more officers walking towards him, he made a couple of phone calls. One to his partner, one to DC Bird, and one to Mick Steele, where he had just come from after picking up ten kilos of cannabis. Nicholls was nicked, then Steele, then Whomes, and a few others, including Russell Tate, and Steele's partner Jackie Street. It is not clear why Nicholls rang Steele. In Bloggs 19, Nicholls said that a few weeks prior to the arrests Steele had offered to take him up in a plane. Nicholls agreed. But when Steele and Whomes turned up, he had a terrible feeling they were going to push him out without out a parachute. Just the night before the arrests Nicholls said he was threatened by Whomes. Just before the arrest he alleged Steele called him, shouting and swearing as some of the cannabis had gone missing. As such, it seems strange to call a man trying to kill you to warn him he might be getting arrested as well? In his first police interview Nicholls does not mention any of this. For all questions about the drugs he replied "No comment." At 11.35pm Nicholls was further arrested for being involved in the murder of Pat Tate, Craig Rolfe and Tony Tucker. There was a long pause, and then Nicholls quietly replied "No comment."

To be "involved in" was not exactly the same as being arrested for the "murder of." They were telling him they suspected he had played a part; how much was for them to know and him to say. Unfortunately, this is another piece of the puzzle that gets lost as soon as the box is opened. From now on, there are a lot of unofficial chats that take place in-between the numerous interviews. Nicholls states in his book that when the tape machine was turned off, he began to shout at the detective that it was all ridiculous. This is another strange thing, as he seemed to have spent the last few months desperately wanting Steele and Whomes nicked for anything, even if it was made up. And if he believed they were going to kill him as well, why didn't he say something? Then he gets a kick in the balls. He is told the detectives he has been dealing with for the last few months are also currently in custody. The police have evidence Nicholls has been cospiring with them to pervert the course of justice. He he is also the one with ten kilos of cannabis (at this stage he might not even know if Steele and Whomes have also been caught with any drugs).

Nicholls is fucked. His nerves have gone. If he gets remanded, the other prisoners won't take kindly to a grass; especially a paid grass. No, fuck that, a grass that was working with police officers to stitch up other criminals. He needs to think of something. The police inform him that if he gets bailed, word could get out that he tried to stitch up every drug dealer in Basidlon. Even those he has never met will think the last drug raid was down to him. They cannot guarantee his safety. Someone says that there is a way out. It meant fucking Steele and Whomes over, but Nicholls had been intending to do that anyway; and in his current position it was better than getting fucked himself.

The Witness Protection Programme had been around for years. It helped both innocent witnesses,and criminals. It was usually the last resort, mainly because it was so expensive. You had to give someone, and their families, a whole new life. It required authorisation from the Home Office, who would have to have a good reason for him to spend millions on a criminal. If Nicholls fully cooperated of course. There were probably two things that helped him make his mind up. If he continued to say no comment, even about the murders, he would still be looking at a couple of years inside thanks to the drugs and the bent coppers. If he did agree to help, the police had taken so long to arrest everyone for the murders, there was a chance that they might be found not guilty. Maybe there was one more thing. Nicholls mobile, which was now in police custody, put him in Rettendon the night the murders happened. It was time to let his fingers do the talking. After speaking to his partner, he signed over his previous life for a new one.

In another police station, Mick Steele, as was his legal right, declined to speak to police about the drug importation, and a pump action shotgun found in his home. When he was further arrested on suspicion of being involved in the murders. He finally spoke. "Do I understand that I'm under arrest for participating in the murder of Patrick Tate?" When told it is on suspicion of being involved in the murders of all three men, he replied – "I'll make one comment in answer to your arrest or charging against the murders; I'm a totally innocent party."

In yet another police station, Jack Whomes was also being arrested for the same offences. The police knew they had no real evidence. If all three of them went "No comment," the police would have to try and charge them purely on the circumstantial evidence in Donna Jaggers statement; and ironically, its only Whomes and Nicholls phones that put them near the scene. This would never be enough to get Steele to court, especially when you looked at what the three men could use as their defence. Numerous people arrested for the murders, including Billy Jasper, who willingly admitted he was the getaway driver for a hitman working for a well-known London Crime Cartel. Nicholls, a police informant, had never spoke about the murders. If one of them was freed, they could turn around and claim the other two were with them that night. Steele had been under surveillance, yet at no point had he said or done something which gave rise to him being linked to the murders. There was no record of him going to the crime scene, and no record of him trying to distance himself from the murders.

Going back to Nicholls; in his book he claimed that he started to tell the police what happened; and they came back with Witness Protection Programme idea. They also came back with cigarettes, pizza, and hot chocolate. From now on, Nicholls was the most valuable piece of evidence the police had about the murders; as long as he wasn't involved in them. Nicholls told police he thought he was going to meet Tate to sort out another drugs deal. He had not been aware of Steele and Whomes plan to kill before it happened, and so had no way of stopping them. He told them he had not witnessed the killings. But Steele and Whomes had pretty much confessed to him what happened when they got back into the car, both with blood on their hands. Nicholls wrote he was going to tell the police during the five months after the murders (honest), but never got the time.

Steele and Whomes, two old school criminals, kept up with the "No Comment" interviews. This was good news for the detectives, as it meant they could be charged based on their lack of alibis rather than the strength of police evidence. After a few days Steele and Whomes were told that Nicholls has named them as the killers. On the advice of their solicitors, they still continued to say "no comment."

Back in his cell, Nicholls was given a desk and writing equipment to be able to plot out a story that needed to fit with what the police already knew. But although this was a major investigation, things began to disappear, such as every single note Nicholls made in relation to the murders, which should have been kept as evidence, and it's not like he was leaving police custody to take the bins out. Nor in any of the interviews does he say he has remembered something and wanted to add or change what he had already said. It was almost as if he would say something in one interview, the police would go away and check, and if it didn't fit, Nicholls would then change his story. There were also times when his account made no sense at all.

In one interview Nicholls said that Tate had got money for the bad cannabis deal from the Mullock brothers in November 95, and he had told them that it was Steele who had stitched them up. There was one small flaw in this, the Mullock brothers didn't exist. They were invented in February 96 by the police pretending to be the IRA. I have no idea how Nicholls came to know about this, as it should have been top secret. He was still speaking to corrupt detectives in February, so perhaps they told him. And we only know these brothers turned out to be undercover police officers because Steele recorded one of the conversations after his life was threatened. The police were not aware of this recording at the time. But before Nicholls gives his final statement in October 1996, the police know that Steele's defence team has a recording of a phone conversation of the Mullock brothers, giving Steele reasonable grounds to claim the IRA committed the murders. The police then had to admit it was them, and the Mullock brothers totally disappear from Nicholls account. Nicholls never even mentions these made up brothers in his book. He may have been a grass, but only on real people.

There is also an issue with the vehicle that Nicholls was driving that night. In one interview he boasts is able to reel off phone numbers from the top of his head and give directions of travel from six months before as if he is reading a map book. But when it comes to cars it's a bit of a blur. He starts off saying it was driving a works van, then a VW Scirocco, or possibly a white Citroen, possibly a VW Golf, maybe it was a VW Golf convertible, might have been another works van, or a Land Rover, and then decides it was the definitely the Scirocco...possibly. No; too many saloons seen with the Range Rover that night. It must have been the VW Golf convertible. The ideal car for driving through snow and ice in December.

It seems incredible that he couldn't remember in the first interview what car he had been driving on the night three men were murdered. Nicholls, an innocent man, must have been worried about any evidence being transferred from his clothes to his car? Surely most people would have cleaned the car inside and out the next day, and as such remember what car they had to scrub? One answer may be that if he made a mistake and gave details of what he was driving at the very beginning, there was a real fear that witnesses may come forward and name a different time, place and a totally different vehicle. No one can state when and where they saw you driving if you never admit what car you were in.

Nicholls also said he was unable to get a shotgun prior to the murders and didn't know why Steele wanted one (this changes to two shotguns in some of his accounts). He cannot recall when Steele first asks him to get one; but low and behold he obtains one after the murders have been committed. Not only that, he takes it to Steele's home (at least that way if the police find any of his fingerprints, he has already got an answer).

Also, in the first couple of interviews Nicholls states that he drove Whomes along the road and stops opposite Workhouse Lane, so that the lane is to his right, and Whomes has to cross the road to get to it. But by the time we get to the final statement it has Whomes telling Nicholls to turn into Workhouse Lane and then telling him to turn around so he is facing the junction. Whomes then tells Nicholls to meet back at this exact spot when he calls. Nicholls never sees the scene. Problem solved. Speaking of car journeys, let's go back to the time of the arrests.

Word would have quickly got out that people had been nicked on the 13th May for the murders. Bearing in mind the corruption in Essex police was so bad that they had to have an internal investigation; it would be of no surprise if news of the arrests reached a lot of criminals as well. On May 15th John Marshall, an Essex businessman who specialised in buying and selling prestige vehicles, and as associated with Pat Tate and Bernard O'Mahoney, left home in his Range Rover, telling his wife he had to sort out a deal. He had five thousand pounds in cash, and a holdall. After trying all evening to contact him, his wife eventually called police to report him missing. On the 17th May, Steele and Whomes were charged with the murders and sent off to prison on remand. On the 19th May, Kenneth Noye, a man also known to Pat Tate, was involved in a road rage attack and killed Stephen Cameron. He went on the run to Spain, but was eventually caught three years later. It transpired that Noye got his Land Rover through John Marshall.

Steele and Whomes may have wondered what was happening whilst they were on remand. What they needed was a message. On the 22nd May they got one. The body of John Marshall was found in the boot of his car in a street in east London. It is believed Marshall had been shot at point blank range with a shotgun somewhere in Kent on the 15th May. He was then put into the boot of his car and driven to London, where the car was spotted a few days later. There was still five thousand pounds cash in the glove box. Whoever did it wasn't bothered about money. But the holdall, and whatever it had contained, had gone. Police believe two men must have been involved in the murder; as Marshall, a former body builder, had been lifted into the boot of his Range Rover after he had been killed. Even more perplexing, Marshall had been covered up under a large pile of hay that wasn't in the car when he left home. Detectives might have thought that the hay had been used to hide the body. But others who heard the news in prison might have known what it meant…if you're thinking of talking to the police, you will also end up with the other dead grass.

II

In another twist, Tate's long-term partner Sarah Saunders, was arrested on 13th June 96 for attempting to pervert the course of justice, and handling a stolen motor vehicle. This was the VW Golf that broke down and Tate collected on the day he was murdered. When police checked the car that was sitting on his driveway, they found out it was on false plates, and the original vehicle had been stolen. Police say that Saunders was informed of this, but a few days later she sold it to Michael Steele. She was interviewed five times in one day, all without a solicitor present. The police quickly forgot about the car (unless it was to remind her that she could be charged and go to court), and got onto other matters.

Saunders said although Tate had paid the deposit on the bungalow, his name did not appear on the paperwork. But it did on the life insurance endowment policy. If he died, the mortgage on her home would be paid off. Tate was released on 31st October 95. By this time Saunders had started a relationship with someone else, but this was secret. She had become tired with Tate's addiction to drugs and knew it was over. She mentioned Tate getting involved with heroin after he started hanging around with his old friend Ian Spindler (the same Spindler that Steele mentions to Nicholls after the shooting, saying he bet he wishes Spindler was in the car that night as well?). To her it seemed that the man she had once loved was now gone. A few days later Saunders went on holiday to Portugal for a week with her sister. When she got back, Tate had kicked her out of the bungalow. She stayed with her mum until she found a place to rent. She went back on the 24th to clear her stuff, and was helped by both Mick Steele and Jackie Street.

When asked if there was anything between her and Steele, Saunders said no, he was like a father to her. Tate got her a VW Golf (from Doorman?), but it kept breaking down. On the day Tate was killed the Golf broke down again. She called him to complain, but cannot remember if she used a phone box, and where she called from. She did not have a mobile, as she had given it to Tate; who then gave it to Lizzie Fletcher, and he got another one. She managed to get the car started and got to her mum's. In the afternoon he turned up with Tucker and Rolfe. The car started, and Tate became very abusive, causing Tucker and Rolfe to hold him back. Tate got into the Golf, threw everything out, and drove off. Tucker and Rolfe helped pick up all the children's toys, and then left. She never saw Tate again.

At about 6pm she called Tate to apologise. "So, I phoned him up and he couldn't have been nicer and I was really pleased because he said oh don't worry, he said sorry for going mad and everything else, and he said listen, I can't talk at the moment, I'm with people. He didn't say who he was with, he just said he was with people at the moment; which he wouldn't have said if he was just with Tony and Craig still cause he would, well he just wouldn't have said that, he would just carried on as normal sort of thing, and he said oh I'm with people at the moment, and I sort of said oh, I'm really sorry, you know I shouldn't have rung you up, you've got enough to do and all that and he said okay. He said give us a call tomorrow and we'll sort of sort it all out tomorrow, like nicely again, you know, and that was that was that."

Saunders then borrowed her sister's car and went to a wine bar in the centre of town with her new boyfriend. She then spent the night with him at his home. The next day a friend of hers called her and mentioned someone had been shot in a Range Rover, but she didn't think anything of it. Later, a friend rang and said that Tate was one of the men killed in the Range Rover. She looked on the Teletext, but it didn't mention any names.

Later on, she got back her old phone that was being used by Lizzie. She remembered that John McCarthy had called her, but she could not recall any conversation with McCarthy about trying to get another mobile phone back. When questioned further as to why she was so desperate to get his other phone back, and that the police only knew this because Lizzie had informed them that Saunders had told her McCarthy wanted the other phone, Saunders could not remember the conversation. When asked if she believed Steele had killed Tate, she said no. She believed that if Tate was with Mick in the Range Rover, he would have said so on the phone. When she first heard that someone called Mick was involved, she thought it was Mad Mick Bowman.

In the last interview the police informed her that they believed that Steele was the instigator of the murders, and had statements from Donna Jaggers which corroborated this. They had also interviewed Darren Nicholls, who had given an account that put Mick in the frame. After a long pause, Saunders began to cry. She told police that she had gone to the bungalow for some reason (date unknown), and Tate had told her that Steele was going for a trip up north, and would not be coming back. She believed this meant he was going to be killed. She called Mick and met him in a McDonalds some day in December. She remembered that he told her not to worry. Saunders couldn't understand what the problem was, because she had heard that Steele had got a lot of money back for Tate; plus, if Steele was in the Range Rover that night when she called, Tate would have mentioned it. That's why she did not think Steele had killed them. Even after the killings there was never a time when she thought Steele had done it.

It is worth pointing out that this interview comes a few months after Saunders had a series of threatening phone calls from the police pretending to be the IRA; and it's quite possible that both Steele and Saunders phones were bugged in order to hear what they said after these calls. So, when Saunders finally admits she met with Steele on the 4th December to tell him about the threat, the police may already have an idea that it had taken place. But if you are going to pin a triple murder on a threat that comes two days before it happens, you then have to go back and look at the conversation about the cocaine robbery two weeks prior. You then have to go even further back to the bad cannabis deal ten days before that. And if Nicholls thinks that Steele was asking for a shotgun and wanting to buy his car before that, when does the decision to murder actually happen?

The police did not seem too bothered about speaking to Ian Spindler or John McCarthy,. The only fly in the ointment was her insistence that if Steele was in the car during the time she phoned; Tate, unaware of the trap, would have said so.

Meanwhile, the trial for the two men arrested over buying the ecstasy pill that caused the death of Leah Betts had collapsed, and so a new one was ordered. This was surprising, as the investigation had involved thirty-five detectives working full time for over six months. The cost was believed to be nearly half a million pounds. Although the police clearly knew who the main dealers were, they had continued to go after teenagers who had done something stupid. Bernard O'Mahoney gave evidence at the trial; but only to say that he never saw any drugs been sold when he was at work. Mark Murray, the real dealer, stayed on the run, and Raquels eventually shut due to lack of business. The media was promoting Ecstasy as the danger drug; and the picture of Leah Betts in hospital almost gave it the same status as heroin. But then it was revealed that the advertising campaign was being run by agencies heavily involved with alcohol companies, who wanted to curb the amount of people going clubbing, but not drinking. The image of Leah Betts was also used by the same companies who financed the backing of a new parliamentary bill to immediately close down any licenced premises where drugs were found. They had no issues of drunken men killing each other in premises which sold their alcohol, but someone caught with a bit of cannabis could close the place down.

Almost unnoticed in the news was the drop in the seizure of cannabis resin being imported into the UK for the first time in years. The smugglers may have followed Steele's advice and just got their own boat. Others may have thought that bringing it in by plane was a better idea. But there was also another reason. Created in America the seventies, it was a weed that got its name because it smelled similar to the animal that lived in the forest regions where it was grown. A developer then took samples of it to the Netherlands in 1982, where it was crossbred, and because of its capability to grow fast and with less light and heat than other crops, it quickly became a favourite with the main cultivators. By the nineties it had been refined so that it could grow even quicker, and you could get a couple of harvests in one year. It was this, rather than the myth about it being ten times stronger than other forms of cannabis, that made it the dealer's favourite. As such, small factories began to be set up across the council estates and disused factories that stretched the country, and England finally had a homegrown that was worthy of standing with its Dutch rivals. It went by the name of "Skunk," and its growth would eventually cause the demise of the last of the great white dope smugglers such as Mick Steele. It is also the first time that black, Asian, and East European gangs didn't need the money or the contacts to import the stuff. The homegrown empire belonged to those who had come from far away; and a new breed of criminals were becoming cartels in their own right.

Chapter 13.

The Prosecution.

Village Boy: "We're ashamed to live here. Our fathers are cowards."

O'Reilly: "Don't you ever say that again about your fathers, because they are not cowards. You think I am brave because I carry a gun; well, your fathers are much braver because they carry responsibility, for you, your brothers, your sisters, and your mothers. And this responsibility is like a big rock that weighs a ton. It bends and it twists them until finally it buries them under the ground. And there's nobody says they have to do this. They do it because they love you, and because they want to. I have never had this kind of courage. Running a farm, working like a mule every day with no guarantee anything will ever come of it. This is bravery. That's why I never even started anything like that... that's why I never will."

The Magnificent Seven.

I

After nearly twenty years inside Downing Street the Tories were looking tired. Opposition leader Tony Blair promised that if he got in, he would be tough on crime, tough on the causes of crime; namely hard drugs (although he might be a bit softer on soft drugs). The Tories rushed through a bill to make it illegal to own handguns, and now anyone caught in possession of one, or other prohibited weapons such as a sawn-off shotgun, would face five years in prison. Blair, perhaps the only man who knew more about lying than the star witness, won a landslide victory.

The law was changed in relation to reporting restrictions for criminal cases. This allowed the Daily Mail to name the five people believed to have been involved in the killing of Stephen Lawrence, even though they had not yet been charged or found guilty in a public court. The chances are they got the right men, but three hundred years of jurisprudence and the presumption of innocence were lost overnight. Doreen Lawrence believed that not only her son had been murdered because of his skin colour; but that the case had so far remained unsolved because of possible links between criminal gangs and corrupt police officers. She would have to wait a couple of years to be proved right. Meanwhile, the phrase "Trial by media," soon became popular. Keyboard warriors now took on the role of circuit judges, missing the irony.

Another death took up all the headlines in August 97 when Princess Dianna was killed in a car crash. There were rumours it was not an accident. Of the three people who died in the car, two of them could have caused a lot of problems to the establishment. Diana had been in a relationship with dark skinned Dodi Fayed, son of an Egyptian, and a Muslim. There were rumours that she wanted to remarry and move the future heirs to the throne out of the country, and that she wanted to expose the hypocrisy of the establishment.

She was killed when the car crashed in a tunnel under Paris after trying to escape reporters. There was a backlash on the way the establishment failed to understand how the public felt about her. It wasn't surprising. The world of public schools and select universities had not changed since the days of the Profumo scandal; even the new Labour prime Minister had gone to Oxford. Around the corner of Buckingham Palace, the trial of two men was about to begin at the Old Bailey.

The trial would be special. It was going to rely solely on the hearsay of a man with a previous conviction for dishonesty; who had been arrested with ten kilos of cannabis, and had been involved with corrupt detectives in trying to fit up other criminals. Things had changed since the last time Steele and Whomes had been in court. This would also be one of the first major murder trials in which the jury were told that Steele and Whomes right to silence and saying no comment to any questions could now be seen as them not wishing to give an alibi until they had been told everything the police knew. The idea of "innocent until proven guilty" needed to be struck from the jury's minds.

The jury were informed of the drug importation offences - "Michael John Steele, Jack Arthur Whomes and Peter Thomas Corry; between the 1st day of August 1995 and the 10th day of November 1995, conspired together and with others fraudulently to evade the prohibition imposed by Section 3(1) (a) of the Misuse of Drugs Act 1971 and Section 170(2) of the Customs and Excise Management Act 1979 on the importation of a Class B controlled drug, namely Cannabis Resin into the United Kingdom." The prosecution had been very clever in not including charges of the drug importation arrests in May 1996. For one, the defence couldn't argue that it was the reason why Nicholls, who had been found with ten kilos of cannabis and could be looking at a few years, would help police and make up a story about Steele and Whomes being murderers. It also avoided the issue of having Pat's brother Russell Tate, as being one of the other defendants in the dock. The other thing was that the 60 kilos of cannabis found at Steele's mum's house would have made it difficult to say he was innocent for the drug importation offences in November 95. As such it gave Steele and Whomes a false sense of security. Rather than just admit their guilt for the drugs, and in doing so weaken Nicholls testimony; they decided to go for shit or bust. The evidence for importing drugs was far stronger than the murders. If they had all pleaded guilty before the trial, the murder case could have collapsed. But Steele and Whomes did not, and it would eventually prove their downfall.

Another interesting point is that the drugs conspiracy went up to the 10th November 95, even though we know that most of the people involved were in a hotel in Ostend on the 18th. The ecstasy pill that killed Leah Betts was bought in Raquel's on the 11th November. The prosecution did not want her name mentioned in court for fear of the deaths being seen as some sort of reprisal, and so giving the defendant's a chance of being found not guilty on the basis the dead men may have deserved it.

Darren Nicholls does not appear on the drugs indictment. He had already pleaded guilty to these. As such he could appear for the court as a witness rather than a defendant. Nicholls explained to the jury that he was just a drugs mule. There were phone records, receipts, card payments for ferries and hired cars, all pointing to his involvement; but Steele was the main player in all this. The proof was in the fact that it was Nicholls who got the ferry back during the bad cannabis deal, but Steele was the one in the boat.

Steele said that whenever he went back and forth across the water, he had no idea drugs were involved. To prove it, at no point had he been found with any drugs during these dates. That was the main thrust of the importation offenses. Steele had been given the chance not to give evidence, but went into the box because he believed the importation offences were weak. Unfortunately, he didn't spot the trap.

The issue of who was in charge of the drug smuggling was not important. What was more crucial were the other names of the people involved. For hidden away amongst drug dealers in Amsterdam and hippies in beach huts were the names of Tony Tucker, Pat Tate, and Craig Rolfe. The jury could now link the man on the boat to the men in the car.

II

Once the drug offences had been dealt with, the prosecution brought out the big guns, and informed the jury, "If you look back to the indictment, we will look at Counts 2, 3 and 4. Counts 2, 3 and 4 are charges against only the first two defendants, Michael Steele and Jack Whomes, and that is for the crime of murder. The prosecution's case is that the defendants Steele and Whomes committed these offences of murder together, with each other, in relation to each of those counts of murder, Counts 2, 3 and 4. The prosecution case is that Steele lured the victims to the farm track at Work House Lane by arrangement with Whomes. He knew Whomes would be waiting and that Whomes then fired fatal shots into each victim. As to whether Steele fired any, and if so, how many shots, it is not necessary for the prosecution to do any proving as to that if you are satisfied that what they were involved in was a joint enterprise. What does a joint enterprise mean in law? The law is this: where a criminal offence is committed by two or more persons each of them may play a different part, but if they are acting together as part of a joint plan or agreement to commit it, they are each guilty."

This is interesting because it goes slightly against Nicholls account of Steele also shooting Tate. The prosecution didn't care if Steele never fired a shot; he had set it up, he knew what was going to happen, and was just as much to blame as if he had pulled the trigger. As the jury took stock of what they had just been told, there was another charge. "We also can turn now to Count 5, the charges against Steele only, possessing a firearm when prohibited, contrary to Section 21(1) and (4) of the Firearms Act 1968. The particulars of offence being this: "Michael John Steele on a day between the 1st day of January 1996 and the 14th day of May 1996 being a person who had been sentenced to imprisonment for a term exceeding 3 years, had in his possession a firearm, namely an 8 shot pump-action shotgun." The jury might not have picked up on the fact that the dates did not match when the killings took place. The prosecution did not have to say it was the murder weapon, or why on earth Steele did not dispose of it ages ago. All they had to do was show the jury a shotgun. Not only that, an eight-shot pump action shotgun.

And so, the prosecution set off on a journey to prove Steele and Whomes were guilty of murder. There was the means. Both men had criminal convictions. Both men were involved in drug dealing, and they might come across people of a nefarious character who could get them a shotgun. Nicholls had pointed out that at some time before the murders took place, Steele had asked him to acquire not one, but two shotguns.

For Motive, there seemed to be plenty of choices. Because of the bad drugs deal, it is alleged Tate had threatened to put Steele on his knees, make him beg for forgiveness, and then blow his head off. Although how this story came about, and who first told it, now seems to have faded away. Sarah Saunders, the former partner of Tate, had told Steele on the 4th December that she had heard Tate say that Steele was "Going to take a trip up North, and wouldn't be coming back." The jury were told that it put Steele in the position of either having to kill, or be killed himself. The police had asked Saunders if there was a sexual relationship between her and Steele. She said there was not. But Nicholls claimed (in his yet unpublished book) said that he always thought there was. When Steele was in the Range Rover as Saunders called Tate; and the way she spoke all lovey dovey to him, made Steele decide to carry out the murders. This was also a good way of getting in how crucial phone calls would be to this case; although Nicholls trips himself up at the start by saying the call had taken place whilst the car was driving up Workhouse Lane, not realising the lane is six hundred yards long, and the phone call lasts four minutes. Let's not forget money. Nicholls explained that when he and Steele went to Amsterdam and get the money back, Mr Stone, the dealer, told Steele that a third of it (which Tate somehow got all off) was good (and then proceeds to hand all the money back?). Did Steele feel as though he had been ripped off twice?

The prosecution moved on. Opportunity. If Nicholls account was true, and that Tate had been telling people that Steele's head was going to pop like a cork when he put a bullet into the back of it, then surely this was going to be soon. What was never explained was when exactly Steele thought his life was in danger? If he only heard about the threat from Sarah Saunders on the 4th December, it doesn't give him much time. But then does that mean the cocaine robbery story was actually true? If it is, who was setting Steele up to land the plane? This same story was corroborated by Donna Jaggers when she gave evidence.

The jury saw a woman who had lost her partner, and her daughter had lost a father. They were not aware of any dealings she may have had in relation to the death of Kevin Whitaker, and how much she knew about the machine gun Rolfe obtained from Mickey Bowman. It was pointed out that although Supt Dibley said he was told about "Micky the pilot" just a day after the murders, Jaggers waited a few months until her memory of events had improved. Even though she had only met Mick Steele in passing, she was able to point him out a year later in an identity parade. Her statement seemed to explain how opportunity was going to knock for everyone that night of the 6th December with a story almost too good to be true; and it was. Jaggers statement is only a witness statement in that she claims to have heard Rolfe say it; and she either has a photographic memory, or was keeping notes. Strangely, Jagger never mentions if she tries to phone Rolfe, or Tucker, or Tate when Rolfe doesn't come back that night. But the prosecution argued that of both phones found, not one of them answers or makes any calls after 7pm; and the reason for that would be explained by a man who was up next.

Chapter 14.

Darren Nicholls.

"I don't have to sell my soul
He's already in me"
The Stone Roses.

Barrister. 'Mr Nicholls, are you a truthful man by nature?'
Nicholls. "I don't think you could say that I am."

I

Before the trial Darren Nicholls had pleaded guilty to four offences. The first was importing cannabis between the 1st September 1995 and 31st October 1995. The second was between the first and tenth of November 1995. He also pleaded guilty to selling a firearm, namely a pump-action shotgun, to Michael Steele, who he knew was prohibited from owning one. The fourth count to which he pleaded guilty was one of having in his possession on 13th May 1996 (the day he was arrested) ten kilograms of cannabis, with intent to supply it to others. He had not yet been convicted for any of these offences whilst the trial was happening; as such, he ran the risk of doing a couple of years even if Steele and Whomes were found not guilty. The police were watching him in the witness box as if he was still under surveillance. It's a shame they didn't do it whilst he was in custody. From his arrest in May 96, there are five months and twenty-six shredded statements until we get to the one given to the jury. The first part of the statement deals with the drug importation offences, but we will join it when Nicholls starts talking about the murders:

"14th October 1996. The witness Darren Charles John Nicholls upon oath states: I went through Rettendon the latter part of 1995. I remember an occasion when I was there with other people, they were Jack Whomes and Michael Steele, I remember that day. I was at work that day, I was working at Sunbury on Thames, my mobile was with me. Michael Steele rang me that day, he wondered where I was and would like to meet me, we did not discuss where we would meet because I was at work, I agreed to meet him later on that day, at Ron Parkinson's motorcycles, Marks Tey at 5 o'clock, I drove to Marks Tey, in I think my Golf Convertible, I have been to Ron Parkinsons before, it sells motorcycles. When I arrived, I parked in the flats opposite, Mr Steele wasn't there when I arrived. When I arrived, I went into the motorbike shop, I bought something for my old motorbike it was either a battery or a light bulb, I then put it in my car.

Whilst I was walking back to my car, I saw Mick, I waved to him I said I was just putting something in my car, and then I got in his pick-up truck. The pick-up truck was a red Toyota it was an M registration, I think. When I got in, I sat in the passenger seat, he said they were going down to do a deal with Pat, him, and Jack. I said "where is Jack", he said "he'll be here in a minute," I don't recall anything else he said. Then I noticed Jack had pulled up behind us. Jack was in a beige Volkswagen, it was a B registration, I had sold the car to Michael Steele. When he pulled up, he got out and spoke to Mick. I don't recall what was said, then he got back in his car, then we pulled off onto the A12 heading towards London. I was with Mick in his Toyota and Jack behind using his Volkswagen. I can't recall exactly what was said, but he said we would meet Pat and there was going to be a drug deal or we were having a drug deal. I can't remember. At that time, I didn't know where we was going. Mick said Jack would show me where the deal was going to be, he said did I know this place but I'm not sure, he said don't worry Jack would show you where to go. Nothing happened on the journey, just normal chat. He told me I was going to swap cars and I was to get in the car with Jack and he was going to meet Pat on his own. We stopped in a lay-by near the Halfway House, which is a pub restaurant on the A127. When we stopped in the lay-by I got in the car with Jack, Mick was going to the Halfway House with Jack. We got to the far end of the lay-by gates, we swapped drivers. Jack was to swap the number plates. I got my feet wet; Jack was wearing overalls and wellies. I remember the wellies more than the overalls because they were new. When we stopped Jack got out to stick the new number plates over the existing plates but they wouldn't stick as it was too wet. I saw the number plates he was trying to stick; they were B registration as well and they were brand new. When the plates couldn't be stuck, they were put in the back of the car, and he said drive down to the Halfway House pub. I had been to the pub only as a child or driving past on the way to Southend.

When we got to the pub jack told me to park at the back as far away from the A127 as possible which I did. I could see Mick's Toyota parked in front of us to the left, after we parked Jack changed his mind and said no don't park here park as close to the A127 so I moved the car. I could still see the hi-lux which was in front again but to my right. Then we had to leave the car running because the windows were misting up because of the weather, I said shall we have a drink and Jack said no. Then he said we were waiting for Pat to arrive and go to a meeting point, shortly after that he said right go. I saw a dark coloured Range Rover when he said that. The Range Rover drove and parked next to Micky's hi-lux, I couldn't see who was in the Range Rover. Jack then told me to drive off and up the slip road by the pub and back down the A127 to Southend, that is what I did. then he gave me directions down the A127 and on to the A130 to Chelmsford I think, which I am familiar with. A130 goes from the A127 all the way to Chelmsford, but we went to the Rettendon Turnpike, which is a roundabout with traffic lights on it. I went straight over to carry on towards Chelmsford, on the other side of Rettendon turnpike and up the hill and back down hill and out the other side.

Jack then said slow down and take the next right, which I did. It was a lane not a road, then I turned left into a gap to turn the car round, the head lamps were facing the road back towards the A130. Jack told me he would ring me when he wanted picking up, I had my mobile with me, he got out had a bag and a coat from the back, the bag I think was a canvass sausage shape bag, I didn't notice it in the car before, I might have done but it didn't register. He told me he would ring me when he wanted me to pick him up, so I pulled off and went right towards Chelmsford, I drove down the road to the first point I could turn round to a petrol station, then I drove back up the road and parked in a pub on the left hand side of the road. I left the engine running and checked my phone to see I had a lousy signal, so I moved to get a better signal up the road.

The pub I was in had a bright pink Morris Minor, the next pub I parked in past the lane and up the hill and took the first left turn, went up that road turned around and first left up there, then came up and parked outside the first house on my left and waited for him to ring. I didn't wait there very long, my phone rang, Jack said come and pick us up and hung up I think I might have said ok. I turned right went back down the road, and had to wait for a few cars to go past so I could turn right into the lane, then turned the car round to face the road again. I didn't see anyone and after a short period of time the back opened and Jack got in. I didn't notice the interior light come on.

I said "where's Mick" he said he won't be a minute he's dropped something. Jack was sitting between the back seats talking to me then Mick opened the passenger door of the car and the interior light came on. When the light came on, I was looking at Jack. I notice he had surgical gloves and I saw something on them like blood. Mick said turn the interior light off, Mick had shut the door about the same time, then he said "let's get going." He said go left towards Rettendon turnpike, so I pulled out, something clicked in my mind something had happened. I pulled out in front on a car, Mick asked if I was ok, I said yes I was, and as we drove up the road towards turnpike. Mick said they won't fuck us about no more, and Jack said yeah, it was quite funny cause when Mick had shot one of them the gun fell apart, he kept asking me if I was ok several times. I realised what happened but not to who, so I said I hope I don't fall out with you two. Mick said no you won't fall out with us. Micks started to hand over to Jack parts of the gun. I saw the barrels. I don't know the names of the other parts; I definitely saw the barrels. I was driving, I was a bit confused at the time.

From the Rettendon turnpike we went back down the A130 to Southend, then at Rawreth traffic lights I turned left, straight to the bottom of that road, we turned right and then took another right turn on or two roads later. As we went up the road there was a pub on the right, the Hungry Horse or Hungry Hippo something like that. I drove into the car park of the pub and parked next to Mick's Toyota which was on the left and stopped the car. They got out and I was still sitting there. Mick had opened up his Toyota. He told me to go and get in the Toyota which I did, then they were getting changed sort of thing, Mick was taking off his wellies and overalls off over his wellies, then slipping his shoes on. Boiler suit and wellies were put in the pickup truck and Jack did the same I think, and then we drove off. Mick drove the hi-lux with me in passenger seat and Jack was behind us in the Passat. We drove past the Rettendon lane, then Jack overtook us on the dual carriageway as we were driving slower.

There was some conversation in the car with Mr Steele. He said Jack was very cold hearted I said why, he first of all said when they stopped down the lane a gate had been shut so I got out the Range Rover I didn't know where Jack was, then Jack leant into the range rover and shot all three of them. Jack handed Mick a gun and Mick shot them, then he said once that had happened Jack reloaded his gun and shot them all in the back of the head. I can't recall anything else that was said. I did say can we stop and have a drink. Mick originally said yes good idea, as Mick looked shaken up, but when we got to Marks Tey he said best get home straight away. Then I got in my car and headed back to Braintree.

Afterwards I was working at Mick's new house, like a cottage and there were things spoken there with Jack and Mick. In conversations Mick told me that when he was driving to the lane with them in the Range Rover that Pat's girlfriend Sarah had rung Pat on the telephone all lovey dovey which he hated, not like when Sarah talked o Mick and Jackie. He was concerned Pat might have said he was with Mick now but he didn't. Then he hung up the phone just as they were at the lane. I don't know if it was Mick or Jack said when Pat was shot in the back he started to squeal like a baby and his hand had come up and put his hand through the window. Also, Jack had said to me at some point Mick was really excited when he shot them and saying "give me some more cartridges, give me some more cartridges." Afterwards Mick said that he hadn't felt bad about it as Pat deserved it, he was such a bastard, who would give a fuck that pat was dead as nobody liked him which was quite true probably. There was conversation as why it happened with Mick. Roughly it was that when the money had been returned from the bad drug deal a lot of the money Pat had put into it wasn't his he had borrowed it and that what Pat decided to do was not pay the people back and blame Mick to say he hadn't paid them back. Mick knew this because Sarah had told him Pat's ex-girlfriend. Pat was telling them he hadn't been paid back and if he wasn't paid back, he would kill Mick."

Let's pick out certain points of interest. "Michael Steele rang me that day." It is Nicholls who rings first on the 6th, four times in fact. "I drove to Marks Tey, in I think my Golf Convertible." At the time Nicholls had access to at least six other vehicles, so it seems strange that he would be driving around in a small convertible when it was snowing. There is not mention of him going home to change clothes or cars. He meets Steele, and then sees Whomes driving the VW Passat. "I had sold the car to Michael Steele." Although Nicholls cannot remember any more details, what it does do is put his fingerprints all over that car.

A Passat is later recovered, but I don't know where or when, or even if Nicholls ever identified it as the one he used to own.

Before they reach the first pub, he and Whomes get out to try and stick false plates on the Passat. We know this because Nicholls states "I got my feet wet." Although he doesn't say it; if the defence suddenly produced a set of false plates with Nicholls fingerprints on it, he can claim that he was still not aware of what was going to happen. I also think the getting his feet wet gives him an out in relation to the two phone calls between Steele and Whomes; one at 6.03pm, and one at 6.09pm. Nicholls does not mention them, which would be strange if he was sitting next to one of them in the car. It also means that he does not hear any of the conversations. But if he is outside trying to fix false plates at this time, we are now on a countdown to get to Workhouse Lane before the call at 6.59pm. If they are still trying to fix the plates at ten past six; it doesn't give them much time to get to the Halfway House pub, and then drive all the way to Workhouse Lane. And this has to be before Tate arrives at Workhouse Lane at 6.44pm.

They wait near the Halfway House pub, until a Range Rover comes in. "I couldn't see who was in the Range Rover." He is the only witness who can't describe anyone in a Range Rover. Nicholls and Whomes then drive off towards Rettendon, whilst Steele takes the Essex boys to the Hungry Horse pub in Rawreth; which gives Whomes a ten-minute head start before the Range Rover arrives. Whomes tells Nicholls to pull into Workhouse Lane, and turn around using a gap on the left-hand side. To me this reads that Nicholls has driven up Workhouse Lane and used the track road on the left that leads to the Wheatsheaf pub. Whomes picks up a coat and canvas bag and gets out. A pump action shotgun is nearly four-foot-long and would have taken up the whole back seat. The coat on top of the holdall may be a way for Nicholls to not see the outline of a gun when he gets into the car, and when the false plates are put into the back.

But let's get back to the time. They need at least ten minutes before the Range Rover arrives. 6.35pm gives Whomes time to

WHO KILLED THE ESSEX BOYS?

walk up the lane in his wellies and find a place to hide. The Range Rover is on its way. If we say that the call from Saunders ends as they arrive, Nicholls has already had time to drive to the Wheatsheaf pub, check his voice mail, and the signal strength on his phone, which is lousy, and decides to move. For some reason he avoids parking in the large forecourt outside White-house farm shop next to workhouse Lane, even though the shop is closed, its dark, and he believes it's only another meeting to sort out a possible drug deal. He also drives past the empty Parish church car park on the right of the main road. Instead he turns left, drives up Meadow road and waits outside a house. "I didn't wait there very long, my phone rang, Jack said come and pick us up and hung up I think I might have said ok. I turned right went back down the road, and had to wait for a few cars to go past so I could turn right into the lane, then turned the car round to face the road again." We know that the Range Rover was in Rettendon when Tate finishes the call saying he is "with people." Even if Nicholls had dropped Whomes off at the latest of 6.40pm, it is still another twenty minutes before Nicholls gets his call to come and get them. But his little tour of Retten-don would take under ten minutes at best. We also have him getting the phone call, then driving back onto the main road, waiting for a few cars to pass before he can turn into the lane and turn around. First, there are two calls to Nicholls, the first possibly doesn't connect, so Whomes probably moves to get a signal; which means it's been a minute since the shootings. Then, Nicholls has to drive back and collect them. That takes about three minutes. Why are they not waiting together when he arrives? If I had just carried out a triple murder, I might have got a wriggle on. Whomes and Steele, both large men wearing wellies, might have been a little out of breath. And don't forget, they are not at the edge of the junction, "then I turned left into a gap to turn the car round," which means Nicholls travels up the lane again to turn the car around again and collect the two men. Why are they not together?

When the fifty-five-year-old Steele arrives, he gets in the

front, and the interior light turns on. The same thing happens to Nicholls brain, especially when he sees the surgical gloves covered in blood and the pieces of a shotgun barrel that Steele is holding. Nicholls makes a point of thinking aye up, somethings happened here. This is just a piece of verbal signposting for anyone reading the statement: I knew nothing about the murders until after they had happened. Interestingly, in Nicholls first couple of police interviews he mentions that Whomes returns with a holdall, and then Steele gets in with his own holdall. As Nicholls drives away, he sees what looks like a sawn-off shotgun. But six months later, both holdalls and the coat have gone, and now both men are wearing surgical gloves. It's almost as if Nicholls has been told a sawn-off shotgun doesn't match the evidence, and there are no fingerprints at the crime scene. Getting rid of the holdall and putting on the gloves from the middle set of interviews onwards resolves both problems.

Here's a question. How do you get someone to confess to murder? You don't, you get their mate to do it. "Mick said they won't fuck us about no more, and Jack said yeah it was quite funny cause when Mick had shot one of them the gun fell apart." The gun falling apart is irrelevant, but it allows us to know Steele killed at least one of them. When Steele takes Nicholls back in his Hilux to collect his car. "There was some conversation in the car with Mr Steele He said Jack was very cold hearted, I said why, he first of all said when they stopped down the lane a gate had been shut, so I got out the Range Rover, I didn't know where Jack was, then Jack leant into the range rover and shot all three of them, Jack handed Mick a gun and Mick shot them, then he said once that had happened Jack reloaded his gun and shot them all in the back of the head."

And now we have Steele making Whomes guilty of murder. The interesting thing about this conversation is that Nicholls is recounting what Steele told him in person. It should read "Jack handed me a gun and I shot ***." Surely if the gun broke after one shot, Steele would know who he was looking at? Also, we never actually get Steele or Whomes directly confessing to Nicholls what they had done (even during the five months before they are arrested, neither Steele or Whomes wants to talk about what happened to the only other person who knows). Whomes reloading the gun also implies that a pump action shotgun wasn't used; and that nine shots were fired.

We also get a few more confessions. "In conversations Mick told me that when he was driving to the lane with them in the Range Rover, that Pat's girlfriend Sarah had rung Pat on the telephone all lovey dovey, which he hated, not like when Sarah talked to Mick and Jackie. He was concerned Pat might have said he was with Mick now but he didn't. Then he hung up the phone just as they were at the lane. I don't know if it was Mick or Jack said when Pat was shot in the back he started to squeal like a baby and his hand had come up and put his hand through the window."

Again, we get the time issue. Tate ends the phone call at 6.47pm. So, do we have over ten minutes waiting before the rear door of the Range Rover is opened, Steele to get out, Whomes to come down and fire, Steele to fire, pick up whatever he's dropped, and Whomes to call Nicholls. Or, does the shooting happen straight away, and then the two men spend the next ten minutes admiring their handywork? Perhaps this is another example of Nicholls statement giving details of the crime scene to help validate his story. But in some of the early interviews Nicholls states that Steele told him Tate got the phone call at 6.44pm as they drove down Workhouse Lane. Now this would make sense if Nicholls did not know how long that phone call lasted. It would also mean that when Nicholls leaves the Halfway House pub at 6.30pm, he has to drive the fourteen miles in the knackered Passat to reach the lane, let Whomes out, and then leave, all by at least 6.40pm. That's good driving, especially as it should take nearly twenty minutes in rush hour traffic, in the dark, with snow on the roads. So, Nicholls changes his story to Steele telling Tate received a phone call whilst they were driving "towards" Workhouse Lane. It's almost as if someone has gone through those first accounts, and then got Nicholls

155

to tweak the times in order to fit the evidence.

Another thing that Nicholls is not aware of is the carbon deposits left under the exhaust pipe, which could only have happened if the engine had been running for quite a while. And these minutes can't include the shootings as there is not enough time. "Also, Jack had said to me at some point Mick was really excited when he shot them and saying "give me some more cartridges, give me some more cartridges." But all the evidence points to a pump action shotgun being used. "Afterwards Mick said that he hadn't felt bad about it as Pat deserved it, he was such a bastard; who would give a fuck that Pat was dead as nobody liked him, which was quite true probably.

There was conversation as why it happened with Mick. Roughly, it was that when the money had been returned from the bad drug deal a lot of the money Pat had put into it wasn't his; he had borrowed it, and that what Pat decided to do was not pay the people back and blame Mick to say he hadn't paid them back. Mick knew this because Sarah had told him, Pat's ex-girl-friend. Pat was telling them he hadn't been paid back and if he wasn't paid back, he would kill Mick."

This is certainly more than what Saunders told police when she was arrested and interviewed in June 96. Her account was that Tate told her Steele was going to take a trip up north, and wouldn't be coming back. This was taken to mean Steele was going to be killed; but at no point does Saunders mention anything about Tate ripping off his investors and then telling them that he would kill Steele over it? Why didn't Saunders say that to the police at the time? Who was Tate telling this to; and if Steel only found out this information on the 4th December, why was he asking Nicholls to get two shotguns at least two weeks before the bad drug deal?

Nicholls continued to add to his story whilst he was in the witness box. He said that when Steele had called him to meet at 4pm, he replied he could probably be able to meet at 5pm, and Steele agreed. Nicholls goes on to say he had stopped at a pub with his workmates, then dropped them off, then went home for a short while before going to meet Steele. He remembers that he got to the bike shop at MarksTey about five, and has then travelled back down with Mick in the Hilux; although at no point did he ever think to ask why he has just driven thirty odd miles North, only to drive back another thirty miles South. Surely, he could have left his car in the Halfway House as well? He describes the attempt to change the registration plates, and then the journey Workhouse Lane, getting there at around 6.30pm.

He drove away, going to the Wheatsheaf pub, then going back past Workhouse Lane to the village; and then after a matter of minutes he got a phone call from Jack: "Come and get us." He might have said "okay". Then he turned right down the A130 towards the lane. He could not turn straight into the lane because there were cars so he had to wait. Then he turned the car into the track and again did a three-point turn to face towards the road. He had headlights on and when he pulled in, he did not see anything or anyone as he drove into the track and turned round. Once he had turned in almost immediately the back door on the passenger side opened and Jack got in (he must have been hiding in the field). Nicholls said, "Where's Mick?" Jack said, "He won't be long, he's dropped something." After a couple of minutes at the most (the same time it took to carry out the shootings?), Steele opened the front door, got in, and told them to go. Nicholls pulled out too quick and a car nearly drove into them. Steele said, "For fuck's sake pull yourself together." Nicholls said at the time he was a bit shocked. Mick started to hand a gun over to Jack in the back. Nicholls told the jury: "I saw, I think, a set of side-by-side barrels, not under and over. They were quite short; perhaps as short as a foot long or a little bit more (which would make it a sawn-off shotgun).

Nicholls tells the jury that he rang his friend at quarter to eight to go for a drink, and at this point the defence barrister pointed out that it was yet another call that was not in the telephone schedule as it was deemed not important by the prosecution. Some members of the jury must have wondered what other phone numbers were also not on the schedule because someone had deemed them as "not important."

In relation to the shotgun, Steele had asked him some time before the murders if he could get him a gun. Nicholls asked around, couldn't get one. It was only after the murders that a shotgun was delivered, and Nicholls subsequently took it to Steele. Nicholls told the jury that over the next few months he was desperate to tell the police. He was literally on his way to the station to tell them about the murders when he got arrested. Now it was the turn of the defence to ask questions.

II

The first thing that was pointed out to the jury was the numerous "off the record" conversations between Nicholls and the police that bordered on a conspiracy. Halfway through one interview was a twenty-minute toilet break. There was a "welfare visit" that lasted nearly eight hours. During another interview, Nicholls was heard to say "I've fucked the story up again." The jury were showed how the early statements had changed, giving more and more details as the weeks went on. Pretty much the opposite of how the memory works. The barrister went back to the custody record. He noted that the officers who were interviewing Nicholls were the same ones conducting welfare visits. This continues until the 21st May, at least ten interviews later, when Nicholls is de arrested for the murders and is now treated as a witness. His black and white television in his cell is replaced by a colour one. the visits continue on a regular basis. When asked in cross examination what these conversations, some lasting two hours, were about; Nicholls replied that he often just used to play cribbage.

Barrister: "Over the page into June it goes on. Lots of cribbage, lots of welfare. Mr Nicholls, you can see that right up to 6th June having been visited for hours day after day by DC X and DC Y, you are still being interviewed, are you not?"

Nicholls: "Yes."

Barrister: "What was DC X talking to you about?"

Nicholls: "He was just someone that played cribbage and went down the shops with me and got all my food and things like that."

Barrister: "Kentucky fried chicken, Taco chips, hot chocolate before you went to bed."

Nicholls: "Yeah."

Barrister: "It must be wonderful to be arrested."

In one example of how much is story changed, the jury were told how Nicholls account of Whomes actions on the night became more involved as the weeks progressed. In the first accounts Nicholls says he drops Whomes off on the opposite side of the road from Workhouse Lane; and yet when he gets the "Come and get us" call he is able to realise that they want him to pull into workhouse Lane and turn the car around so it is ready to go, even though he has no idea what has gone on. This changes in later interviews for Whomes to tell Nicholls to turn onto Workhouse Lane and then explain to Nicholls what he wants him to do. In relation to vehicles, Nicholls originally said that he might have been in an old works van. But that could easily draw the jury's attention to the statement made by Mr Tarbuck when he says that around 8pm of the 6th he sees what he believes to be a white coloured Escort type van pulling quickly out of Workhouse Lane. An hour later than the alleged time of death. This might also make us aware of the statement by Mr Kowalenski, who at around the same time had seen a white male, about 5ft 8 in height, wearing a black balaclava, quickly running out of a field next to Workhouse lane. During one interview the 5ft 7 Nicholls was asked what he was wearing, to which he replied it definitely wasn't trainers. Next to the Range Rover was a footprint which had been made by a trainer, about shoe size 7.

In the police station Nicholls was given a desk, filing cabinet, and writing paper to make notes about what he remembered. Unfortunately, he said in court that he threw every single piece of paper away. When Nicholls was asked why in none of the interviews he is ever recorded as producing any of those notes, or at any point says that he had remembered something whilst in his cell and wanted to change his story; Nicholls replied that once something had come back to him, he didn't need the paper anymore.

It was put to Nicholls that the twenty-sixth statement, his final version, was after he had been guided in the story by police officers. He denied it, and said he had always told the truth. He then had to admit that he and a corrupt detective had lied to senior police officers about the bad cannabis found in an old pit. He said he never gave DC Bird any hint that he knew about the Rettendon killings at the time; but then admitted to speaking about setting Steele and Whomes up and get them arrested, but not for murder. He was going to steal the cash when it was on a ferry, or get them nicked when they came back with cannabis. Nicholls later confirmed that he was made aware that the corrupt police officers had been arrested before he informed anyone about his knowledge of the murders.

It was pointed out that whenever a motor vehicle was used for an illegal purpose, it was owned or hired by him. VW Scirocco, used for alleged drug run into Holland. VW Golf cabriolet, used to take drug money into Holland. Peugeot 406, used for alleged drug run into Holland. Seat, used for alleged drug run Holland. Mondeo, used for alleged drug run Holland. VW Passat. owned by Nicholls and then allegedly sold to Steele. Jaguar XJ6, Transit van, Land Rover, all owned by Nicholls. And in the early interviews he stated he was driving a white Citroen that night. Nicholls was asked when he sold the VW Passat. He could only answer that he never kept any records, but it might have been a few weeks before the murders. He could not explain why he had not filled in the log book or notified the DVLA when he believed Steele only wanted it for legal purposes. Nor could he answer why Steele would want to buy such an old banger, surely not as a getaway car? Perhaps the strangest thing was that the two cars Nicholls claimed he was in that night, a VW Passat and a VW Golf, were also the same two cars, in make and models, that Tate had also been in that day. He had taken the Golf from Sarah Saunders, and picked up a Passat from Barry Doorman's showroom. And the Polo left outside Basildon Tyre services seems to disappear as well.

The defence then spoke about Nicholls going into the bike shop in Marks Tey, and whether it was a battery or a light bulb he had bought. In his original account Nicholls had bought a bike battery and was putting in the back of his works van when Steele turned up. But by interview number 14 it had become a light bulb, and he was in one of his own vehicles. The reason being that the police had attended Ron Parkinsons bike shop to confirm Nicholls account, and found that no battery had been sold on the day of the 6th.

Barrister: "How come that you had been thinking about it subsequently, and lo and behold the battery is a light bulb?"

Nicholls: "Well, 'cos I could never like actually remember which vehicle I was in. I was always unsure which one it was."

Barrister: "Anyway, here we have got the light bulb, it is for aerial 3 - right?"

Nicholls: "Yes."

Barrister: "You have bought some light bulbs - right?"

Nicholls: "Yes."

Barrister: "So, on that day you went to Parkinson's you bought some light bulbs for your aerial 3."

Nicholls: "Yes."

Barrister: "What did you do with them? Did you put them in your aerial 3?"

Nicholls: "No, I didn't actually. The rear light bulb to the aerial 3 was actually the same fitting as a rear Land Rover light on the number plate light."

Barrister: "You dropped you voice. The rear light bulb on the ariel 3 was what?"

Nicholls: "The same fitting as the Land Rover rear light. So, before I took my Land Rover for an MOT, I took the back out of it, and put it in my Land Rover, but I didn't ----"

Barrister: "---- because you know, do you not ----

Nicholls: "I didn't realise it was 6 vaults on the Land Rover and it blew immediately so I had to go back and get another one. The aerial 3 is 6 vaults and the Land Rover is 12 vaults so the bulb blew."

Barrister: "Because it would appear that you are saying that you bought one bulb that was for the bike and you put it into the Land Rover."

Nicholls: "Yeah."

Barrister: "Let us just go then to the next thing. We have got the battery that turns into the light bulb. Then what, Mr Nicholls, the vehicles change, do they not? Because we start off, do we not, with a van at interview 7. "It might have been my firm's van." Talk about it being the sort of beaten up van."

Nicholls: "Well, I'm just presuming. I presumed it was the van."

Barrister: "Sorry, it is not a presumption, is it? "I put it back in the van, then I think I sort of going back to the van, he's (Steele) pulled up and sort of beep, beep, beep. I had to sort of go, 'Hang on a minute, I'm putting my battery in,' because they say keep it upright for an hour." There is no doubt that you are saying it is the van, is there, keeping it up on the back of the van?"

Nicholls: "Like I said, I thought it was the van so I presumed it was the van."

Barrister: "Mr Nicholls, the truth, if you say I thought it was the van, fair enough."

Nicholls: "Which I did originally."

Barrister: "If you then say, "And Steele came up as I was putting the battery in the back of the van and I said, 'Hang on a minute, hang on a minute, it's got to stand up for half an hour,'" that is not thinking it is a van, that is embroidering. That is giving more of an account about the van, is it not?"

Nicholls: "I suppose so, yes."

Barrister: "How he has come along and you say keep it upright. That is the point I want to ask you about. You are being certain it's a van because you are giving a description of what Mr Steele is doing in relation to you and the back of the van and the battery, are you not? You are giving a description. Do you agree or not?"

Nicholls: "I agree that is the description I'm giving, yes."

Barrister: "All that description goes out of the window, does it not? The description goes out of the window, does it not?

Nicholls: "Well, I mean in the description I said I put the battery in the van, and I don't see where I put it in the back of the van; but perhaps I said that somewhere."

Barrister: "Did you say, "Hang on a minute, I'm putting my battery in," or not on 6th December Mr Nicholls?"

Nicholls: "Yes."

Barrister: "It is all untrue, is it not?

Nicholls: "Well, I know I didn't buy a battery then, but I did buy a battery when I met Mick on an occasion."

Barrister: "Was there another occasion when you said, "Hang on Mick, I'm putting in my battery before I go fishing," or something?"

Nicholls: "No."

Barrister: "Anyway, there we are, interview 7 in a van. By interview 14 the van has become the convertible, has it not?"

Nicholls: "Yes."

Barrister: "This van or battery has been put in is now a convertible. We can see you have already got the light in interview 14, and lo and behold, "I have also had a thought of what car I was driving that night as well. Do you want me to tell you what I thought I was driving? I was driving a Golf convertible."

The barrister moves on to the details in Nicholls story (or should that be stories?). One example is in interview 4, in which Nicholls says he and Whomes leave the Half Way House pub, drive along towards Rettendon, and then stop to change the registration plates. He gives a long and detailed account about him and Whomes not being able to change the plates. But a few interviews later Nicholls changes his account to say that the stop to put on the false plates takes place as they are driving from Marks Tey towards the Halfway House pub. He gives the same long and detailed account about him and Whomes not being able to change the plates. The barrister points out that the memory does not work like that. You cannot recall all the details of an event in sequence, and then suddenly realise that every little thing you remembered actually happened in a different time and place but in exactly the same order. In front of the jury the barrister asked Nicholls if he can remember saying, "The trouble with telling a lying story is it's difficult to remember it." Luckily, Nicholls could remember saying that.

The shotgun he only got because Steele said he wanted one. He believed the request had come a few weeks before the killings. Nicholls gave a couple of dates, starting from the time Tate was released, to a week before the murders, none of which fitted Saunders telling Steele abut the threat from tate. Nicholls told the jury he got one a few weeks after the murders from someone called "French." The "French" gentleman came to court and said that Nicholls had never asked him to get a gun.

Nicholls could not account as to why his memory was exceptionally good in some aspects of what had happened nearly six months prior, but very vague on others. He said he "Had told the absolute truth about the lead up to the events of 6th December, what happened that night, and the absolute truth about buying the shotgun for Steele at his request." Nicholls admitted he had kept some things to himself during some interviews, as he had been made aware that two police officers he had been conspiring with for the last six months had also been arrested on suspicion of corruption. He agreed he had been a paid police informant, but denied that he conspired with an officer to carry out a number of illegal activities. Nicholls also admitted that in one interview he said, "I fucked the story up here again." In another, "I've lost the plot. I don't know if I'm off the track." In another, "I'm hoping you will remind me of things I can't remember." One thing was clear, Nicholls had certainly gone out of his way to remind the jury how many times he was telling the truth.

There are many people who believe that the defence barristers should have challenged Nicholls a lot more strongly; for example the phone call at 6.69pm. It is only Nicholls who has ever said the deaths occurred between 6.47 and 6.59pm. There is no other evidence to support that fact. The barristers could have asked what time the first missed call was to either Tucker or Tate's phone. If it was, for example, 7.10pm, that gives us the same time to carry out the murders, and the call from Whomes was to signal that things had started rather than it had ended.

But there is the trap when asking Nicholls any question; and possibly why the prosecution only gave the defence the edited phone calls. Both Steele and Whomes had said not only that they didn't do it, but they were not even there. To question Nicholls in detail about what happened on the night of the murders might cause more grief for Steele and Whomes.

On a final note, although the jury were not aware that Nicholls was speaking to a publishing company and a television company, clearly in breach of court procedure, he is able to remember even more after the trial. His book, Bloggs 19, contains descriptions and conversations that he had somehow forgotten until a few years later. Knowing he was not going to be cross examined again, he was able to portray himself as an ordinary bloke caught up in an extraordinary situation. But it was the statement in this book that the jury heard, and it would be this statement that would decide if Steele and Whomes were guilty.

III

On 4th December 1996, almost a year after the event Police re-trace Nicholls journey, with Nicholls. There would be a driver, Nicholls giving directions, and an officer making taking notes. The only thing I would say when reading this is that I don't know if Steele's call to Whomes at 6.09pm could have put him in the Halfway House car park.; and the comments in brackets are the officers. -

1. Marks Tey to Thorndon Country Park, 39 miles, duration 1 hour. N.B. traffic on the A12 was fairly free flowing. No snow on

the ground. Weather conditions good. (1700 – 1800hrs)

2. At the Country Park, drove to the gates, which were closed. There was a sign on the gates which said "Gates Close at 4.30"

3. From Country Park entrance, drove to the Half Way House Pub. This was only approximately one third of a mile from the Country Park on the back road. This took about two minutes. (1805hrs)

4. Short consultation at the Half Way House to discuss the lay-out of the car park in the dark. Lighting very good. However, it was not possible to recognise people in their cars.

5. Depart Half Way House to Workhouse Lane, Rettendon. 14 miles, duration 25 mins. Throughout this journey, drove on major roads at 50 mph (where dual carriageway available) where there was single carriageway, speed on some bends on the A128 was approximately 20 - 30 mph. (1830hrs)

6. Then drove 1.5 miles to the Wheatsheaf public house which involved having to do a U turn at the central reservation near the Bell public house in Rettendon. This journey took approximately 5 minutes. At the Wheatsheaf public house there was a reasonable mobile telephone signal. (1835hrs)

7. From the Wheatsheaf, drove to Meadow Road, passing Workhouse Lane on the left-hand side before the hill. This journey of about a mile took approximately 3 minutes. (1840hrs) By Nicholls account this should be 1859hrs, as this is when he gets the phone call.

8. Meadow Road to Workhouse Lane, about half a mile, took about 3 minutes, which included waiting for a gap in the traffic before being able to negotiate the right turn into the lane. N.B. the entrance to the lane was completely shrouded in darkness.

(Another issue, if it has been three minutes since the phone call, why are Steele and Whomes not together; he's only meant to be picking up part of a shotgun, not waiting for a bus?)

Chapter 15.

Defence.

"And the men who spurred us on
Sit in judgement of all wrong
They decide and the shotgun sings the song"
The Who

'Alibi' - A defence by an accused person that he or she was elsewhere at the time the crime in question was committed

I

In the early nineties the first trial of O.J. Simpson made news
around the world. The evidence was pretty good, but mostly
circumstantial. The defence team knew that Simpson, a big
lumbering man who spent his college years running rather than
reading, would probably trip himself up at some point. So, they
made the decision not to let him anywhere near the dock to
speak. We never got his account of what he did on the night his
former wife and her friend were brutally murdered. Instead, the
defence attacked police procedures and discrepancies in witness statements, hoping the jury would remember the mistakes
rather than the bodies.

In England a defendant also has the right not to give evidence.
That way the defence barristers could tear into the police failing to get a time of death, and then go after the testimony of
a convicted liar who only agreed to help after he had been arrested and then put on the Witness Protection programme. And

apparently that was the plan. But after Steele and Whomes had watched Nicholls give his evidence, they decided they would also have their say.

Steele started by telling the jury of his previous convictions. Again, perhaps it's not a wise move to tell a jury that you did three years for large scale cannabis importation when one of the charges you are in the dock for is large scale cannabis importation. The reason he did so was simple; here was a man who had been ducking and diving since Moses was in shorts. Theft, fuel tax fraud, and cannabis, were all on the list going back to the sixties; but no armed robberies, no GBH's, nothing to say that he would use violence to solve a problem. If anyone was involved in the murders, it was Nicholls. Steele said that there was an incident when Tate was in hospital and Nicholls visited him. Whilst there Tate bullied Nicholls and tried to get him to fight with someone. When Nicholls next saw Steele, they spoke about Tate getting shot, and Nicholls said that he could shoot someone if it came to it. Steel thought Nicholls was a bit of a Billy Bullshitter, and forgot about it.

When the bad cannabis deal went wrong, Tate had threatened to kill Nicholls if he saw him. Steele acted as mediator, getting the money back and handing it to Tate. As for his personal relationship with Tate, Steele said that Tate had changed since becoming addicted to drugs, but he had never been afraid of him. He was aware Tate was having problems with Sarah Saunders, and helped her move out of the bungalow. He admitted that he had spoken to Saunders on the 4th, but did not take Tate's comments about him taking a trip up North seriously.

On the 6th December he and his partner Jackie went down to collect the trailer from Whomes uncle's address in Bulphan. At no point did he use any telephone box. Steele said it was Nicholls who called him at 4.39pm, wanting to know if Whomes was picking up the Passat. Steele left his home address with his partner Jackie at 4.45pm in a Renault 21 (was it ever checked to see if it had a towbar?), rather than the Hilux, as it was full of building equipment. He stopped on the A113 to get petrol, signing the receipt at 5.01pm. At 5.10pm he drove to the nearby Tesco, where Jackie did some shopping for sausage rolls and champagne. Whilst waiting he got a call from Whomes at 5.12pm. When Jackie returned, he then drove to Bulphan. At 6.03pm he rang Whomes to confirm his uncle's address. When he arrived, Steele knocked, but there was no answer. He called Whomes again at 6:09pm to tell him he had the trailer, and drove away. At no point did he go anywhere near the Halfway House pub, nor Rettendon, nor the Hungry Horse pub in Rayleigh.

They arrived home at approx. 7.25pm. Phyllis Stanbrook and her daughter Gemma arrived at 7.30pm, and stayed until 9.15pm (the case would have been dropped if Jackie Streets phone had been subject to cell site analysis during this time; but Steele did not give his alibi until over a year after the murders, and the information had gone). At 8.18pm Steele made a call from his landline to his mobile to check if his phone had a signal. He then rang Whomes from his landline at 8.21pm. Then from the landline to his own mobile again at 8.39pm. He then rang Whomes again. Steele said this was him trying to fix the handset on the landline.

It is Nicholls who rings Steele the following day on 7th December, at 5.19pm, about some electrical work. Steele believed the television and newspapers named Tucker, Tate and Rolfe on the 8th December. The next call from Nicholls is on the 9th December at 6.40pm. Steele believed the discussion was about the murders. At some point he may have even mentioned that he had said he had spoken to Sarah Saunders, who had said she had phoned Tate on the night.

He denied killing all three men. As for the shotgun. At no point did he ask Nicholls to get him one, and could not have hidden it in the loft when Nicholls said, as he was renovating the property and there was no ceiling at the time and he had photographs to prove it.

Steele then says he started receiving phone calls in February 1996 from two brothers, "Billy and John Mullock," claiming to be the IRA. The brothers claimed that Tate had owed them money. As the calls began to take on a more threatening nature, Steele decided to record them. Steele can be heard saying he thought Tate had borrowed the money from the Blundell brothers. He continued to be threatened by the IRA, until he simply tells them to do what they've got to do, as he couldn't give a fuck (that's some pair of balls). The Mullocks stop phoning. Whether this was because they knew they had gone too far when Sarah Saunders went to the police because she was petrified, or they realised they had got nothing from the threats, we do not know.

The police were not able to produce any of their phone calls for public security reasons, and not one single police officer was available to stand in court and explain the reasoning behind their actions. I don't know if the jury were informed that in spite of all these threats, not once did the police manage to get anything which linked him to the shootings, or if Steele and Saunders phones had been bugged. Steele believed that corrupt police officers had decided he was going to be blamed for the killings as it fitted the story of Tate making a threat about him; even though someone had come forward and pretty much confessed to being involved in January.

As for Craig Rolfe, Steele said he never had a conversation with him in his life. With Tony Tucker, he had been to his address a few times to help with some building work, but that was it. When he found out about the murders, he thought he would definitely be interviewed by the police, as he considered himself to be a friend of Tate's; but was surprised when he had not heard anything from the police.

When arrested for the murders on 13th May 1996 he gave "No Comment" answers to all questions on the advice of his solicitor. It was put to him that he could have given an account which would have given him an alibi. It was put to the jury that under English law every man is innocent until proven guilty, and that it was the job of the prosecution to prove his guilt beyond all reasonable doubt.

Steele's most important witness, his partner Jackie Street,

had severe depression and could not attend. It was agreed by prosecution and defence that her statement would be read out to the jury; re affirming the fact Steele was driving the Renault 21 that day, and that she was with him at the time the murders are meant to have happened.

The edited phone lists from the police suggests that the Steele landline was not used throughout the late afternoon and early evening; perhaps backing up the fact Steele was telling the truth. Steele argued the list of calls shown to the jury had been heavily edited by the prosecution to make it look as if he only called a select few people during the build-up and on the day of the offence, and that his defence barrister had repeatedly asked for a full list from all the phones in the investigation, but had been denied. It is not known if Steele was asked if he ever called Tate after 7pm of the 6th December, or at any time on the 7th December.

Nicholls had claimed the killings took place between 6.45pm and 7pm. But not a single gunshot was heard during that time, despite experts saying the noise should have been audible a mile away. However, at about midnight, an independent witness heard about six gunshots in the area of Rettendon. Again, it is not known if the police carried out any cell site work on Steele's phone to show where he was at this time.

And in relation to time, there appears to be numerous witnesses who see a Range Rover at various times in Workhouse Lane with only three people in it. We can give the police some leeway when it comes to the cars, as they only knew which other vehicles were involved when Nicholls told them six months after the investigation had started. But from the very beginning not one witness ever came forward to say they saw three men in a Range Rover following a red Hilux truck, nor anyone in a VW Passat driving erratically that night, trying to fix number plates in a layby; and most importantly, no one had seen a Passat go into the lane and come out on two occasions within fifteen minutes (and Nicholls had even said he had to wait for a space in the traffic to turn in; and then almost crashed when he tried to turn out).

Phyllis Stanbrook had known Steele for a number of years, as Steele had been previously married to her sister. She and her daughter went to the address in at 7:30pm, and remembered seeing a Renault with a trailer in the driveway. They stayed for a few hours, eating, drinking, and then left. There appeared to be nothing out of the ordinary about Steele that she could recall. In cross examination Stanbrook was asked how she be so sure of the date. She replied that she hadn't been, until Steele's defence team had told her the date.

II

Jack Whomes was a big heavily built man with size 12 feet, but could barely read and write. He denied the conspiracy to import cannabis. In relation to the murders, Nicholls had said Whomes was wearing brand new Wellington boots when he was dropped off at the lane, but not a single footprint was found which could match that of Whomes - or even Steele for that matter. The defence argued that a man of his size would have clearly left some trace, especially if he had been hiding behind some bushes with a coat and a bag; and had then gone down at least ten steps to the car and shot the three men. Quite possibly he had then gone back up to get the other shotgun (it is Nicholls who states that both men had guns, rather than the evidence pointing towards one shotgun being used); and then when it was all over, he must have gone back up behind the bushes to collect the holdall (again, in the first interviews Nicholls tells police that both Steele and Whomes come back to the car with holdalls).

The two occasions that Whomes tried to call Nicholls must have meant having to move around quickly in the dark and walking back up to a high point in a field order to get a signal. And yet again not one single Wellington boot print was found (if both men were wearing brand new boots, and had gone from the gate down to where the VW Passat is waiting, they could have left hundreds of footprints). The argument was he simply wasn't in Workhouse Lane.

Whomes went on to describe the 6th December. He was on the docks that day until about one o'clock, then got back to the yard at about two. Colin Bridge, a friend of Nicholls, arrived, and asked to borrow the trailer as Nicholls VW Passat has broken down along the A130. Whomes told him that he needed the trailer to take a small tractor to Micks, but he would pick up the Passat later (Bridge attended court and denied meeting Whomes on that day). Bridge being at the yard would also explain the phone calls made from the Sorrel Horse Inn, as it is just down the road from the yard Whomes worked in.

He arrived at Steele's home at 4pm, then took the mini tractor over to Meadow Cottage. After that he went to Sudbury and spoke to someone about a JCB. He believed he went through Fordham, then onto the A12. Along the A130 he came to the pink Morris Minor that stood outside a pub and saw the Passat. He winched the car up, then tried to ring Nicholls but didn't get through and hung up. He was asked, why ring? He said, "I rang to tell Darren I'd got the vehicle." He said that at about 7pm he turned round and went back to the yard at Barham.

A few days later, he rang Darren and told him that the gear box was slipping. Darren said he was not that bothered, then asked if Whomes could lose the vehicle and he'd claim on his insurance. Whomes told the jury there was a scrapyard nearby with a crusher, and it would have been fairly easy for him to make a getaway car for a triple murder disappear; but the next day he gave the vehicle to John O'Connor who did stock car racing. The Passat then sat in the yard for about a week before O'Connor took it. Hardly the actions of someone wanting to get rid of the evidence.

At this point I should also say that I could not find any record of when and where the Passat was seized by police. A Passat was recovered, and it was examined for any traces of blood; but none was found. Gun residue was found, but it did not belong to a shotgun (I'm not sure what this means. Again, it could be argued that the police were not aware of the vehicle for six months, and it could have been used by a lot of people. But let's remember that Nicholls had said he had sold the vehicle to Steele sometime before the murders (he couldn't remember when), but from what we know of Steele, he would have checked to make sure it was a decent motor (especially if he wanted it as a getaway car). And if he had driven it around for a few weeks, looking in the boot and under the bonnet; and Whomes had driven it on the night, why was there not one piece of forensic evidence that linked them to the vehicle or the murders? Missed by the jury was the fact that no one seemed to know what had happened to thePassat that Tate had collected an hour before he died.

It was put to Whomes that he cold-bloodedly killed three men. Whomes said, "I couldn't cold-bloodedly kill anybody. I couldn't kill a sparrow. Anybody who knows me knows I'm not capable of it. I don't care what the prosecution say." He said he'd never known Tucker or Rolfe before. After the murders there was plenty of conversations, with Steele believing that Nipper Ellis had done it (Whomes could have said anyone, as there was not a single shred of forensic evidence could be produced against the two defendants.

The defence barrister brought up the issue of corrupt police officers, and wanted DC Bird and DS Stimpson to attend court. But they couldn't as Operation Apache, which had started in 1996, was still continuing, and it was argued it might expose confidential police procedures.

One witness for the defence was Dennis Whomes, Jack's uncle. He had visited the yard in November and saw Steele's trailer for sale. He offered to take it home to Bulphan and try and sell it there. After Dennis had given evidence and left, Whomes was then asked about his trip to his uncle's house the night before the murders (cell site on his mobile phone had put him in the area). Whomes told the jury he had gone to his uncles to get the trailer, but it was locked, and no one was in. He remembered calling through the letterbox, then leaving a note. At this point the jury were shown a photograph of his uncles' door. It didn't have a letterbox. It was on the wall. The defence pointed out that the door and letterbox looked new, and that his uncle should be able to come back and tell the jury if they had been bought in the two years since the murders had occurred, but they were overruled.

III

The jury were informed that Billy Jasper was currently serving a long prison sentence for other matters. Jasper didn't want to give evidence in public, and refused to name the people he had mentioned in interview. He agreed he had told police that he and a few associates were talking about how they had been ripped off by Tucker. There was talk of a cocaine deal, and robbing the Essex boys, or even getting rid of them permanently, but Jasper thought nothing of it. Then a short time later he was offered the job as a driver. Jasper thought it was another drugs deal when he picked one associate up in a stolen car and they drove to a part of East London. The associate got out, and another business associate got in, this time with a holdall and what Jasper believed was a sawn-off shotgun. Jasper was given directions to Rettendon. The associate, wearing a tracksuit and trainers, got out and said he would be back in a bit.

The associate came back with what he said was a couple of kilos of cocaine. It was not until the next day that Jasper realised what he had been involved in. He may have initially decided to talk about the murders in the hope of getting a lesser sentence. His account matched some of the witnesses who believed they heard shooting around midnight, but without an official time of death, this seemed to be irrelevant.

Later, we shall talk about Operation Tiberius, the largest ever investigation into police corruption in London and the south east. It included Mr Jasper and his connections with serving officers. Basically, even though his account was about as credible as Darren Nicholls; Billy was the one who had police and thieves in high places. In another twist, at the time Jasper was giving evidence, Jesse Gale, the man Jasper had named in interview as being involved, but refused to say his name in court, was killed after being hit by a car

One of the things the jury were still not clear of is when the plan to murder took place? Was it on the the 4th, when Mick Steele possibly said "Fuck it," and decided he wasn't going to run? Was it on the 3rd, when Billy Blundell warned Tate to be careful if he stayed with Tucker? Leah Betts was buried on the 1st December. On that day the Government proclaimed that drug dealers would be brought to justice.

How about the last few weeks of November when Tate kicked Saunders out of her house, and the only way she was getting back in was if he left in a box? Or O'Mahoney after he had walked away from Raquel's? The 17th November, when Steele handed back all the money for the bad drugs deal, knowing that a third of it was good? This was when Steele told Tate that a London Crime Cartel wanted him to bring back a plane load of cocaine, and that the Essex boys should rob it.

This is the same week that Leah Betts dies after taking an ecstasy pill from Raquels. Tate crashing Tuckers Porsche and being arrested for drunk driving. Even though he is on licence he somehow isn't recalled back to prison. How about the 6th November, which is just one of the dates that Steele asks Nicholls to get him a shotgun?

The 5th of November, when the Essex boys organise the cannabis deal. The first week that Tate is out of prison, when Saunders decides she cannot live with Tate anymore. This could also be when either Tucker or Tate contact someone in the London Crime Cartel about the drugs dropped into a reservoir near Rettendon. It must also be in the same week Tate is getting money to put into the cannabis syndicate.

The 31st October, when Tate gets out of prison. If someone

wanted to kill him and Tucker, they would have had to have waited a year. That must be the last date that we can really say the murders must have been planned, surely?

What about September, when the plane load of cannabis that was found near Rettendon, and Tucker suddenly moving to a new address and trying to obtain a shotgun licence. The green Range Rover that Tucker used to own now disappearing. Tate in prison asking Steele to take his twenty thousand pounds that Tucker was holding to pay Saunders, and for Steele to give her money on a weekly basis.

The stories of Tucker and Rolfe robbing drug dealers, and even killing one of them with an overdose. In truth we could go back years. There are plenty of unsolved murders and attempted murders in Essex and the east end that we could attribute to Tucker, Tate and Rolfe having at least some knowledge of. Real revenge is timeless. If your planning on killing someone and getting away with it, make sure you pick the right moment.

Let's not forget to go forward a few years as well. Whoever finished off the Essex boys probably started off taking over at least one of their clubs. But a jury doesn't deal in probable's; they have to believe beyond all reasonable doubt in order to convict.

We finish on the forensics. The plain truth was that there wasn't any. There are also no reports of SOCO finding areas on the car that showed signs of being wiped clean. Without getting too Quincy, there is nothing to suggest that there was someone sitting in the rear of the Range Rover that night. As such, the defence barrister had a real chance of putting doubt in the jury's mind about Steele being at the scene. And if he wasn't there, then the trial was over.

The pump action shotgun found in Steele's barn was compared with the small firing pin marks on the cartridges from the crime scene, and they did not match. There was the expert opinion that the cartridges all came from the same shotgun; which was different from Nicholls account of two weapons being used – eight shots, but only seven cartridges found; perhaps one got stuck in the other gun? Steele had denied any knowledge of asking Nicholls to get him a gun, or that he had ever seen the found shotgun before.

To be fair to Nicholls, it would have been quite easy for him to say he got Steele the gun before the murders took place, but he never. He always maintained that he got it after the killings. He was, after all, the only honest criminal in court that day.

Chapter 16.

The mobile phone evidence.

"We shall defend our island, whatever the cost may be. We shall fight on the beaches, we shall fight on the landing grounds, we shall fight in the fields and in the streets, we shall fight in the hills; we shall never surrender."
Winston Churchill.

.   I

If you have ever read the terms and conditions for a mobile phone, then you are a better man than me. In 1995 mobile phones were a lot simpler, but trying to explain to a jury how they worked was always going to be difficult, especially when at that time there were two types of mobile phones. Analogue, which were similar to walkie talkies; and digital, which would be the way forward. Both worked on the principle of triangulation. If you were to stand in a field, your phone would find the nearest three masts. It would then connect to the one which had the best signal; and it would also give your location on a map to within half a mile. The phone would change masts as you moved around In 1995 it wasn't an exact science. Masts could cover a radius of about thirty miles, allowing a sixty-mile gap between each one, far away enough so that the signal could often be lost. Sometimes swapping over the phone from your left to our right hand would cause the signal to switch to another mast. These were heady days.

Both Steele and Whomes were within thirty miles of the murder scene, if you believed the killings took place when Nicholls said they did. The prosecution stated that it seemed slightly strange for two men who lived over fifty miles away both happened to be near Rettendon that night. The defence argued that half the population of Essex were within thirty miles of Rettendon on the 6th December. Steele's defence was that he was with his partner, coming back from Bulphan after picking up a trailer. In relation to Whomes, he said he was in the Wheatsheaf pub picking up Nicholls broken down VW Passat. The call he made to Nicholls saying he had got it went to the phone mast nearest to the pub rather than Workhouse lane, and helped prove his alibi.

In order to show the evidence, the prosecution gave the jury a series of maps of where the masts were, and an area of where the phones were. There was also a list of various phone numbers, the time of the calls, and who was called.

But there was a highly contentious legal issue before they were shown to the jury. The phone list had been redacted by the prosecution. They had decided which calls they believed were relevant to the case. This would now be considered a miscarriage of justice, but in 1997 no one was aware of just how important mobile phone technology would be. The defence team did request to see all the phone calls before the trial; but then came another issue. The police were only wiling to send them the phone records for Tucker and Tate up to 7pm, when they believed the killings had happened. By the time the defence asked for all the information, over a year since the deaths, the phone companies have got rid of their records.

The prosecution refused to hand over all the phone records. This could be because one of the numbers had connected to another number which had been deemed to be highly sensitive; and to give a full record of all the phones apart from one number would imply someone was possibly passing on sensitive information.

We then come to the last issue in relation to the cell site evidence. Between December 95 and August 97, extra transmitter masts had been built, changing the signal strength of a phone in a certain location. To recreate the same tests even a year later to try and match the results from the night of the 6th would be flawed.

Going back to the list, some of the numbers also related to landlines; so, the name of the person paying the bill might not be the person holding the phone. For example, someone using Rolfe's landline number may be speaking to his partner Donna Jaggers; and Jackie Street might be using Steele's landline to call Mrs Whomes. The Police also included some calls made from payphones because they believed that these were made by people linked to the trial, either the victims or the defendants. Here we have the edited list of the calls made on the 6th December.

Time	Number ending	Caller	Number	Person called
09.02	7327	TUCKER (Mobile)	0213	ROLFE (Landline)
09.20	7131	TATE (Landline 49 Gordon rd)	7327	TUCKER (Mobile)
09.26	7131	TATE (Landline 49 Gordon rd)	0213	ROLFE (Landline)
09.55	7327	TUCKER (Mobile)	7679	GARWOOD (Landline)
09.56	7679	GARWOOD (Landline)	7679	GARWOOD (Landline)
09.59	8162	TUCKER (Landline)	0213	ROLFE (Landline)
10.21	7327	TUCKER (mobile)	7679	GARWOOD (landline)
11.21	1430	NICHOLLS (landline)	7288	NICHOLLS (mobile)
11.31	7327	TUCKER (mobile)	0923	TATE (MOBILE)
11.43	7327	TUCKER (mobile)	0537	Basildon Tyre Services Ltd
11.46	7131	TATE (landline 49 Gordon rd)	7327	TUCKER (mobile)
11.50	8327	SAUNDERS (landline)	1979	STEELE (landline)
12.21	8162	TUCKER Landline	7327	TUCKER (mobile)
12.22	7679	GARWOOD (landline)	7679	GARWOOD (landline)
12.51	7288	NICHOLLS (mobile)	1979	STEELE (landline)
12.52	7288	NICHOLLS (mobile)	3978	STEELE (mobile)
12.53	7288	NICHOLLS (mobile)	2729	STEELE (mobile)

12.54	7288	NICHOLLS (mobile)	1430	NICHOLLS (landline)	
12.54	7288	NICHOLLS (mobile)	3978	STEELE (mobile)	
12.59	1979	STEELE (landline)	5646	WHOMES (mobile)	
13.23	7327	TUCKER (mobile)	8162	TUCKER (Landline)	
13.24	0923	TATE (mobile)	8162	TUCKER (landline)	
14.00	3978	STEELE (mobile)	7288	NICHOLLS (mobile)	
14.02	8162	TUCKER (landline.	7327	TUCKER (mobile)	
14.11	3978	STEELE (mobile)	5646	WHOMES (mobile)	
14.14	0923	TATE (mobile)	0537	Basildon Tyre Services Ltd	
14.22	0537	Basildon Tyre Services Ltd	7327	TUCKER (mobile)	
14.23	7131	TATE (landline 49 Gordon rd	7327	TUCKER (mobile)	
14.29	1430	NICHOLLS (landline)	7288	NICHOLLS (mobile)	
14.29	0370	Payphone, Sorell Horse Inn, Ipswich	7327	TUCKER (mobile)	
14.32	0370	Payphone, Sorell Horse Inn, Ipswich	010*	Payphone Timberlog Lane. Clay Hill Rd, Basildon	
14.32	0370	Payphone, Sorell Horse Inn, Ipswich	7327	TUCKER (mobile)	
14.52	0370	Payphone, Sorell Horse Inn, Ipswich	7288	NICHOLLS (mobile)	
14.56	1430	NICHOLLS (landline)	7288	NICHOLLS (mobile)	
14.56	1430	NICHOLLS (landline)	7288	NICHOLLS (mobile)	
15.06	3978	STEELE (mobile)	7288	NICHOLLS (mobile)	
15.08	3978	STEELE (mobile)	5646	WHOMES (mobile)	
15.50	0923	TATE (mobile)	0213	ROLFE (landline)	
15.57	1979	STEELE (landline)	7288	NICHOLLS (mobile)	
16.04	7679	GARWOOD Landline	7679	GARWOOD (landline)	
16.36	7288	NICHOLLS mobile	1430	NICHOLLS (landline)	
16.39	7288	NICHOLLS mobile	3978	STEELE (mobile)	
17.09	6495	WHOMES landline	5646	WHOMES (mobile)	
17.12	5646	WHOMES mobile	3978	STEELE (mobile)	
18.03	3978	STEELE (mobile)	5646	WHOMES (mobile)	
18.09	3978	STEELE (mobile)	5646	WHOMES (mobile)	
18.34	8327	SAUNDERS (landline)	0049	MR M Hood. (landline)	
18.44	8327	SAUNDERS (landline)	0923	TATE (mobile)	
18.59	5646	WHOMES mobile	7288	NICHOLLS (mobile)	

19.19	1430	NICHOLLS (landline)	7288	NICHOLLS (mobile)	
19.55	7288	NICHOLLS (mobile)	51430	NICHOLLS (landline)	
20.18	1979	STEELE (landline)	43978	STEELE (mobile)	
20.20	1979	STEELE (landline)	5646	WHOMES (mobile)	
20.27	8162	TUCKER (landline)	7327	TUCKER (mobile)	
20.36	8162	TUCKER (landline)	0213	ROLFE (landline)	
20.39	1979	STEELE (landline)	3978	STEELE (mobile)	
20.39	1979	STEELE (landline)	5646	WHOMES (mobile)	
21.07	6495	WHOMES (landline)	5646	WHOMES (mobile)	
21.11	8162	TUCKER (Landline)	7327	TUCKER (mobile)	
21.22	1430	NICHOLLS (landline)	7288	NICHOLLS (mobile)	
21.49	5646	WHOMES mobile	6495	WHOMES (landline)	

What is noticeable is that Steele never makes any calls to Tucker or Tate's mobiles. Most of the calls in the morning seem to be domestic or business related. It is not until lunchtime that we get the impression that something is happening, when Nicholls makes numerous calls to Steele. The prosecution put it to the jury that it is Steele who uses a public telephone box at the Sorrell Horse Inn, near Ipswich, as he lived about twenty miles away from it. Although it would be more obvious for Whomes to make those calls, as he worked only a short distance away. In court, Whomes says that it is around this time Nicholls friend Colin Bridge comes to the yard to ask about using the trailer to collect the broken-down Passat; to which Whomes says that he will collect it instead.

The payphone makes a call to Tucker's mobile. Then a call from a payphone near Tate's bungalow, which is also just around the corner from the carpet shop Tucker had recently been in, calls back the payphone in Ipswich. Soon after that the payphone in Ipswich makes another call, this time to Nicholls mobile. Steele argued that it simply was not him. Part of Nicholls defence was that he was working near Heathrow on that day, and a cell site on one of is calls proves that. He remembers Steele calling him whilst he was at work, but it cannot be this call, as Nicholls is already driving home by now. At no point in his statement does he mention getting a phone call whilst driving; and it is not known if any cell site work was carried out on this particular call. If he is still in London, he cannot make it back to be at Marks Tey for 5pm.

When we look at the calls between Steele and Whomes, there is the one at 5.12pm. This would be when all three are travelling down from Marks Tey; but Nicholls fails to mention Steele getting any calls when he is sitting next to him in the Hilux. If we stick strictly to Nicholls account, it must mean Whomes had not yet arrived, or is just about to. And what this does is shift the time forward by fifteen minutes, so the hour it takes to get to the hallfway House means they will not arrive until at least 6,15pm. We can also include the calls at 6.03, and 6.09pm, Nicholls does not mention them in his statement. It could possibly be that the conversations were about the killings, and as such, it would destroy Nicholls basis of knowing nothing about them. But let's say that the calls take place when Nicholls and Whomes are trying to put on the false registration plates. Nicholls doesn't hear them because he's getting his shoes wet. Again, I have not seen the cell site locations for these calls. This now means they have to get to the Halfway House, wait for the Range Rover, and then to Rettendon, which is twenty-five minutes away, in under fifteen minutes.

The defence claimed the two calls were Steele and Whomes sorting out directions to pick up the trailer in Bulphan. The prosecution said that if Steele was in Bulphan at the time, his phone should have pinged from a transmitter mast that covered ninety percent of the area. Instead, it pinged off the mast that only covered ten percent of the area. Meaning he might not be exactly where he said he was, or he couldn't get a decent signal. But that doesn't mean he was lying. If Derick Whomes did not live in Bulphan, neither Steele nor Jack Whomes would have an alibi.

Nichols believed that the call made by Sarah Saunders to Tate at 6.44pm happens as they reached Workhouse lane. This call lasts four minutes. That is four minutes in which Tate never mentions he is with their old friend Mick Steele; the man who was apparently good friends with both of them, and was now going to solve all of Tate's problems. To be fair, Tate does not say he is with Tucker and Rolfe either; he merely mentions that he was "with people," which is something you might say if you were with a group of men you didn't really know.

This call has always felt like one of those calls that you keep going because you are waiting around, both passing the time until whatever you were expecting arrives. In relation to Saunders, she was about to go on a date with her new boyfriend. In relation to cell site, the opinion was that at the time of the call Tate was at least in Rettendon. Four minutes later, 6.47pm, and the jury are told that was the last phone conversation the three men had. The Range Rover has travelled the five hundred yards up to the gate. From Nicholls account, Steele gets out, shots are fired, and then we have ten minutes until Whomes makes the call to Nicholls at 6.59pm to come and get them. It is with this phone call that Whomes becomes more important than Steele.

The prosecution made the jury aware that there was a call just before this which lasted one second, which was not on the list, in which Whomes tried to call Nicholls but didn't connect. The first call went to the transmitter in Ingatestone, about ten miles away to the west of Rettendon; the second call goes to the transmitter in Hockley, again about ten miles away from Rettendon, to the east. The prosecution argued that it showed Whomes in Rettendon, possibly walking through a field trying to get a reception (for a big man in brand new wellington boots he must have been very light-footed). The defence argued that it showed Whomes in the area picking up Nicholls car, and that the transmitter mast the phone pinged to was the correct one if you were in the car park of the Wheatsheaf pub. The distance between the pub and the crime scene was less than a mile. When Nicholls gets the call, he is in Meadow Road; the distance between there and the crime scene is also less than a mile in the other direction.

On another point, Nicholls had said that Steele was in the

Range Rover at the time that Tate speaks to Saunders; but at this time Steele's phone signal is picked up by the transmitter mast in Wickford, which puts him further away from Workhouse Lane than either Whomes or Nicholls, and would be correct if he was on his way back from Bulphan after collecting a trailer. It is estimated the best time he could have reached Workhouse Lane would be 7.11pm.

Both prosecution and defence had their own experts, whose opinion differed slightly on whether the phones put the defendants in the Rettendon area at the time police believed the killings were carried out. And here was another issue for the jury; they had never been given an estimated time of death by a medical practitioner. There was also the issue of Nicholls making a phone call at 6.48pm, which went through the Rettendon beacon. This is not on the list, as the defence claimed it was Nicholls calling his voice message service.

The defence scored another point with Nicholls when his account that he had to move out of the Wheatsheaf pub car park was disputed, as he should have got a very good signal. The expert witness for the defence stated, "In my opinion the evidence in respect of calls received on Mr Nicholls' mobile phone suggests that at 6.59pm on 6th December 1995 he was within the geographical area served by the Orange network cell site at Basildon Essex. That evidence is not, in my view, consistent with Mr Nicholls' claim that at 6.59pm on 6th December 1995 he was in Meadow Road off the A130 near Rettendon." So, the jury were made aware that the man whose account tied the whole thing together, may not have been where he said he was. Ironic, as the only person who is actually claiming he went to Workhouse Lane that night is Nicholls.

Before we move on, there are two other interesting points to note. The jury were also given a phone list for the 5th December, which the prosecution had to admit it had also been edited. And the night before there were similar calls.

| 05/12/95 | 17.45 | 1430 | NICHOLLS (Landline) | 7288 | NICHOLLS (Mobile) |

05/12/95	18.07	5646	WHOMES Mobile	1979	STEELE (Landline)
05/12/95	19.16	1430	NICHOLLS (Landline)	7288	NICHOLLS (Mobile)
05/12/95	19.20	7288	NICHOLLS (Mobile)	1979	STEELE (Landline)
05/12/95	19.21	5646	WHOMES Mobile	6495	WHOMES (Landline)

The prosecution put it to Whomes that the call to Steele at 6.07pm was a dry run for what was to come. That Whomes was in Workhouse Lane seeing if it was a suitable location for what they had to do. Whomes claims he was in Bulphan trying to get the old trailer back. It is not known if any cell site work was done on Nicholls mobile for the 5th. Which again, seems strange. If he had been in the Rettendon area as well it would blow the theory that he knew nothing about the shootings the next night. Unfortunately, by the time the defence have been handed the list, they are told the cell site evidence had gone. And from the phone list it could be argued that Nicholls, who knew Bernard O'Mahoney, who knew Kenneth Noye, who knew corrupt detectives, is the one calling Steele the night before to see what plans he had the next evening. He is also the one calling Steele on the 6th. The defence argued that perhaps it was not Steele who was organising the murders to take place that night.

For the edited phone list on the day after the murders, there was something that the jury may not have spotted.

Date	Time	Number	From	To	Number
07/12/95	12.04	7404	ROLFE (Mobile)	0213	ROLFE (Landline Jaggers)

Did a dead man in a car surrounded by police call home? This is the only occasion that Rolfe's mobile phone appears in the schedule. It would be amazing if a busy drug dealer only made one call on his mobile on the last three days before he died. And if Rolfe had told Jaggers to get a new dress as they were going out that night, surely, she would have called to to find out where he was after he didn't pick her up? What we don't know is if any cell site work was carried out for this phone, which you would

189 WHO KILLED THE ESSEX BOYS?

think would be vitally important.

I still believe that Rolfe had a phone on him, but this was a business, or "burner" phone used solely for Tucker and Tate to sort out deals. Having a phone like this meant that if Tucker or Tate were ever arrested, there would be nothing on their phones to link them to drugs. Rolfe, who had no qualms about collecting a machine gun, would think nothing of carrying this mobile; and the killer took it because they must have known it would link them to the murders. But who called using this mobile on the day after the murders?

We also have a police print out from the 8th December, in which Rolfe has a mobile number ending 4913. This is not the same as Rolfe's mobile on the phone list, which ends 7404.

Sometime after the deaths, Sarah Saunders was questioned about Tate having a second phone which she seemed desperate to get back. Her reply was that John McCarthy, had asked her to try and get it, for reasons unknown. This was the same McCarthy who had been involved in the cocaine deal, and had offered the Essex boys a million pounds if they got the drugs. It was also the same Mr McCarthy who had paid for Tate's funeral, so he must have had some contact with Saunders immediately after the killings. The defence could have also looked into why McCarthy wanted Tate's other phone. Jaggers had said he was involved in the drug deal, Saunders had said he wanted a phone back after the murders, and the police did...well, nothing. This is very surprising as Essex police were about to start Operation Apache, the investigation into links between corrupt detectives and high-ranking members of London Crime Cartels. Here was a man who had a million-pounds available for drugs, and probably enough clout to have the Essex boys ironed out for less than half the price.

Perhaps the jury, confused about this new technology, just wanted to know who was in Rettendon at the time of the murders. The prosecution couldn't put anyone in the lane; but the defence couldn't say they were definitely not in the area. With no forensics, no other evidence; nothing apart from mobile phone data which was at best fallible; the only solid account came from Nicholls. He said he was in Rettendon, his broken-down VW Passat was in Rettendon, and his phone put him in Rettendon at the time the police said the murders took place. But did that mean when he pressed the answer button on his mobile, he also pointed the finger at the two men in the dock?

Chapter 17.

Statements.

"How many special people change?
How many lives are living strange?
Where were you while we were getting high?"
Oasis.

I

In America the justice system allows for the prosecution and defence to choose each member of the jury. From a pool of a hundred available, each side must agree as to who they want to sit.
For example, in the trial of O.J. Simpson, the defence demanded
that they jury be made up of nine African-Americans, one His-
panic, and two white people, totally opposite the actual demo-
graphic of the country. The prosecution, believing the evidence
would be enough and that people would not be racially biased,
agreed. There was also another aspect about the jury that the
prosecution believed. Out of twelve people, ten of them were
women; and women tend to make their mind up quickly.

Donna Jaggers was going to be very important for the prosecution. She had signed the main statement dated the 14th
March 1996, two months before the arrests. In it she names
Mick Steele as the person the Essex boys were going to meet that
night. The defence would find it difficult to dispute what was
in it, because the important parts all started with "Craig said to
me," like Tom Jones with another Elvis story. It contained detailed accounts of the bad drug deal, the plan to rob a plane of

cocaine, and the build up to the night of the murders.

She mentioned that Rolfe told her the bad weather had held them up, although it is not clear if he meant that the snow which had started on the 4th December had stopped the plane from landing at a certain time. If so, the Essex boys may have gone to Workhouse Lane any time before the 6th to check it out. On the day of the murders she was due to finish work at 3pm. That evening Tucker and his partner Anna, Rolfe and Jaggers, and Tate with a woman named Clare (the waitress from TGI Fridays), were all going to the Global Net Cafe restaurant in Romford. They believed they were coming into money and they were going to have a celebration meal.

Jaggers, probably more than Nicholls, is the one who wins the jury over. She knew her partner was a bad boy, but loved him anyway (she had no choice, she had a child with him). She told the jury about being with him when he was committing crime, but only so he wouldn't end up being addicted to drugs again. She was helping him through the narrow times in the hope he would go straight; the Nancy to Craig's Spike. She knew he was no good, but as long as he needed her, she was willing to suffer; and go out for meals with his friends.

Her statement does not mention why he was at Gray's police station at 4.30pm; but then her timing seems to be out from the afternoon onwards. The being dropped off at Lakeside at 5:45pm goes against pretty much every statement about the Range Rover that the police had obtained so far, including Anna Whitehead's. It was dark, rush hour, and there was snow and ice on the road, so let's assume it would take about twenty-five minutes to drop Jaggers off. You will now have to fight the traffic to go and pick up Tucker, which is also about twenty-five minutes away. Being generous, and if you drove like a loon, you probably could make Tuckers for 6pm, but that doesn't give you much time to collect Tate and make your way to the Halfway House which is forty minutes away. Jaggers may have said 5.45pm because it matched the time frame for when police believed the Essex boys had been killed. Lakeside at quarter to six, Tucker at six, Tate at quarter past, Workhouse Lane at quarter to seven. . And now that she had signed such a detailed statement, it would be impossible to change it.

Anna Whitehead says she sees Rolfe and Tucker drive away from the bungalow in Fobbing around 6pm. For Rolfe to get to Gordon Road to collect Tate would take ten minutes. The Halfway House pub, another twenty-five. This is where Steele meets the Range Rover, and they all drive to the Hungry Horse pub, another twenty-five minutes away. After Steele parks and gets into the Range Rover, we have another ten minutes until they get to Workhouse Lane. It really depends on what witness you wish to believe. So far, we have not heard from anyone who has nothing to lose or gain by telling the truth. A final note about Jaggers. On the 18th July 96, there are two old fashioned identification parades, where people are lined up against the wall, and she recognises the man she knows as "Mickey the Pilot" as Michael Steele. In a second parade she identifies someone as the man she saw once in a passing glimpse in the white car from nine months ago outside Tuckers home when they were collecting some drugs, and states that it was the man she saw with Steele. It is Jack Whomes.

The next important witness was going to be Sara Saunders, the former partner of Tate. But she said could not attend to give evidence for personal reasons. She had been interviewed about the conversation with Tate about Steele taking a trip up north, and not coming back. She had told police about meeting Steele at a McDonalds on the 4th December to tell him about the threat, and him not seeming to take it seriously. Even afterwards she refused to link Steele to the murders. Also, when she called Tate on the evening he was killed, she believed that if he was with his Steele in the car, he would have mentioned it at some point during the four-minute conversation. She did give a statement that on the day of the murders he, Tucker and Rolfe attend her mums address to collect the car he had lent her because it had broken down. They leave around 3pm. Tate in the VW Golf, Tucker and Rolfe in the Range Rover. She later calls Tate at about 6.45pm, and he tells her "I cannot talk to you now, I've got people with me. I'll talk to you tomorrow."

Jackie Street, Steele's long-term partner, was also unable to give evidence due to severe depression. Before her statement was read out to the jury, they were advised that as she couldn't be cross examined, they had to decide if she was telling the truth or not. Her account was the same as Steele's. They had gone to Bulphan to collect a trailer, stopping off on the way there to get petrol, and then at a Tesco to get sausage rolls. They were together throughout the evening.

One woman who did turn up was Donna Garwood. Although Anna Whitehead should have been the more obvious choice, as she was living with Tucker at the time. She told the jury that she had accompanied Tate and others to Ostend on November 16th, 1995. Tate paid for everything including meals, ferry tickets, drinks and hotel bills. When they reached Ostend, they went to a pub and Tate left them to talk to a man. She said: "They came back into the pub together. This guy Michael was carrying a carrier bag." The two men sat at a separate table to the party and talk together for some time and Garwood said later that evening she noticed Tate then had the bag. She also mentioned that before he was killed, Tucker had become very concerned about something that Tate had done, and felt it had caused a lot of problems.

The first thing that comes to mind is that he was the one who was supplying the Ecstasy pill that Leah Betts had taken. If he had bought a load on tick, and then dumped them when he thought they were bad, that's a quick twenty grand you could owe. Or it could have been stitching up those who had given him money for the bad cannabis deal. But Garwood believed something had happened before then. Let's not forget that it would be good for business if the issue with Nipper Ellis was resolved; especially if it was a London Crime Cartel who wanted it to end. The second thing that comes to mind is that Steele is the one handing the bag over to Tate.

The one thing missing from all those weeks of madness is any mention of what Tate felt about his old friend Nipper. Ironic-ally, the whole thing had started because of Garwood. The court heard she was asked to identify Steele in an identity parade at Colchester but failed. Under cross-examination by the defence she pointed out Steele in the dock (bit easy, he was the one standing in-between two security guards). The female jurors might have thought the women had pretty much put Steele in the picture; but there was one more to come.

Rebecca Carr was probably the most important witness the defence had. She was a fully paid up civilian who did not know anyone involved in the case, and came forward after the mur-ders were reported on the news. Carr had finished work at her school and was driving home when she sees the Range Rover with three men in it when they stop at the traffic lights in Ret-tendon at 5:45pm. She identified Tucker in the front and Tate in the back. She is absolutely sure of the time, as she retraced her journey back and could tell where she was at specific points. The three large men in the Range Rover stood out essentially be-cause they were three large men in a Range Rover. She believed they were following a white Sierra, which also appeared to have three people in it. As the lights changed, the Range Rover kept up the Sierra as it overtook a slow-moving transit van (Whomes had a transit van), and then it did the same. They passed Work-house Lane, then both cars quickly pulled into the forecourt of Whitehouse Farm shop and turned so that they both faced the road. Carr is someone who had a clear and unobstructive view of the people in the Range Rover. She is able to give a time and lo-cation. More importantly, she mentioned the white Sierra, even though the public had never been told of another car; and the tyre tracks found at the scene could have belonged to a Sierra Cosworth. Although she didn't see who was in the white car, it did throw serious doubt over Nicholls account of Steele being in the back of the Range Rover at the time he said it was. We should take Carr's statement as the most truthful: three men in a Range Rover near Workhouse Lane.

It is quite possible for them to drive to the Halfway House

soon after, as its only twenty minutes away and would still just fit into Nicholls timeline. But then how can Steele be luring these men to their deaths if they are the ones who are seen at Workhouse Lane an hour before they are killed? The question was, could any other witness back up her claim; or at least put doubt on Nicholls?

II

When was the last time you saw three men in a car? As well as Tucker having a head like a mop, and Tate with biceps like a grizzly bear's legs when its crouching to take a shit; you knew that when you saw them, you knew. You knew that these were not the sort of people you were going to fuck with if they decided to drive at three miles an hour, and they knew it as well. As such, you probably would remember them, if only to make sure you stayed out of their way. You could argue that Steele and Whomes were also two big men; and Steele also had a Range Rover. Bernard O'Mahoney was also over 6ft tall. What car he was driving that night we don't know.

The only person who can't be thrown in with all these big lumps is that little fringe Darren Nicholls. He is the only one you would drive past and then immediately forget. But when you see the news, three men killed in Range Rover in Rettendon; chances are you would remember when and where you saw them. Over the course of the investigation the police took hundreds of statements, although we only have what has been made available to the public. At this stage I am not sure what statements the jury were given in 1997. They would have been given what was called "a bundle," filled with statements and documents for them to read. I have put in what I think are relevant statements in a timeline of events, rather than the dates they were taken. We must also be aware, that unless someone is able to corroborate the time in some way, we have to give a bit of leeway on whatever they call; let's say fifteen minutes either side.

William Theobald owned Whitehouse farm, along with his brother Peter. About twelve years ago he joined a gym and got to be friends with Tony Tucker. They would often give each other lifts, so Tucker knew where he lived. William stated that Tucker began to stop going to the gym on a regular basis when he split up with his wife, and they last spoke a few years ago. William ran the shooting club whilst his brother Peter looked after the pheasants. William only sold mauve and red shotgun cartridges. Workhouse Lane was part of the farm. It led to the fields used for shooting. A small stretch of woodland went around the edge of the fields, and there was a small track that ran alongside it to three ponds and a small patch of land where cars could park. The gate was usually locked when it got dark. In December this would have been before 5pm.

P. Gilmore gives a statement that at some point in September 95 he sees a green Range Rover parked in Workhouse Lane. There was a driver, a passenger, and someone in the back; all of large build. They appeared to be speaking to someone who was standing outside, and looked nervous. There were also two other cars parked on the opposite side of the road. Gilmore only remembered it because he thought there was going to be a fight. We know that Tate is not with them. But it is believed Tucker had a green Range Rover at this time; and let's remember that the plane load of drugs is meant to have been dropped at around this time. It is possible that Tucker was already involved in a London Crime Cartel, and the loss of the drugs.

P. Draper recalls that on the 27th November 1995 he had to take his wife's car to work. At approx. 8.30am he sees a dark blue Range Rover travel through Rettendon. Just after it passed Whitehouse farm it indicated to turn into the track road. He believes there were only two people in the vehicle at the time.

On 4th December A. Grayston is driving past Whitehouse farm on his way to work in the morning when he sees a white BMW on the track road, sticking slightly out of the junction. The lorry in front of Grayston has to slow down to get around it, and so dies he. As he does, he sees a white male walking in the field down towards the car. He was white, well built, 30's, short dark hair, and looked similar to the footballer Steve Bull. He was also carrying a pair of binoculars.

B. Lowe is driving past Workhouse Lane at around 6.15pm of December 5th. He sees a dark coloured Range Rover and a Ford saloon type car. Three men are standing in the lane, and two of them appeared to be arguing with the third. The two men closest to the Range Rover are described as large build. The third man was tall, in his forties, and going bald. This statement is interesting on the basis the prosecution believed that Whomes was in Rettendon at the time doing a rehearsal for the killings.

S. Armstrong worked in the Carpenters Arms pub, Rawreth (just down the road from the Hungry Horse in the next village of Rayleigh). It is a small out of the way pub, mainly used by the locals. He states that on either the 5th or 6th December at around 8pm, Craig Rolfe and another male came up to the bar and ordered drinks. They stayed for about twenty minutes and then left. Armstrong cannot be sure of the exact date. I think we can say that chances are it was the night before the murders; but a note should be made that Workhouse Lane was only a few miles away, and again, the prosecution believe Whomes was in Rettendon on the 5th. The Carpenters Arms pub comes up again during Steele's defence. He claimed that one day in November Nicholls called him as he had been threatened by Tate about some dud cannabis. Steele met Tate in the Carpenters Arms a few days later, where he arranged to help get back the money.

H. Owide was at home in Canning Town, east London, at 11.15pm on Tuesday 5th December. He saw a dark coloured Range Rover in Wanstead Park Road. "My attention was drawn to this vehicle because when it pulled to the offside four large males got out of the vehicle. After seeing their faces in a newspaper, Owide believed one of the men was Rolfe.

B. Thompson lives near Gordon road, Essex, where Tate had the bungalow. He remembers seeing the Range Rover on a couple of occasions, and knew Tate by sight. On Monday evening, 4th December, he remembered seeing a white transit van outside Tate's address. There were two people in the van; one was Tate, the other was another large white male. Then just after midnight of Wednesday 6th, Mr Thompson took his dog for a walk. He saw the transit van outside the bungalow again. As he approached, it drove away towards Timberlog Lane. A few minutes later a police car appeared. Thompson remembered it because he wondered if the police car was following the van.

We are now into the day of the murders. It is quite possible for Steele to fly from Essex to Amsterdam and back within a couple of hours, depending on the weather.

F. Darling goes past Workhouse Lane around 8am of the 6th December, and sees three men standing next to a dark coloured Range Rover. All three men were wearing dark coloured clothing, and looked as if they were waiting for someone. It would seem strange that if you were waiting for someone for a legitimate purpose, why not use the large farm shop forecourt just a few hundred yards up the road?

G. Gilmore drives past Workhouse Lane between 8 – 9am. He sees a Range Rover facing onto the road. One man is standing by the front passenger door. He is white, aged in his twenties, 6ft tall, medium build. There are two other men in the car. Both of them are of a large build. There were two other vehicles parked nearby; one of which is a BMW.

S. Morgan drives past workhouse Lane at around 9.30am. He sees a blue Range Rover in workhouse Lane. There were two men in the front of it, and a man in the back. He could only describe them as white, late twenties to early thirties. looking at the edited phone list, it's quite possible for them to be in Workhouse Lane, and that Rolfe is using Tuckers mobile to call home. Liz Fletcher could also be calling Tucker's mobile if Tate did not have a signal. But we come a bit unstuck for the call at 9.26am, as it is Tate's landline calling Rolfe's landline; unless Liz is still trying to get hold of Tate, and calls Rolfe's home to see if he is there.

Mrs Theobald lives at Whitehouse farm, and on that day

was working in the farm shop. Workhouse lane is a few hundred yards down the road. Sometime before 10.30am she sees a white car pull into the forecourt, quickly followed by a Range Rover, with a group of large white males inside. She remembered it because they looked like bailiffs. Neither vehicle stops fully. Instead, they seemed to get in line, headed towards the exit, and then out towards Workhouse lane. We know that the gate was unlocked at around 8am every morning. As these statements were taken days or a few weeks after the murders, it is highly likely that police would have checked who was using the fields that day for fishing or pheasant shooting. But there is no evidence to suggest that three innocent men were in a Range Rover at that time. Surely five separate witnesses can't be wrong? Anyone of the Essex boys could make Workhouse Lane within thirty minutes, so it not impossible for them to keep coming back to the Lane. The question is why?

Mr A. Reynolds was a mechanic for Basildon Tyre Services (the place that keeps popping up in the phone list). He remembers he was called by Tucker and Rolfe prior to the 6th in relation to the repair of a Vauxhall Vitara that belonged to Tucker's girlfriend. Then on the 6th December between 10.00-11.00am, Tate and a female known as Liz arrive. Tate is driving a Mercedes, and Liz is driving a VW Polo. They agree to take the Vitara, leaving the VW Polo to be repaired. An arrangement was made to pick the polo up before 6pm, if not it would be left on the forecourt for someone to collect. Tate takes the Vitara and Liz drives away in the Mercedes.

V. Thurlow was at home at 11.45am on 6th December. From his bedroom window he sees a blue Range Rover heading from West Road to Gainsborough Drive, with just one occupant. It was being followed by a white Ford Granada type car with lots of spoilers, and possibly six people inside. The speed of the vehicles and the nature of their driving made him concerned. He believes he then hears the sound of gun shot. When he looks out both cars are driving at speed. We only have Peter Cuthbert's statement that he was driving a Mitsubishi Shogun on the day.

Workhouse Lane is about a twenty-minute drive away.

E. Guiragossianlapage was a neighbour of Rolfe's. She has seen Rolfe drive numerous cars since he has lived at his address, including a white van, a Mercedes, a jaguar, and a Peugeot. At around midday she sees Rolfe drive off in the blue Range Rover.

Peter Cuthbert states that he met Tucker Tate and Rolfe at the Eastern garage about midday to sign for the finance on the Range Rover. They then all get into Cuthbert's Mitsubishi Shogun and drive to TGI Fridays, where they stay for about an hour. They then go to Diamond Close, near Rawreth, as Tucker wanted to speak to someone, but they are not in. Cuthbert then drives all of them back to Eastern Garages, where Tucker, Tate and Rolfe speak to someone in the showroom office. Cuthbert believes they all leave the garage sometime between 3 and 4pm. He had been asked if he and his wife wished to join everyone for a meal at the Global café that night, but declined as he had to get up early the next day.

Barry Dorman stated that on the 6th, Tucker, Tate, Rolfe and Peter Cuthbert turned up at his car showroom near the Five Bells Roundabout, roughly twenty minutes away from Rettendon, sometime before lunch. Cuthbert was going to be the named person paying back the finances on the Range Rover, but Tucker was paying off the money; and Dorman was told that the payment would soon be paid off in one lump sum. They filled in the forms and then left. Tate had also been looking for a car to give to Sarah Saunders, and had agreed on a white VW Passat that Dorman had got on the 25th November as a part exchange (from a Mr Bowman who had been there the day before perhaps?). Tate mentioned that he was still going to buy it. Dorman does not mention them returning after lunch.

L. Wolfe worked at TGI Friday's. She states that she spoke to four men sat at a table at around 1pm. Tucker and Tate introduced themselves, and at some point, Tate asked Wolfe to get another waitress, Claire Carey, to ring him. Everyone (apart from Cuthbert) appeared to be in high spirits and was messing around. She believes Tucker had to use Tate's phone as his couldn't get a signal. They left after an hour.

M. Harding of L. T Carpets, Timberlog Lane, gives a statement in which Tucker, Tate and Rolfe arrive in a blue Range Rover between 1.30-2pm, to pay off a bill for a flat that was being renovated by Tucker. Harding states that although all three men came into the yard, only Tucker came in the office to pay off the bill. He does not mention if Tucker received any calls on his mobile. What is obvious is the clear discrepancy between this and Peter Cuthbert's statement. Cuthbert states that they are all in his Shogun until at least 3pm. We now have the phone calls from the payphone in Ipswich, Tucker's mobile, and a payphone in Timberlog lane. These are all around 2.30pm.

Sarah Saunders says that at around 3pm, Tucker, Tate and Rolfe come over to her mum's because the VW Golf has broken down. Tate has an argument with Saunders, causing Tucker and Rolfe to hold him back from attacking her. If we assume that this is the VW Golf that Saunders sees on the driveway of Gordon Road and sells it to Steele after Tate has died, then let's say that it was driven back there this afternoon.

DC Pullinger sees Rolfe driving along Brooke Road and then parking outside Grays police station at 4.30pm. DC Pullinger knows Rolfe, and reminds him to get Jaggers to come in and give a statement. DC Pullinger then gets back in his car and drives away. If DC Pullinger knows Rolfe, why is he not arresting him for driving whilst disqualified? Why does he want a statement for Donna Jaggers, and what is it for? Finally, where is Rolfe going? This time fits if we make the timeline of Rolfe picking up Tucker at 5pm, picking up Tate at 5.30pm, and being at Workhouse Lane at 5.45pm. In fact, if it wasn't for witness statements from people who knew them, this would be perfect. But DC Pullinger mentions that Rolfe is wearing tracksuit bottoms and a puffa jacket, so he must go home and get changed.

Barry Dorman left his car showroom sometime around 5pm. As he was driving, he got a phone call from work saying that Tate had turned back up. Tate spoke to Dorman and explained that he wasn't going to give the Passat to Sarah as they had an argument, but would still take the car as he had agreed to buy it. He told Doorman that he would pay for it in the morning as he had "a lump of money coming," and then took the vehicle. Tate lived about five minutes' drive away, but we don't know how he got to the showroom, and why he needed the Passat if he wasn't going to give it to Saunders? Tate has so far been in a Mercedes, a Vauxhall Vitara, a Range Rover, A shogun, a VW Golf, and a VW Passat.

Colin Bridge, the man in the van who was stopped with Nicholls when he was arrested in May, is also the man who allegedly attends Whomes yard to ask about using a trailer to collect the broken-down Passat on the afternoon of the 6th. He does not give a statement until months after the murders, so is a bit vague on the details. He believes that on the day he has been picked up by Nicholls first thing in the morning, and they have driven into London. He believes Nicholls was driving a white VW Scirocco. They worked until about 1.30pm, and then driven back to Essex, where they went into The Cock pub, and stayed drinking for a few hours. Bridge drives Nicholls back to Nicholls home, and leaves him and the car at the address at around 5pm, making it impossible for him to reach Marks Tey at the time he said he did. Then again, perhaps he didn't need to drive all that way. On another note, this is the same pub where Nicholls claimed he was approached by a corrupt detective and asked to be an informant.

At around 5.15pm, A. White has left Basildon and is driving eastwards along the A127 towards Southend and the turn off for the A130. A dark blue Range Rover in front of him keeps pulling out into to road, possibly to see what is ahead of the traffic. There are two people in the back, aged mid 30's, and he describes them as scruffy looking (boiler suits?). One of them was wearing a black reefer type coat with large lapels (is this the black coat Whomes takes from the back seat of the Passat?). He could not see if there was someone in the front passenger seat. The driver is described as having short dark hair and being clean shaven. The Range Rover then turned off and headed south on the A130. This is the first time that we possibly have four people in the Range Rover. The roads Mr White is describing are a series of dual carriageways. The A127 goes over the A130. When White states they then head south, they are heading towards the roundabout, which will enable them to head north on the A130, towards Rettendon, and Workhouse Lane, approximately fifteen minutes away. Or, you could continue south towards Gordon Road, again, only fifteen minutes away.

Mr Hassell, Tate's neighbour, hears the sound of a car horn at 5.30pm. He looks out of his window to see a Range Rover turning in the road. He does not think that it's the same green coloured Range Rover that he has seen before (would this have been Tucker's old Range Rover?), but at this time it is already dark. He then hears someone coming out of Tate's address, and the car driving away. Workhouse lane is twenty minutes up the road.

D. Burrows is driving past Whitehouse Farm at approx. 5.30pm. There is a dark coloured saloon car in front of her driving very slowly. When it reached Workhouse Lane the car suddenly turned left into the lane without indicating. She could not see how many people were in the car.

R. Carr has already stated she saw the Range Rover in Rettendon at 5.45pm, and it seemed to be following a white car, possibly a Sierra. Both of which both pull in to the forecourt of Whitehouse Farm shop. She is able to make a positive identification. Although Darren Nicholls has never been able to remember exactly what car he was driving on the night of the 6th, we have to wonder why he would be so far out on his timeline. The only thing we know in his statement that is correct is that he receives a call from Whomes at 6.59pm. That cannot be disputed. We also have the phone call from Sarah Saunders. So, the only other answer is that the Essex boys have gone to workhouse Lane before Nicholls states, and then left.

Mr Reynolds closes the garage bang on 6pm, leaving the VW Polo outside, and drives away. About five minutes later he sees the blue Range Rover, with Rolfe, Tucker, and Tate in the back. He believes they are heading towards Cranes Close to pick up the car. Workhouse Lane is about a fifteen-minute drive away. At approx. 10pm, Reynolds drives past the garage and sees that the Polo has gone. Which begs the question, who picked it up, and where did it go? (If we assume it belongs to Liz Fletcher there is a possibility that she picked it up.)

K. Coppins was walking between the Carpenters Arms pub in Rawreth and the Hungry Horse pub, between 5 and 6pm. She has a good look at a Range Rover coming towards her, as she is interested in them. The car stops, and she sees the man in the front passenger seat. She describes him as a large man with receding hair, who appeared to be in his late forties, wearing a white shirt and dark jacket. The driver was also a large man, and she believes that there were two men in the back. She recognises the car when it appears on the news one or two days later (there is an issue with this statement, in that it is not taken until the 17th May 96. As such she cannot recall the exact date, and so it may even be the night of the 5th, which would possibly coincide with the statement from the barman in The Carpenters Arms).

At approx. 6pm R. Mantle is driving home when he stops to let a Range Rover cross the road to turn into Workhouse Lane (in his statement he refers to it as Millhouse lane). He believes the driver was wearing a white shirt. He could not recall anyone in the front seat, but remembered there was a rear passenger.

With so many witnesses seeing a Range Rover apparently going back and forth, you could argue that one of them has to be the Essex boys. Its now after 6pm; and we have no independent witness who can verify Nicholls account as to what happens in the next hour. There are no witnesses who saw the Range Rover in the Halfway House pub car park in Horndon. No witnesses who saw the Range Rover in the Hungry Horse car park in Rayleigh. Only K. Coppins comes close to putting four men in the Range Rover.

S. Carey gives a statement. She knew Tate as he was seeing her daughter Claire, who worked at TGI Fridays at Lakeside. "The last time I had any contact with Tate was on Wednesday 6th when he phoned me at home around 6pm (she doesn't say if its landline or mobile). He had rung several times earlier in the day asking for Claire and on the final occasion Claire still wasn't back from work and Pat said that he had to go out for about half an hour but asked that I tell Claire to hang on as he would be back. Pat didn't sound concerned or worried on the phone." This statement is relevant as it highlights the fact that the phone lists handed to the jury were either edited, or Tate was using more than one phone. More importantly, if he was already near Rettendon by 6pm, he would certainly be back within thirty minutes.

R. Wright's statement is that at approx. 7pm he is driving through Rettendon when he has to stop as two or three cars ahead have stopped. He sees a Range Rover, possibly green in colour, waiting to turn right into Workhouse Lane. He believes at least three people were in the car, possibly four. The man in the back was wearing a fawn light-coloured top (interestingly, the photograph of Steele and Nicholls at the waxworks museum shows Nicholls wearing a light fawn coloured top). As the vehicle turns, Wright notices that the rear lights are covered by a grille, and that the car keeps going down the track road. The Essex boys Range Rover did not have light guard grills.

M. Strelleyupton lived on a farm near Workhouse Lane. On the 6th he was outside and heard what sounded like rapid shots fired; but cannot recall if it was around 7.30pm or 9pm.

R, Reid stated that at approx. 7.30pm he was travelling through Rettendon when he sees a dark coloured Vauxhall Cavalier in front of him with one person in it. The car makes off at speed, overtaking a slow-moving white van. On the other side of the road, a dark coloured Range Rover pulls into a lane and turns back out in order to turn right. Reid believes there was at least 3 people in the car. In front of him, the Cavalier then turned off. At this stage let's remember Donna Jaggers statement regarding the machine gun, dated 08/02/96, she mentions meeting Bowman, who was driving a white VW Corrado. Also present was another male, and he was driving a green Vauxhall Cavalier.

K. Tarbuck was driving home in a white Sierra. At approx.

7.40pm that night he drove past Whitehouse farm on his left-hand side. A white escort van suddenly pulled out from Workhouse lane, causing Tarbuck to break suddenly. He goes on to say, "The reason I remember this is that in pulling out in front of me, it caused me to brake and because it was icy and snowing, I thought what an idiot he was." We can only guess if Tarbuck made any gestures in relation to the other persons standard of driving. But this is the closest we get to anything that matches Nicholls account about just missing a car as he drove out of the lane. The only difference is that we are now nearly an hour behind. Mr Tarbuck could not see how many people were in the van, and we do not know if he is talking about a van with just front doors and side panels, or if it is a four-door type estate escort as used by decorators and electricians. Tarbuck goes on to say that the driver accelerated away very quickly, and by the time Tarbuck reached the turnpike, the other car had gone. It is another incident almost an hour after Nicholls had allegedly dropped Whomes off. In his first couple of interviews Nicholls believed he had driven to Marks Tey in his works van, as he remembered putting a bike battery in the back of it. A few interviews later, both van and battery have gone.

Tarbuck is also another witness that the police did not wish to call. The reason may be because of the time he sees the van. We only have Nicholls statement that the three men were all dead before 6.59pm (not even a pathologist was able to corroborate this). And we only know this because of Nicholls claimed the 6.59pm call was to pick Steele and Whomes up. When he does, both were covered in blood. There is always a possibility that Nicholls has got his sequence of events wrong again, and that the murders happened after the phone call.

At around 8.15pm, A. Kowalenski is driving through Rettendon, when he sees someone running from the field near Workhouse Lane. He describes the person is around 5ft 7, medium build, wearing a dark coloured balaclava. The man stops running and starts to walk when he reaches the Lane. Mr Kowalenksi also comments that at the time the snow is falling, and settling. Although when the Range Rover is found in the morning, there is no snow or ice on the windows. But here is another strange thing, the convoy of Range Rovers that seemed to converge on Rettendon before the killings now seemed to have disappeared. Apart from one more strange incident, which may or may not be relevant.

At around 8.30pm, V. Townsend hears shouting outside her home, which is about a mile away from Workhouse Lane. She looks out and sees a Range Rover. Behind it was a small white car. At some point a male goes to the Range Rover carrying what she believes to be a dog, which he puts into the boot, and then gets into the back of the car. The Range Rover then quickly drives away. Well, what can we make of this? The simple answer is that a group of people have been looking for the family dog perhaps all day and half the night, and that quite a few people in Essex have Range Rovers. But let's be honest, the key statement for me is from R. Carr. She gave a statement within a few days of the murders. She was in her car when she clearly saw Tucker and Tate in the Range rover less than six feet away. The Range Rover was heading towards Workhouse Lane, and Carr checked the time to confirm it was 5.45pm. No if's, no buts. And she has nothing to lose or gain from the police. That is not to say that Steele or Whomes wasn't involved, but it gives reasonable doubt to Donna Jaggers account.

Before we finish, there are a few more statements of note. S. Asker lived near the farm. At approx. 11.45pm she heard a series of loud bangs similar to a shotgun.

S. Rogers, who also lived near the scene, stated he was outside feeding a foal when he heard gunshots at around midnight. He remembers it because there is sometimes rabbit shooting in the darkness, but these are usually in twos from a small calibre rifle. This was approximately six shots in quick succession, possibly from a shotgun, and they came from the direction of Whitehouse farm.

On the 7th December, D Reeves drives past Workhouse Lane before 7am. He sees a white Ford Cosworth in the lane, as if waiting at the junction, but believes there was no one in it.

The next witness was Peter Theobald, who drives up the lane at 8am that morning with his friend to feed the pheasants, not realising that one of the men in the Range Rover was an old friend of his brother's. And that is the end of this timeline.

I don't know how many of these statements were given to the jury in order for them to make a decision; I can only say that we know Rolfe was driving a blue Range Rover, we know that Steele had a blue Range Rover on the 8th November 95, we know Tucker used to have a green Range Rover up till abut September 95, and that John Marshall bought and sold Range Rovers, as well as other prestige cars, and his body was found in a black Range Rover in May 96. When it comes to make and models of cars, we don't know if people get it right in their statement. For example, someone could say it was a Range Rover, when it was really a Land Rover, such as the one Peter Theobald was driving, or the one Kenneth Noye used; or even the one that Darren Nicholls had. Some people could also mistake an early 1990's Mitsubishi Shogun for a Range Rover.

And when it comes to cars, Pat Tate certainly gets around. He leaves home in a Mercedes, and returns in a Vitara. He could possibly get into the Range Rover before lunch. Cuthbert meets all three at the car showroom., and then Tate then gets into Cuthbert's Shogun. There is a discrepancy as to what vehicle he gets into after lunch; as Cuthbert puts him in the Shogun until around 3pm, and another witness sees him in the Range Rover before 2pm. We know that Tate is at Sarah Saunder's mum's around 3pm, and he drives away in a VW Golf. Two hours later he is back at the car showroom after suddenly deciding he is going to buy the Passat, even though he is not going to give it to Sarah. What happens to him, and the Passat, after this, is a mystery. Certainly, at no point does Saunders ever mention that when she spent a couple of minutes talking to Tate on the phone does he say anything about getting her another car. This Passat should have been a vital part of the police investigation.

We can give the police some leeway in relation to the second Passat, because Nicholls does not give an account until five months after the murders, and the police are grabbing at straws when trying to find evidence which helps corroborate parts of his story. But among all the items after Jasper and Nicholls had been arrested and interviewed, there is an interesting statement from 23rd July 96.

P. Mayhew was clearing the Rettendon church car park, which is a few hundred yards away from Meadow Road. In the bushes he finds what appears to be a sawn-off section of a side by side shotgun barrel (as per Nicholls initial accounts to police, and Jasper's). He also finds a set of front and rear number plates. It is not known if any fingerprints were on them, but only one person has ever claimed to have handled false number plates on the night of the murders.

Court witnesses.

The jury heard evidence from the forensic scientist John Burns. He said all three men were shot at close range. The cartridge cases were all 12-bore vantage cartridges. The firing marks on the cartridges showed that all of them were fired using the same firearm which there was a strong possibility of being a pump-action or self-loading 12-bore shotgun. He concluded that 8 shots from a 12-bore shotgun appeared to have been fired at the scene: Two into the right-hand side of Tucker, and one into the back of his head. Two into the right side of the head and face of Rolfe; and three at Tate: One into the right torso, one across back of the head and one into the left side of the head.

He thought that most of the shots appeared to have been fired through the open rear off-side door of the vehicle. One of the shots to the head of Rolfe having first passed through the right-hand corner of the driver's head rest. The shot fired across the head of Tate appeared to have passed through the glass on the rear nearside door. The shot into his head appeared to be fired from the nearside of the vehicle through the same glass. The angle of the shot into his right torso suggested that he was in a position similar to where he was found when the shot was fired. The likelihood of a large capacity magazine and the appearance of the fired wads suggested the use of a gun with a full-length barrel. But Burns could not discount the use of a gun with a lesser magazine capacity, something that would have required reloading. As for only one weapon being used, that was based on the cartridge all having a similar mark from the weapon's firing pin. But we have to remember that it was eight shots, but only seven cartridges; so, there is a possibility that one of the shots could have come from a different shotgun.

Pathologist Paula Lannas gave an account of attending the crime scene and seeing the bodies in situ, but did not go into the Range Rover to get a time of death. She noticed that tyre tracks went up to the gate and beyond, and that blood had seeped down to the gate as well. Later that day she carried out an autopsy on each victim. Even though we are still possibly on the twenty-four hours window, in which it is the easy to carry out certain tests, she still does not give a time of death. She would certainly have been able to put the time within a few hours, and possibly get rid of any doubts about the killings taking place at midnight.

For a start she could have done a simple rigor mortis test. That happens about two hours after death, and lasts for twelve hours. Blood pooling, or liver mortis, was also an option. As soon as someone dies then gravity takes over. Without a heartbeat to keep the blood pumping, it settles in the lowest part of the body, and reaches its maximum eight to twelve hours after death.

A full autopsy was then carried out; so again it is surprising no time of death is recorded. The blood, stomach and vital organs would have been examined. Certain foods ingest at a certain rate. We know what Tucker, Tate and Rolfe were eating and drinking at around 1pm on the 6th. The food would have stopped digesting the moment they died, and so what was in their stomach would have told us what time they were killed. A simple alcohol test on the blood sample would tell us if they had been killed within six or twelve hours from drinking a beer. Dr Lannas could only answer that she didn't believe she was ever requested by the police to give a time of death.

Even though there were a lot of statements that cast doubt on what had gone on that night in Workhouse Lane, the jury were left to rely on the prosecution telling them what time they believed the killings had happened because Darren Nicholls had told them so. The phone call, Greenwich meantime 6.59pm, could not be disputed. As for me, I think the statements taken soon after the event give a more accurate account than those taken a few weeks or even months later. That is not to say we forget those significant events in our lives even years after they happened. We don't. But memory is a liquid jigsaw. As soon as you try and put one bit into place, it sucks and slurs as you try to resurrect what you think happened. Time passes; the memory slips even further out of the frame until some pieces disappear altogether. The longer you leave it, the more you have to rely on your imagination to put the picture together. But like the lane, you can never really go back.

Chapter 18.

Summing up.

"You're born, you take shit. You get out in the world; you take more shit. You climb a little higher, you take less shit. Till one day you're up in the rarefied atmosphere and you've forgotten what shit even looks like. Welcome to the layer cake son."
Layer Cake.

I

Crown Court is an act of theatre. The main players all wear a costume. The judge in a white wig, the barristers in black gowns, the defendant in a cheap suit. Witnesses who have only been to church three times in their life swear to tell the whole truth as they hold up a Bible. The jury sits; interested at some points, bored at others. Soon they will be requested to make a decision that could change someone's life. Before that, the prosecution and the defence barristers get to make their closing speeches. But in this trial the judge unexpectedly breaks away from the script and explains that this particular case is special. "Nicholls is a convicted criminal who was engaged in drug abuse and the importation of drugs into this country. You must bear in mind it was in his own interest to become a prosecution witness... he hopes to get less time to serve." This is a very strong statement to make, and certainly not the usual procedure.

The barristers summarised the first charges; the conspiracy to import drugs up to November 1995. Nicholls admitted being involved in smuggling, and said he did it along with Steele, Whomes, Tucker and Tate. Steele and Whomes claimed they never knew what was in the box. When a cannabis deal went wrong, Steele stepped in to help calm the waters, as he feared Tate was going to hurt Nicholls. In Ostend the money is returned, and we get the promise of a cocaine deal, along with a robbery, but it was all a front to commit murder.

The jury were reminded that on the morning of the 7th December 1995, it took a long time for two farmers to defrost their car, which had been parked since 5pm the night before. At 8am they drove up Workhouse Lane, over snow and ice puddles, none of which had been broken. Turning the bend, they saw the Range Rover parked in front of the gate. Realising what was in the vehicle, they called police. The police were not yet using a computer system, and listening to the call you can hear the operator having to write everything down. The two farmers had attended court and were shown tyre marks on the other side of the gate. They said that they looked recent, but could give no explanation as to how they got there. Both agreed the Range Rover had no frost or snow on the roof or the windscreen; and that none of the windows were steamed up.

When police arrived at 8.17am, a crime scene was started, and a cordon set up. The first police doctor arrived at 9.20am. When asked why he did not give an estimation as to the time of death, he said he was told not to in order to stop cross contamination. The jury were reminded of Dr Paula Lannas. She had been a pathologist since graduating in Africa in 1974. When asked about the time of death, she replied "I was not called to make an assessment of the time of death."

Forensic scientist John Burns gave evidence. He said that there were puddles of blood near the gate, but could not account as to how they leaked from the car. He believed all the shots came from the same weapon, although he could not discount that the shotgun may not have been a pump action, nor could he confirm if the shots were fired from a sawn-off shotgun, depending on how much of the barrel and the stock had been removed. As to the injuries to Tate's head, he said he thought the offside shot struck Tate's head first before striking the window, but the other nearside shot into the head was fired through some of the glass in the window. He added, "There would be a very loud noise and a total of 8 shots. They would have been heard for a distance certainly greater than a mile."

Detective Inspector Hughes gave evidence in relation to the vehicle. He said the Range Rover was an automatic, and was set in drive with the hand break down when it was seized. The tank was a third full when it was checked, and the ignition of the Range Rover was off. A carbon deposit mark under the exhaust pipe would have meant the vehicle would have been stationary with the engine running for a period of time. There were numerous tyre tracks found at the scene, but no vehicle that had been recovered matched those marks. It is believed one set of marks belonged to a prestige vehicle, such as a Sierra Cosworth. None of the tyre marks matched those of the VW Passat which was recovered some months later. There was a footprint, as if someone had been standing talking to the front passenger, which police had identified as belonging to a specific brand of trainers, possibly adult size 7 or 8. No wellington boot prints were found.

Another officer gave details of what had been seized from the car. As well as Tucker and Tate's mobile phones were their address books. Rolfe, although he did not have a mobile phone, also had an address book. There was £1,430 cash in total. In the boot was a Head sports holdall, which was empty.

There was Darren Nicholls account. He had got a call from Steele to meet up for another drug deal for around 4pm on the 6th December. So innocent was he in all this, he said he couldn't make that time, but would be free for about 5pm. Steele, the man alleged to have planned the triple murder with clockwork precision, readily agreed. Nicholls, who couldn't remember what car he was driving, was able to recollect the details of the journey. From Marks Tey they drove to Thorndon Country Park, where he and Whomes try to put the false registration plates on the VW Passat. Unable to, they put the false lates in the back in the car. They then park near the Halfway House pub in Horndon. When Whomes sees a Range Rover come into the car park, he tells Nicholls to go, and gives directions towards Rettendon. He then drops Whomes off, drives around, gets a phone call, and picks both men up. At this point he sees the gun parts and the blood on the gloves.

Steele agreed he had met Sarah Saunders at McDonalds at Barham on the 4th December after getting a phone call from her. He was not concerned about Tate's threat, although he was aware that Tate had a drug problem. He said he never used any telephone box on the day of the murders; but agreed he had decided to drive to pick up a trailer during rush hour in bad weather, and that he had not asked for Whomes' uncle's telephone number before setting out on his journey, and so would not know if he was at home or not, even though he had guests that night.

When it came to why he had answered "No comment" in his interviews rather than give an account, the jury were told he had taken advice from his solicitor. The prosecutor told the jury that Steele's alibi for the murders could have been said at the time he was arrested; and under new laws, advice from a lawyer not to comment on certain matters could imply an element of guilt. The rock-solid alibi of the petrol receipt was not as good as first thought. It could have been obtained by anyone and signed by Steele at a later date.

Whomes account was summarised. Weeks before the murders he had given a trailer to his uncle Dennis to try and sell. Jack Whomes went to Bulphan to collect it on the 5th, but his uncle was not in. On the 6th Whomes told Steele he was going to pick up Nicholls car, and that he should get the trailer. Whomes drove down onto the A130 until he saw a pub with a pink Morris Minor outside. He winched the Passat onto the trailer and then tried to call Nicholls just before seven to tell him he had it, but all he could hear was static. He then took the car back to his yard, where a few days later Nicholls told him to scrap it if it couldn't be fixed. Instead he gave it to an old friend to go banger racing in.

Billy Jasper associated with major criminals who dealt with

cocaine worth hundreds of thousands and had no inhibitions about shooting each other if they fell out. He said he took a man to Rettendon to sort out a drug deal, and had no idea the murders were going to happen; although the man did have a holdall containing a sawn-off shotgun. The police believed that Jasper was a fantasist and did not investigate his account or the people he said he was with.

As the summing up drew to a conclusion, the jury were told, "To the murder charges, the defence of Whomes and Steele is one of alibi. They say they were not in Work House Lane at the time the deceased were killed and had nothing to do with it. They draw attention to the lack of scientific evidence as to the time of death. They say the evidence of Rebecca Carr as to the time she saw the Range Rover, the evidence of Kevin Tarbuck, as to what he saw, mean that the prosecution cannot disprove their alibi. They point to the evidence of William Jasper and Steven Rogers as raising the possibility that someone else killed those men at about midnight. As to Count 5 against Steele, the shotgun, he says that Nicholls could not have put the shotgun into the roof when he claims to have done. Had he done so; it would have fallen straight down because there was no ceiling there then. Steele says that the progress of the work was such that it was not possible to hide the gun where and when Nicholls said he did."

Then the judge gave his summing up. "The prosecution case as to Count 1 is that there was an agreement to smuggle cannabis resin; that it was an agreement between each of these three defendants (Steele, Whomes and Corry) and that there is the clearest possible evidence of it in their landing at Felixstowe ferry in the early hours of 8th November, and in what each of them said and did not say to the police and customs that day by way of explanation for their appearance there. The prosecution say they have proved five trips across the North Sea, the middle three being the ones when drugs were bought back on the boat: The first making the contact with John Stone and leaving the money which was used for the second; the last being the trip to retrieve the money that had been paid for what has been known as the duff cannabis.

As to Count 2, 3 and 4, the prosecution case is that there was a falling out between Steele and Tate and a threat by Tate on the life of Steele. They say that Tate, Tucker and Rolfe were lured by Whomes and Steele to that lane on 6th December, and were then killed by shotgun cartridges fired into the back of their heads. As to Count 5, they say that after the killings Nicholls, at Steele's request, got him a fresh shotgun, fresh because the one that had been used was said to have been ground up, and took it to him at Meadow Cottage. They say it was in December or January that Nicholls last touched the gun and that was in the roof of Meadow Cottage. Thereafter, Nicholls did not do anything about the gun, and in particular did not tell the police about it. He said it was no plant. In relation to all the counts in the indictment, the prosecution case is that despite all the legitimate criticism that can be made of Darren Nicholls, that criticism is valid; but his evidence from the witness box was reliable and can be believed. The defence of Whomes and Steele, in a nutshell, to the allegation of agreement to smuggle cannabis is there was no such agreement. Steele never took the boat across the North Sea on any smuggling trips; the boat was bought as a diving vessel and was to be used as such when it had had sea trials. The trip which ended on 8th November was a trip for sea trials which was daubed by mechanical failure. It was not a smuggling trip. Their case is that the account given by Nicholls is a lying one. They point that all that is to be said against Nicholls is a matter that you should consider everything, including his previous criminal activities; both those for which he has convictions and more particularly for those that he has not, his later and more recent criminal activities including the criminality with Detective Constable "A". They point to the taped conversations with Detective Constable "A". They point to what Nicholls said in the third interview; having been told he had to tell the truth but nonetheless minimising his involvement by not telling it. They sum up in their arguments what you heard for days quite rightly because it is necessary to test matters in the evidence that Nicholls gave in this court. They urge you to say that you cannot believe Nicholls in the light of those facts. They refer to the great caution that I advised you to use in looking at Nicholls's evidence at the beginning of this summing-up. They say that Nicholls has blended fact and fiction; and been prompted or guided by dishonest police officers in the interviews, and the taking of the statements. They suggest that the telephone schedules are deliberately dishonest. They say that there are not innocent errors; the errors are made deliberately to be misleading. As examples of that they point to telephone calls that are not there, admissions on the telephone schedule in relation to calls on the 5th and 6th November: One at 8.46pm and one at 4.36pm. Those are examples that they put before you of omissions. What they say about the omissions are that they are deliberate and meant to mislead. I remind you as a matter of law as I have done already, and this will be for the last time, that the word alibi means someone was elsewhere. I remind you of the direction of law that the prosecution has to prove the defendant's guilt so you are sure of it. He does not have to prove he was elsewhere. The prosecution must disprove the alibi. Also, I remind you that coming to the conclusion, if you do, that the alibi is false would not be the end of it. Even if you conclude the alibi was false that does not of itself entitle you to convict the defendant. It is a matter you may take into account, but you have to bear in mind that an alibi is sometimes invented to bolster a genuine defence.

You have to decide, and this was the legal direction I gave you, first, whether the defendant, in each case Whomes and Steele, whether a defendant did tell those lies. Were they lies? If you are sure in either or both cases that they were lies you go on to consider another matter, but if you are not sure in either case that they were lies then you ignore the matter. If, however, you conclude in the case of Whomes or Steele, or both, that they were lies, consider why a defendant lied. The mere fact that a defendant tells lies is not in itself evidence of guilt. A defendant may lie for many reasons; they may possibly be innocent ones in the sense that they do not denote guilt. For example, there can be lies to bolster a true defence, to protect someone else or out of panic and confusion. If you think there is or may be an innocent explanation of those lies then you should take no notice of them. It is only if you are sure that a defendant did lie and did not lie for an innocent reason that his lies can be regarded by you as evidence going to prove guilt in supporting the prosecution case. I have given you all that direction before and it is convenient that I have repeated it now."

And there it was. Who had stood in the dock and told the truth, the whole truth, and nothing but the truth? As the jury left to discuss a verdict, what they did not know was that for the last few months Nicholls had been in contact with a publisher and a television producer. Nicholls had gone through all the statements so many times he could probably recite them in his sleep. And if you wanted some bedtime reading, they were in luck. In the summer of 1997 Bernard O'Mahoney published his book "So this is Ecstasy?" In it he detailed his career as a doorman at Raquel's nightclub, including the death of Leah Betts, and the death of the Essex Boys. As such, when the jury walked out of the Old Bailey, they could have walked into a newly opened bookshop to help them come to a decision.

Chapter 19.

The Verdict.

If the glove don't fit...you got to acquit.
Trial of O.J. Simpson.

I

There was one question not asked of the jury: With the same evidence, namely, no forensics, no eyewitnesses, very primitive mobile phone data, and just the word of a convicted criminal facing ten years in prison for drug offences; would the police have been able to charge someone else? If Nicholls had named Mickey Bowman, Billy Jasper, Bernard O'Mahoney, Kenneth Noye, or Nipper Ellis, for the murders, would they have stood in the dock?

Bowman was mentioned as mixing the cocaine after the robbery; and the best time to pick up the stuff would be straight away. Jasper gave an account as good as Nicholls; perhaps even better, as at least his timeline included the sound of gun shots, and that the killer was wearing trainers. O'Mahoney was holed up in a hotel around the corner. Easy enough to slip out of a window and head off to a pub car park to open the boot of a vehicle not registered in your name. Noye becomes very agitated two days after Steele had been arrested for the murders, perhaps he was worried about being next? Just a day after Tate's business associate John Marshall had been murdered and found in the back of his Range Rover. He stabs a man in a road rage attack and flees to Spain. It was later revealed that Noye had help in escaping justice by a corrupt police officer. Nipper Ellis claimed he was hundreds of miles away at the time of the murders, although we still have no idea what time the murders took place.

The jury might not have realised how many others were possible suspects. They did not hear about the arrest of Leah Betts father, or Barry Dorman being confronted by Billy Blundell just a few days before the killings. They never heard about the meeting Tate had with the Blundells, or what that conversation was about. The police themselves avoided scrutiny because they told the judge Operation Apache was still ongoing, nearly two years after it had started, and so were immune from public interest. The London Crime Cartels were too powerful to have their names mentioned. Between the murders and the trial someone had taken over the doors to the clubs the Essex boys used to run, someone had continued to supply cannabis, someone had continued to supply cocaine and ecstasy; but by now the police had stopped looking.

It was January 1998. The trial was over. That was it. The prosecution believed the two defendants had committed the murders because they feared Tate was going to kill them. The defence had said there was reasonable doubt in the case to say that Steele and Whomes did not pull the trigger. Darren Nicholls had given an account which matched only a few details of the police investigation, and the prosecution had decided that his statement was the bigger picture.

On the 15th January the jury of eight women and four men retired to a hotel to consider their verdict. They had been told by the judge that in the future he might be prepared to accept a majority verdict of ten to two, but for now he expected a unanimous verdict. Either everyone thought they were guilty of murder; or, if one person thought there was reasonable doubt, the two men would walk free.

The first night was difficult. What if someone believed Nicholls was telling the truth about the murders, but lying about the gun? What if someone else thought Steele was innocent in the killings, but involved in drug smuggling? They had been asked to look at each count individually, but everyone knew it was impossible. The prosecution had created a beginning, middle, end; drugs, murders, gun, each offence was linked to the next one.

The drug smuggling was strange. How can you convict if no one actually caught them with anything? But the prosecution pointed out that it didn't matter; this was a conspiracy to import drugs. The police also had the dud cannabis found in a disused pit that Nicholls said he had dumped. Again, it doesn't matter how strong the stuff is, as long as the smugglers believed it was cannabis. The jury also had to remember it had been found because Nicholls was working with a corrupt police officer.

Nicholls, who had a previous conviction for dishonesty, lied to senior police officers about how he knew the drugs were in the pit. Was he the man in charge? All of them knew Pat Tate, who the press had labelled as a drug dealer. Steele's account of being in the hotel in Ostend was because he was trying to stop Tate from threatening to kill Nicholls. It went back to the question; do you believe Steele and Whomes when they said they knew nothing about smuggling cannabis?

The next day the jury returned. They had not reached a decision. The judge sent them away. Another drive back to the hotel. More questions. What about the cars? The Range Rover would have been noticed; and apparently a lot of people did. But this big blue lump of metal was not the TARDIS; it couldn't be in two different places at once. The fact was, a blue Range Rover with Tucker and Tate in it had been seen near Workhouse Lane at the same time Donna Jagger was being dropped off at the shopping centre twenty miles away. It then appears near a Tyre centre when it should be on its way to the Halfway House Pub. And if the Essex boys already knew where Workhouse Lane was, why would they need Mick Steele to give them directions? If they were planning to go out for a meal later that evening, why not tell him to drive to Workhouse Lane, and then everyone can go their own way when the meeting was over? After all, its Steele who is meant to setting the trap, isn't it? Lets remember that soon after the murders the police recived information that the Essex boys were going to hire a hitman to take out a rival dealer, but were double crossed. Was Steele the rival dealer? Had he been the one who was lured to the lane to be killed; but the Essex Boys were killed instead? They had seen their killers, perhaps even watched them come to the car; but had no fear because they believed it was Steele who was going to be killed?

Three large men in a Range Rover seems plausible. But two large men and a little guy in a VW Passat? No one sees a big bloke in overalls and a little dumpy guy trying to fix something onto the front of the car when it stops in a layby. No one sees it driving around, or almost causing a crash as it pulls out of Workhouse Lane after the shooting.

Perhaps it's the timing that's wrong? Rebecca Carr was adamant that she saw Tucker and Tate in the Range Rover at exactly 5.45pm in Rettendon? She was only a few feet away, the light was good, and she gave a statement within a day of seeing the news. But then she also believed it was following a white car? If her statement is true, it means all the the people who knew the Essex boys and saw them earlier are mistaken.

On Saturday morning the jury went back to court with still no unanimous decision. The judge told them they were allowed to call friends and family to tell them they would not be home for the weekend, but were not allowed to discuss the case. Time to think about the phone calls, and Tate's movements on the day.

Just after midnight of the 6th. A white transit van is seen outside Tate's bungalow. A few minutes later a police car arrives and drives past. Gordon Road is technically a close, as the end is a large turning circle. What were the police doing?

9.20am. There is a phone call from Tate's bungalow to Tuckers mobile. We cannot assume that it is Tate making the call; it maybe that Liz Fletcher has tried Tate's mobile but couldn't get through.

9.26am. Tate landline calls Rolfe's landline. Does Fletcher know Donna Jaggers?

Between 10-11am Tate drives a Mercedes and Liz drives a VW Polo to Basildon Tyre Services. They leave the Polo, and tell Andrew Reynolds that someone would collect it later. Tate then drives away in a Vauxhall Vitara that belongs to Tucker. Fletcher in the Mercedes. Reynolds states that at around 6pm he leaves the VW Polo in the forecourt with the keys inside.

11.31am. Tucker calls Tate, mobile to mobile.

11.36am. Tate's landline calls Tuckers mobile.

Morning - lunchtime. Barry Dorman is at his car showroom at the Five Bells roundabout. Tucker, Tate, Rolfe and Peter Cuthbert arrive to sort out the finance payments for the Range Rover.

1pm. Tate is with Tucker, Rolfe and Cuthbert at TGI Fridays at Lakeside. The waitress states that Tucker was having problems with his mobile phone, and so used Tate's to make a call.

1.24pm. Tate's mobile phone is used to call Tuckers landline. This may be another signal problem. In 1995 snow could disrupt certain phones from connecting.

1.30- 2pm. Tate, Tucker and Rolfe attend L.T Carpets in Timberlog Lane, Basildon.

2.14pm. Tate calls from his mobile to Basildon Tyre Services.

2.22pm. Basildon Tyre services call Tucker, even though Tate has the Vitara.

2.23pm. Tate's landline calls Tuckers mobile.

2.29pm. Payphone at Sorell Horse Inn calls Tucker's mobile. It is not known if Tate is present for these calls. It seems strange if this is about the cocaine robbery when it has always been Tate's idea.

2.32pm. Payphone at Sorell Horse Inn calls a payphone at Timberlog Lane, which is just around the corner from Tate's address.

2.32pm. Payphone at Sorell Horse Inn calls Tucker's mobile again.

Afternoon. Tate attends Sarah Saunders parents address after she called him to complain that her car had broken down. The call from Sarah does not appear in the phone schedule given to the jury, and in one interview she thought she may have used a payphone. He turns up with Tucker and Rolfe, has an argument with Sarah, and takes the VW Golf.

3.50pm. Tate's mobile calls Rolfe's landline. Rolfe then drives to Gray's police station.

At about 5pm Barry Dorman receives a phone call from his showroom to say that Tate had returned. He was going to take a VW Passat they had spoken about a few weeks ago, and would pay for it in the morning has he had a large sum of money coming. You would think that a man involved in a million-pound cocaine robbery and about to become very rich, might not be that bothered about picking up an old banger. The only thing of note would be that the car wouldn't be in his name, and if he was stopped, he could say he had only just bought it, and not have a clue of there was anything in the boot. Plus, if it ended up getting crushed, there was nothing that could come back to him.

5.30pm. Tate's neighbour hears the sound of a car beeping. He looks outside and sees a Range Rover turning around. They think it might be a different Range Rover than the one that has picked him up previously. A short time later he hears Tate's door closing, and the Range Rover speeds away.

S. Carey gives a statement to say that Tate had called a couple of times on the 6th to try and speak to her daughter. The last call was at around 6pm. Tate was taking her daughter to the Global Café. He told Carey that he had to go out, but would be back in half an hour. This is not on the phone list, and so we don't know if it was on the landline or a mobile. Tate said he was thinking about leaving a note, but might not bother now, which made Carey think he was still at home. Carey is told to tell her daughter to wait, as he would be back within half an hour. (This statement is made on the 6th February 96.)

6.05pm. The witness Reynolds is driving away from Basildon Tyre Services and has reached Cranes Farm Road just around the corner, when he sees the Range Rover with Rolfe driving, Tucker in the passenger seat and Tate in the back, going towards the garage. Rettendon is approx. twenty minutes away. Reynolds later drives past the garage at around 9pm, and sees that the VW Polo has gone. As it was Liz Fletcher who drove it to the garage, it's quite possible it's her car and she picked it up (no statement?).

6.44pm. Saunders calls Tucker. The conversation lasts four minutes. At the end Tate says he has to go as he is "with people." The jury are told that the phone signal showed it was most likely in the Rettendon area. Nicholls stated this call happened when they reached Workhouse Lane. The police said the call finished just as the Range Rover got to Workhouse Lane. If both believe they are right, Tate and the others only have a further twelve minutes to live. If that is the case, Steele has only thirty minutes to get back to the Hungry horse pub, get changed, drive to Marks Tey to drop Nicholls off, and then get home before witnesses arrive. A journey that should take well over an hour and a half.

II

On Monday there was still no unanimous verdict. Reporters claimed the killings could have been retribution for the death of Leah Betts, a gangland hit, and even an old crook who had fallen in love with the victim's young girlfriend. For a jury that had no idea how the criminal world operated, it all sounded just like the films. You had people whose actions seemed to be without consequences. Shootouts in the wrong side of Southend, guns under hospital beds. Buying bungalows for two hundred grand in cash; and drug smuggling trips which sounded more like an episode of Only Fools and Horses. There was also the story of the half a million pounds worth of cannabis dropped from a plane; and the plan to rob a million pounds worth of cocaine from another plane. Another link to "Mickey the pilot." Tate threatening to shoot Steele, and Steele asking Nicholls to get him a shotgun; although no one was sure of the date when it all started. On one occasion it was even before the bad cannabis situation, which doesn't seem to make sense unless Steele already had something planned? And then on other times Steele asks Nicholls to get him two shotguns. Why didn't Nicholls ask what they were for? And if the request came after the trip to Ostend, why wasn't Nicholls concerned for his own safety? Surely the request for a shotgun must have come at the same time as buying the VW Passat? If Steele wasn't bothered that day in McDonalds, it must have been because he had already had something planned. But that means someone must have told Steele about the threats before he went to Amsterdam and got the money back. Who was it, and what did they hope to gain?

Tuesday. Still no unanimous verdict. Don't forget, this is not about being innocent, it's whether or not the prosecution can prove beyond all reasonable doubt that a person is guilty of the offence they have been charged with. Nicholls account of the killings had come from the alleged killers themselves. The police must have hoped that the judge would change his decision to a majority verdict. The longer it went on, the more doubts they must have had about winning. Instead, the judge told the jury to go back again and see if they could reach a unanimous decision. For now, it was another night on a mattress that you didn't own, and more questions that remained unanswered.

The evidential phone schedules not including all the phone calls during the relevant time seemed very strange. The prosecution could have agreed with the defence to black out names and numbers that both agreed were not important, but they never. Then you had an expert claiming it was highly unlikely that Steele was in Rettendon at the time police say the Murders were committed, but may not have been in Bulphan at the time he made the call to get Whomes uncles' address. Likewise, the cell site for Whomes supported his alibi of being in the Wheatsheaf pub car park rather than workhouse Lane; even though in one police interview he said he was nowhere near Rettendon on the night of the murders.

Nicholls mentions Whomes taking a holdall with him, but cannot recall bringing one back. Was this the holdall found in the Range Rover, was it ever tested for gun residue? And if this was going to be the biggest drug heist in history, why doesn't

Tucker or Tate get any phone calls from Steele for at least twenty-four hours before the alleged killings take place? There is the argument about Steele being a phone box man, but this was a payphone near to where Whomes worked. What was it the judge said? "Joint enterprise." It didn't matter who pulled the trigger; if they were both involved then they are both as guilty as each other. Both of them claimed to have driven over fifty miles away from home: one to pick up a trailer; the other to pick up a broken-down car, at the same time the Essex boys are going up and down Rettendon like rabbits. And that phone call. "Come and get us."

What everyone agrees on is that Nicholls admits to being in Rettendon on the night, and the 7pm phone call from Whomes confirms this. Using the call as a basis of fact, we have a couple of options.

1. Steele and Whomes were not involved in the murders in any way. Steele was collecting the trailer in Bulphan, and Whomes was picking up the Passat from the pub. The phone call is in relation to this, and Nicholls has made the whole thing up. As to why he would be in Rettendon as well, that is another matter.

2. Nicholls, Steele and Whomes are innocent of the murders; but Steele arranged a meeting with the Essex boys about a drug deal. Nicholls and Whomes have gone as back up in case Steele get's into trouble. others arrive, and things go pear shaped very quickly. What's done is done. The three men are in trouble. If they say anything they could also be killed. But technically, Steele, Whomes and Nicholls are innocent of conspiracy to murder.

3. Nicholls is innocent, whilst Steele and Whomes conspired to murder the Essex boys along with others, but they did not pull the trigger. It plays out almost as Nicholls describes it; but he never says anything to the police about the mystery hitman.

4. Nicholls is innocent of the murders, whilst Steele and Whomes conspired to murder the Essex boys, and events played out exactly as how Nicholls wrote them in his final statement.

5. Nicholls, Steele and Whomes were all involved in the mur-

ders. The meeting in workhouse Lane was planned, and all three knew that the murders were going to take place, irrespective of their role in the actual killings.

Perhaps it didn't matter who got them? A lot of people thought the Essex boys deserved it. Hadn't they been linked to the death of Leah Betts? But then you could look up at the ceiling and realise you have lost sight of the real issue. Three murders. Three people blasted to death in what would only be described as a pre-planned ambush. Three men, all fathers, none of them saints, but can any man say that he is when he decides to take control of his future? Each one shot with no chance to escape. They would never hear their children tell them that they love them. They would never stand in the dock and have to account for their previous actions. They should have also faced justice for the things they did. But murder is still murder. Perhaps the time for talking was over?

It is not known if the judge had set a time limit on how long the jury would take on making a decision; or if he had changed the verdict from unanimous to majority it would have made any difference. After four months of the trial and a week of being trapped in a hotel, the jury once more were driven to the Old Bailey. They informed the judge they had reached a unanimous verdict on all counts. Steele, Whomes and Corry were brought back from the basement cells and up into Court 2. All three stood as they were found guilty of conspiracy to import cannabis into the UK. The defendants must have wondered how? For the dates they had been convicted of, only 262 micrograms of cannabis had ever been found. But when the establishment decides that your time is up, it's up. The judge then requested Corry to be taken back down.

The jury were asked for the next decision, and quickly gave their verdict. On the second, third and fourth counts, Steele and Whomes were guilty of conspiracy to murder Tony Tucker, Pat Tate, and Craig Rolfe. It didn't matter who had pulled the trigger; the two men had been involved in some way, and their alibis were not strong enough to prove beyond all reasonable doubt that they hadn't. It was over. And then almost as an after-thought, on the fifth count, Steele was found not guilty for the illegal possession of a pump action shotgun. Which is strange as it was the only real piece of evidence the police had.

Steele and Whomes were given a minimum of fifteen years before they would be eligible for parole. Five years for each death seemed less than if they had killed just one person. But it is just one of the many strange things about this trial. And as the defendants, the jury, and members of the public left the court-room, they must have wondered if it was really all over?

Chapter 20.

Twenty-Twenty vision.

"Life is too short to hold grudges? I think life is too short to let people keep getting away with the same shit."
Peaky Blinders.

At the time many people felt that the convictions were unsafe. There were a lot of unanswered questions. These have grown over the years, and over twenty years later many still remain unanswered.

1. Why were the Essex boys not arrested before the murders? After the death of Leah Betts the police must have known that Tony Tucker was involved in drug dealing at Raquel's nightclub, and he should have been tugged quicker than the end of my balloon. Craig Rolfe, already linked to the death of Kevin Whitaker, was now driving around in a Range Rover even though police knew he was disqualified. Pat Tate was nicked for drink driving after crashing Tuckers Porsche. He was also still on licence after being released from prison a week earlier, but it is not known if he was charged or bailed for these offences. We do know that he assaulted the manager of a pizza parlour the night before he was killed, and that the police knew it was him. But the manager is told not to press charges, and Tate carries on the next day as if he knows the police are not going to arrest him. Were they under surveillance during this time? Police knew about

Tuckers threats to O'Mahoney. Perhaps there is also another possibility. Tucker knew he wasn't going to be spoken to because he was already having informal chats with the police. Rolfe was clearly going to speak to someone when he pulled up outside the police station. And the fact that Tate didn't seem to care about getting arrested might have been because he knew later that night he wasn't. The issue could have easily been solved if all of the phone records had been put in as evidence.

2. Just how high up were the Essex boys in the criminal underworld? Were the rumours of them robbing other dealers of thousands of pounds worth of drugs, being involved in debt enforcement, and stealing traveller's cheques true? Being a legend in your own lunchtime means fuck all to the man that eats when he wants. The Essex boys expected to have their cake and eat it. They didn't see someone waiting to blow out their candles.

3. Is the cocaine story true? Did Steele make it up, or someone else? The robbery idea first seems to stem from Tucker after a load of cannabis is found in a nearby reservoir just after Tate is released. We have from the 9th November to the 17th for Tate to say that Steele is ripping people off and should be shot; but we have no proof he was saying it during this time. Jaggers believed the plan happened in the hotel, but Steele gets all the money back, and Tate is very happy. So where is the motive to kill? At this point Steele wouldn't know that Tate wasn't going to hand the money back, unless someone told him, and even then, he could have buggered off to Benidorm and saved himself the hassle of cooking bacon in prison.

4. Why the 6th December? Ironically, this tends to lend weight to Sarah Saunders claim she met Steele in a local McDonalds on the 4th December to tell him that his life was in danger. But if Steele had been planning to kill Tate since the 17th November, wouldn't he now think that if he went through with it, Saunders could tell the

police about this meeting? The prosecution put it to the jury that this gave him just enough time to organise a hit. But Nicholls claimed that Steele was asking for a shotgun about a month before the killings, and can't remember when he sold the VW Passat to him. Even Donna Jaggers claims that the supposed cocaine robbery had been held up because of the weather (it started snowing on the fourth). Billy Blundell warned Tate on the 3ʳᵈ about Tucker, and then appeared the next day at Barry Dorman's car showroom. Was the 4ᵗʰ meant to be when things were going to happen?

5. How many Range Rovers in Rettendon? In the area, and on the day, they become so numerous that they throw serious doubt on Nicholls account of Steele being the one who lures them to the lane. And so many Range Rovers with three men inside. It's more likely that Tucker had chosen it as the meeting place. Someone else with a Range Rover waiting to meet a friend could have easily parked in the farm shop forecourt, the Wheatsheaf pub, or the parish church car park up the road.

6. Why Workhouse Lane to carry out the killings? If Steele only had a problem with Tate, he could have easily killed him when he was alone in his bungalow. The police probably would have gone after Nipper Ellis. Or if Tate had simply disappeared the police would have thought it was connected to Leah Betts and he had done another runner to Spain. To set up such an elaborate sting with the danger than one of them might say something to someone (like Tate did to Saunders) seems strange from what we know about Steele.

7. How can all the witnesses be telling the truth? In every statement we should look for a couple of things: how long after the event was the statement taken, does the person have something to lose or gain from not telling the truth, and is there anything in the statement that can be corroborated by facts? R. Carr makes her statement

on the 9th December. We can be pretty sure the account she gives is still fresh in her mind. You could argue that Donna Jaggers has a lot to lose as she is in possession of a machine gun and could get five years. In Nicholls statement we have the phone call from Whomes at 6.59pm, and this is proved by checking his phone bill.

8. Let's go back to the other phone call. Remember when you first start going out with someone and you could chat about anything? Then what? A couple of years later the best you can manage is asking them what's for dinner. You don't need to listen to the shit about their day and how the new supervisor is out of order; you've moved on. Tate was seeing Saunders for six years, and now they were separated. On the day of the murders he had to be held back from attacking her. That night Saunders, who was going out on the town with her new boyfriend, called Tate. She must have asked where Tate was and where he was going, just so they wouldn't bump into each other (unless she was going for a date at a Pizza parlour). But what have they got to say to each other that takes four minutes? Tate had said earlier in the day that he was taking the VW Passat, but wasn't going to give it to Saunders. And if you're involved in a million-pound robbery, would you really be speaking about fixing the clutch on your ex-girlfriend's shit heap? Saunders doesn't mention about Tate getting her another car. Perhaps she was doing all the talking for four minutes?

9. Why is there no forensic evidence? For Steele and Whomes not to leave any trace whatsoever is an amazing stroke of luck. Steele, who is in the Range Rover for nearly thirty minutes (not wearing surgical gloves), leaves no trace. Whomes, an 18 stone man in a brand-new pair of Wellington boots, should have definitely left at least one footprint. The only mark found was a distinctive trainer shoeprint left in the mud on that side of the Range Rover, possibly a UK size 7 or 8, so definitely

not Steele or Whomes.

10. Could it have happened the way Nicholls said? The key is the phone call at 6.59pm. He needed to give an account as to that call, and why he was not involved. The key factor would be saying the killings took place before the call rather than after. For that you would have to know what time the first missed call took place.

11. Why were the full phone lists never revealed? There is mention of Tate having two phones; and two weeks before the murders we know Rolfe had his own mobile. Let's also remember that the prosecution believed Whomes tried to make a call from the crime scene but couldn't, so he had to move higher to get through to Nicholls. If this is the case, did any phone expert go to the lane with banks on each side, sit in a car, and actually see if they could get a connection?

12. Why a VW Passat? Nicholls bought and sold second hand cars, and this one wasn't up to much; so why would Steele want it a few weeks before the murders? Nicholls is unable to give a date of when he sold the car to Steele (before the bad cannabis deal might be important), how much it was worth, and any record of the sale. For a man who can memorise mobile phone numbers, he not only forgot what car he was driving that night, but also any details for the Passat, even if it was a saloon or an estate? Nicholls claims that he turned the VW Passat around in Workhouse Lane on two occasions, effectively leaving four sets of tyre prints going across the lane, and yet none were found that would have matched a Passat. Nicholls could have said he drove away in any car. He must have thought the Passat had been crushed, as he never mentions it again. Whomes could have said he was collecting any car. This VW Passat seems vital as evidence and alibi; so how did the police find it? Did Whomes tell them? A forensic examination takes place, but there seems to be no record of it in the court exhibit list. Could it be the

other VW Passat that Tate picks up from Barry Dorman? We know that cars are a form of currency – Bowman hands over a machine gun, and the VW Passat appears on his forecourt a day later. Tate hadn't collected it after 5pm on the night of the murders to give it to Sarah Saunders, so where did it go? The Wheatsheaf pub car park perhaps?

13. Superintendent Bright, who was head of surveillance and the drug squad at the time, gives a statement a few years after the murders to confirm that he did receive a phone call at approximately 6.30am from a detective on the drugs squad to say that three men had been shot dead in a Range Rover, and names Tony Tucker, and Pat Tate. How did the police know about the murders an hour and a half before the bodies are officially found?

14. When did Steele become the main suspect? The police say they were given information about the Essex boys meeting "Mickey the pilot" just a day after the murders; but that wouldn't have been enough. There would have to be mention of the bad cannabis deal to at least get a motive. That could have come from a number of people; Barry Dorman, Donna Jaggers, Peter Cuthbert, Sarah Saunders, Bernard O'Mahoney, Donna Garwood, Nipper Ellis, Liz Fletcher, all could have said something. And if more than one said it then it would certainly be possible to put Steele at the top of the suspect tree. The phone records showed no calls between him and the Essex boys on the day of the murders; but if you could just find that connection you knew the pieces would fall into place.

15. When did Nicholls become a police informant? He says that it is just after the murders, when a detective tells him he knows he is a drug dealer. But Nicholls had never been arrested for drug offences (as far as we know). Operation Yewtree started in 2012, and was the investigation into historic sexual offences committed by celeb-

rities in the 70's and 80's. One of the people arrested was radio presenter Paul Gambaccinni. He was on bail for nearly two years before the case was dropped, and he was eventually paid compensation after the accusation turned out to be false. It is quite possible that Nichols could have been on bail for a year before he got arrested in May 96. We will never know, as all his previous records have been erased.

16. Why was Sarah Saunders considered a suspect? For Operation Century to have been authorised, which could have included the bugging of her telephone, there must have been reasonable cause to suspect she was involved in the murders. It is quite possible that by February the police had become aware that the mortgage on the bungalow would now be paid off because Tate had taken out a life insurance policy; and that the VW Golf (which had turned out to be stolen) had been sold by Saunders to none other than Mick Steele. But strangely, in February they would not have been aware of the pair meeting two days before the murders took place.

17. How many other police officers were arrested for Operation Apache? We know that two were on the same day that Steele, Whomes and Nicholls were all arrested in May 96. But was Operation Apache an investigation into police corruption, or just corrupt detectives involved in the Essex boys murders? And if it was, why did it continue until after Steele and Whomes lost their first right to appeal in 2001?

18. What if the London Crime Cartel was more than one gang? Operation Deenside was an investigation into corrupt police officers and the Bowers family, who ran part of their business from Peacocks gym in Canning Town. This involved large scale drug importation, hijacking lorries and money laundering. It is believed they had links with Mickey Bowman and Billy Jasper. Eventually this and other investigations went under

the one title of Operation Tiberius; after all the evidence of police corruption and a crime cartel was destroyed. The new operation also included the investigation into David Hunt, who was the leader of another crime cartel from North London. He also was involved in large scale drug importation. He took over a lot of clubs in London and Essex, including Epping Forest Country Club. The Adams family were another crime cartel, believed to have links with Kenny Noye, and Tony Tucker. The Blundell family had originated in London, but moved most of their business to Essex.

19. Who were the other people whose name appeared during the investigation? Saunders believes Ian Spindler and Tate did hard drugs together. He was at the hospital when Nicholls went to see Tate, and Tate said that if they had a problem with each other they should fight. Nicholls says that Steele mentions him as someone who should have been in the Range Rover as well that night? Terry Ball owned four houses in Essex, but suddenly decided to move to the West country just before Tate was released. After the murders his partner Linda Millard complained to a friend that she had overheard Terry talking on the phone about the killings, and what was said shocked her so much she went to stay with another friend. It is alleged that a few weeks later, Terry found out where she was hiding; and a few days after that, Linda disappeared, leaving her car and her shoes on the edge of a cliff. John McCarthy had a million pounds in cash to buy cocaine. Did he also know Mickey Bowman and was in on the scam to cheat Steele out of deal by mixing his share of the drugs? Did he also have a motive to pull off a gangland hit in a field full of pheasants; leaving Tucker, Tate and Rolfe well and truly plucked.

20. Where is the rest of the investigation material? From the very start, there seems to be large chunks of information missing. Most of the information in this book

has come from the public domain. I don't know if John Whomes has anymore paperwork. Perhaps the simple answer is if the Government, solicitors and the police, say you cannot have access to something, or it cannot be made public, then what are you going to do? For every question you ask, they have the ultimate answer: The investigation into the Essex boys murders has already been solved.

II

Post 95 Timeline.

1996 –

Start of Operation Apache, a secret investigation into police corruption in Essex constabulary.

January - Billy Jasper arrested for a separate offence. In custody he tells police he was with Jesse Gale and a man named Paul. They were aware the Essex boys were going to rob the canning Town organisation, but it was a double cross, and Tucker and Tate were going to be set up. On the night of the 6th they meet, with Paul carrying a Head sports bag. Jasper directed police to Rettendon and gave details of what happened.

7th Jan - Burglary at Meadow Cottage, London Road, Clacton, a property belonging to Steele, who reports it on the 09/01/96. A shotgun is later found in the loft in May.

10th Jan – Simon Renoldi, a colleague of Jason Vella, is sentenced to six years and eight months imprisonment after he was convicted of conspiring to supply Ecstasy, amphetamine, sulphate and cannabis, and false imprisonment. Vella got 17 years for various drug offences. With Vella and Tucker gone, Essex was now wide open for a takeover.

11th Jan – Donna Jaggers contacts D.I. Florence and gives him the machine gun that Rolfe had got from Mickey Bowman at end of November/start of December.

30th Jan - O'Mahoney gives a statement regarding drug dealing at Raquels.

8th Feb – Donna Jaggers gives a statement in relation to Rolfe getting a machine gun from Micky Bowman.

9th Feb – Essex police call Steele pretending to be the IRA. Over the next few days, they continue to call Steele and Saunders saying they had given money to Tate and now they want it back. When they start making threats, Steele records one of the conversations, and Saunders goes to Essex police. The phone calls stop, and Essex police have never explained the reasoning behind the threats, or what else was said, as they claim they did not record all of the calls.

15th Feb – Police arrest Mickey Bowman on suspicion of murder and possession of a machine gun.

13th March – Mass shooting of schoolchildren in Dunblane, Scotland, by man who owned numerous handguns. Act rushed through parliament for the possession of handguns/prohibited weapons to carry a minimum 5 year sentence.

January/February/March/April/May – Nicholls meets corrupt detectives, gets paid for showing them where he dumped the dud cannabis. They talk about arresting the people who buy the drugs off him, stealing cash from Steele, and creating a drug factory

14th March - Donna Jaggers gives a statement to police in which she names Steele as the person Rolfe was going to meet on the night he died. There is no mention of Nicholls or Whomes.

26th March. Surveillance team see Steele in company with Russell Tate, his new business partner for another drug deal.

Minesh Nagreecha, 24, stabbed 12 times at his home in Hemel Hempstead. House then set on fire. Former doorman and member of Adams family gang, Stephen Marshall, is arrested for murder, then later released without charge.

14th April – car hired by Nicholls is stopped at customs in Dover. Nothing found, but it is put on the system.

20th April – Dibley retires. Investigation is taken over by Supt Storey.

29th April. Steele is seen in company with Russell Tate. Tate is later stopped and is found to be carrying eight thousand pounds in cash.

1st May. O'Mahoney questioned in relation to a separate murder. He had threatened Danny Marlow in relation to an unpaid debt. O'Mahoney asks officers if they have found the shotgun cartridge that he threw away on Workhouse Lane.

13th May – Nicholls arrested for smuggling 25k worth of cannabis. Once in custody he is arrested for the murders

Steele arrested for being concerned in the importation of drugs. When interviewed on 14th May, on the advice of his solicitor he gives no comment answers about the offence he has been arrested for. After a search at his homes, five thousand pounds in cash, and a pump action shotgun capable of holding 8 cartridges is found. No comment to these questions. At the end of the interview he is further arrested on suspicion of being involved in the murders of Tucker, Tate and Rolfe. At this point Steele comments that he is innocent.

Whomes arrested for drug importation Whilst in custody he is then further arrested for the murders.

15th May – John Marshall goes missing. He had previously had dealings with Tate, O'Mahoney and Kenneth Noye.

17th May – Steele and Whomes are charged with the murders.

Nicholls stays in police custody. As per PACE, his custody record is updated when he goes out of his cell, but there are no recordings of the 30hrs worth of conversations he has with detectives in private, and what was said.

19th May – murder of Stephen Cameron by Kenneth Noye in a road rage attack on M25 in Kent. Noye goes on the run to Spain, but is eventually caught three years later.

22nd May – Body of John Marshall found dead in the boot of his Range Rover. The Head sports bag is in the car, but is empty. 5k in cash is in the glove compartment. Police believe he was killed at point blank range by a shotgun whilst he was in Kent. Someone has then driven his car into east London and left it in a side road.

1997 –

Seventy year old Charlie Kray jnr arrested for conspiracy to import cocaine. He claimed he was set up by undercover police officers, who only went after him because of his name. Although the evidence showed he played hardly any part in the conspiracy, he was given a 12-year sentence, and died in prison three years later.

The civil trial of OJ Simpson. Unlike a criminal trial where the defendant has to be found guilty beyond all reasonable doubt, a civil case relies of the balance of probability, a much lower threshold, and Simpson is found guilty. He is not given a prison sentence; but instead is fined millions of dollars for causing the death of his ex-wife and her friend Ron Goldman.

September – Start of the criminal trial for Steele and Whomes

October - Jesse Gale, a man linked to the murders by Billy Jasper, is killed.

1998

20th January 1998 – Steel and Whomes convicted of murder

January 2000

The pathologist in the investigation, Dr Paula Lannas, is herself investigated by the Home Office Advisory Board, due to serious failures in some of her results. She had already been investigated in 1996 for the quality of her work, and placed under close scrutiny. The Board decide it would not be in the public interest to continue with the investigation, and close it without coming to a decision.

October – Reggie Kray dies.

Chapter 21.

Doing Time.

"How do you go on, when in your heart you begin to understand... there is no going back? There are some things that time
cannot mend. Some hurts that go too deep."
The Lord of the Rings.

I

Hindsight is a wonderful thing. When Oasis played Knebworth
in the summer of 96, there were a hundred and fifty thousand people all holding nothing more than a joint. Within a
few years people would spend more time taking pictures than
making memories. At the turn of the millennium the internet
exploded, along with religious terrorists. From a high security
prison Mick Steele and Jack Whomes tried to appeal against
their convictions. But other things were happening beyond
their walls. Tony Blair promised to change the face of Britain,
and he did. He made it worse. During the time he was in power,
the gap between rich and poor got wider, education standards
went down, illegal immigration went up, and Islamic terrorism
overtook the IRA when it came to mass kilings. It was a case of
"Meet the new boss, same as the old boss." The house of Lords,
once home to the landed gentry who cared about the country, was now filled with company directors and political pawns
who only cared about themselves. There were a series of ex-
penses scandals; but when the establishment cover's things up,
they tend to stay covered. Using Parliamentary privilege and
the Official secrets Act, information can be buried for years.

In 1973 Wendy Sewell was attacked in a graveyard and died of her injuries. Stephen Downing, a church groundsman then aged 17, but with a reading age of an 11-year-old, was arrested and kept in custody without a solicitor until he finally signed a confession. Even though he said he didn't do it in court, he was convicted of murder and given a life sentence. After twenty years in prison Downing was told that if he admitted he did it he would be eligible for parole. He said no. How could he admit to something he had not done? His family kept demanding an enquiry, and the Court of Appeal finally reviewed the case. They agreed that his conviction, based on nothing else than a forced confession where he was kept awake by being slapped and having his hair pulled, was wrong. The medical report on Sewell contradicted pretty much everything that Downing had said he had done. The Court of Appeal even went so far as to say that if they had heard the same evidence given at a trial now, he would never have even been charged. They stated they, "did not have to consider whether Downing had proved that he was innocent, but whether the original conviction was fair. The question for (the Court of Appeal's) consideration is whether the conviction is safe and not whether the accused is guilty. What the defence had proved was that there was reasonable doubt about the "reliability of the confessions made in 1973. The court cannot be sure the confessions are reliable. It follows that the conviction is unsafe. The conviction is quashed."

When they police went back to reinvestigate the case, they found that most of the evidence and investigation material had been destroyed. After serving over twenty-seven years in prison, the government finally agreed that a miscarriage of justice had taken place. At the same time John Whomes, Jacks brother, was demanding that their solicitor should sit in the discipline hearing taking place for DC Bird and DS Stimpson, as he felt that much of the evidence being discussed related to Darren Nicholls, and to the Essex boys murder case. He was refused, and the hearing was held in secret. Stephen Downing was released in 2002 and awarded a five-figure sum, just as the original police officers in that case retired.

Those coppers could have spent their time getting a DVD of the film "Sexy Beast." It harked back to the lovable cockney gangsters who were into a bit of dodgy dealing and had a code amongst theives. It also made a healthy profit. People soon realised that British gangster films with a basic story that included drugs, big tits, big guns, a big fight, a bit of cheese you cunt, could line the shelves of Blockbuster's as long as the cover had a picture of Danny Dyer or Craig Fairbrass somewhere on it. This wasn't new. A film about the Krays in 1990 showed that there was an interest in true life crime on the screen.

Around the same time, we saw the rise of True Crime books. They often involved someone who had been there at the time. The first man out of the box was Bernard O'Mahoney with "So this is Ecstasy?" Published in 1997, whilst Steele and Whomes were still on remand, the book was very much about Bernard and how he got to become head doorman at Raquels. It finishes with the death of Leah Betts, and the killings of Tucker, Tate and Rolfe. Bernard waits until the year 2000 to publish an updated version called "Essex Boys," to tie in with a film of the same name. He continues in the same vein with another updated version, "Bonded by Blood" in 2006. In this book O'Mahoney puts the robbing of a large seizure of drugs from a gang based in Canning Town before the bad cannabis deal.

Other books have also been written, such as "Last man Standing," by Nipper Ellis. Published in 2009, it gives details of the feud between Ellis and the murdered men. In it, Ellis puts Nicholls as the man who helps Tate organise bringing over the cannabis. Nicholls is the one who takes the money over, he is the one who collects the drugs, he is the one that goes back to Amsterdam and waits at the hotel for the money to change hands. When Ellis is spoken to by police after the murders, they ask about Tate's mobile phone. Ellis tells them that Tate had four mobile phone numbers. Or more precisely, he had a couple of sim cards, and when he wanted to speak to certain people or conduct certain types of business, he would replace the sim card in his phone, talk to who he needed to talk to, and then swap the sim cards back.

Ellis goes on to say that Liz Fletcher received a call from one of Tate's numbers at 9.45pm on the night of the 6th. For reasons unknown this was not investigated. Nor does there appear to be any statement from Liz Fletcher regarding what happened at Baildon Tyre services, the last time she saw Tate alive, what happened to the VW Polo she left at the garage, what phone number(s) Tate had, and if she received any phone calls, especially from a Mr McCarthy.

"Once Upon a time in Essex," written by Bigfoot in 2016, is a story about a surveillance team who start to investigate the Essex boys after a series of drug raids. It is fiction, and that leads us into our next book.

The first thing we should say about "Bloggs 19" is that Nicholls was already in the process of writing it before the trial. If the defence had found out, they could hammer it home to the jury that Nicholls account of the murders was about as real as Harry fucking Potter's homework. More importantly, the prosecution would have had a duty to tell the court of this matter; but police claimed they knew nothing about Nicholls meeting with agents and publishers whilst he was in custody; how?

In the book Nicholls portrays himself as a man trapped by circumstances; caught up in criminality, rather than being a criminal. Everything is about him being stitched up by someone else; from former work colleagues, to the detective he thought was his friend. He seems more confused than Scooby Doo during the first couple of smuggling trips. When it comes to the bad cannabis deal, Nicholls blames someone else for the fuck up, but somehow still remains involved long enough to go back to amsterdam to sort out getting the money back. And now begins the saga where Tate goes loopy. It's surprising that Tate didn't want to speak to Nicholls during this time. After all, he was the guy on the go with the blow between Amsterdam and the coast, he could have swapped over the drugs, making sure Tate got the good stuff. But we have to remember this is all

Nicholls version of events. He can say what he likes. Steele and Whomes have always denied being involved in the importation of drugs, and the others are dead.

When it comes to the day of the murders, Nicholls account has improved even more over the passage of time. He goes into more detail than what he did in his final statement, and what he said at court. Effectively, there is now a lot more information that corroborates the police's version of events. After the murders Nicholls goes out and becomes a police informant. He is organising getting the drugs and then have his buyers arrested. He is talking about setting up an amphetamine factory with a police officer, using money he stole from the bot of a car when it's on a ferry on its way to buy drugs. There is no talk of wondering if someone is going to grass him up and the police are going to arrest him for murder; just balloon juice of how he begins to think Steele and Whomes might kill him, and he was almost going to go to the police before they all get arrested.

If I was Nicholls would I have told police about the murders? Probably not. Thats not being callous; but if you are living in that worlkd, being a grass never has any happy endings. But if he truly feared for his own life he could have called crime stoppers anonymously and given information; he could have even told the detectives he was speaking to on a regular basis, rather than wait until after getting arrested himself. He could have called police about the shotgun, and that would have at least put Steele away for a couple of years.

Just a day before the arrests Nicholls says he felt Steele and Whomes were definitely going to kill him, and so he was almost relieved when the police arrested them all for the drugs (even though as the police close in, he calls Steele to let him know). In the police station with a solicitor present he gets his moment to do the right thing, but doesn't, even though just like Bowman and Jasper beforehand, there is no real evidence for the police to be able to charge anyone with the murders. But there are ten kilos of cannabis in his van, and there are two police officers he has been attempting to pervert the course of justice with. At this point he suddenly realises now is the time to tell the police what happened. Some say Nicholls didn't need an alibi for the killings, he just needed an editor.

But reality kept fighting back. In 1999 at Epping Country Club in Essex, a doorman who had links with Tony Tucker, and a cartel from Canning Town, was stabbed to death after a fight involving another team of doormen. His murder has never been solved. The amount of murders and missing persons linked to criminal gangs has become a permanent feature across England, its not surprising there are a number of films that are either based on the murders or linked to them in some way.

"The Essex Boys" was released in 2000. "Rise of the Foot Soldier" was released in 2007, and has since gone on to spawn numerous spin offs. "Bonded by Blood" was released in 2010, and tried to tell the story from Nicholls point of view. There have been loads other films which have gone straight on to the shelves in the local supermarket; and like Jack the Ripper, the story changes every few years to get a new audience interested.

Perhaps the biggest growing media platform for those interested in the case was the internet. It had gone from being a hobby for nerds in 95, to dominating every household within ten years. Playstation and Pornhub changed society from a chemical culture to a technological one. Bernard O'Mahone may divide opinion, but his website on the murders has given us far greater access to the investigation than any other search engine. There are some very informative subscription channels on Youtube; such as Crime Scene to Courtroom, Theo Cloud, and Galactic 73. Much of them set out their theories through the numeorus strange facts which haunt this particular case. O'Mahoney also regularly uploads videos about the case on his own Youtube site. Interestingly, in 2020, just as Whomes parole appeal was set in motion, O'Mahoney changed his stance from saying that Steele and Whomes were innocent, to they did it, with the caveat that Whomes had been easily led by Steele, and that he could have walked away, as he had no issues with Tucker, Tate or Rolfe.

Facebook has a couple of sites dedicated to the murders, such as "Essex Boys, The Truth and nothing but the Truth." There is also "What happened in Essex in 1995," which again tries to figure out what happened. Once you start looking, you find so many people feel that a miscarriage of justice has taken place, you wonder why the establishment has refused to take it to the Court of Appeal. Some reporters still like to do things the old way. Various articles have been published relating to the case. Many state that a technologically literate jury of today would not have been so blinded by the flaws in the mobile phone evidence. And in relation to giving evidence, in 2011 laws were introduced in relation to special measures for witnesses, which included, screens in court, or even having your identity and voice masked. People too frightened to speak out at the time may have come forward to give their account if they would not be recognised. They also decided that if anyone in custody were believed to have any issues, including the lack of being able to read and write, they would be entitled to an appropriate adult. Too late for Jack Whomes, he learnt how to read and write from his prison cell.

We should also mention the crime scene photos that ended up on the internet. These were pictures of real people that had been shot dead. The crime scene photos had them still in the car, and laid out in a murtuary. How they got onto the internet is in some ways the story of the internet itself; as humans we have a fascination in out own mortality. Looking into famous killers and murders gives us a window into a world most of us hope we will never enter.

Both men have been involved in other incidents whilst in prison. Steele was attacked by a group of Muslim prisoners after he refused to stop cooking bacon in the prison kitchen. Due to the injuries he received he was given over forty thousand pounds in compensation. Unfortunately, the government then blocked his appeal application at the last minute, on the basis he now had money and so should not have been given legal aid, even though his had already started the process before he was attacked.

It's a shame the justice system is not as stern with those already in power. The Chilcot Enquiry, which looked at the government's role into taking Britain to war against Iraq, decided that it was an illegal war based on lies and deceit. Thousands of women and children had been killed, causing chaos in the middle east that still rumbles on today. The only winners were the arms dealers, the oil companies, and the politicians, none of whom were ever charged or convicted. Dr David Kelly who tried to expose the corruption was found dead; which the police listed as suicide. It seems the establishment is is intent on behaving the same way in this millenium as it did in the last century.

G. Couzens was in the specialist prison unit with Nicholls in October 1996. He recalled a conversation when Nicholls told him he had taken two men in his car to the murder scene. Four men then arrived at the scene in the Range Rover, and after the murders had been committed Nicholls took three men from the scene in his car. Nicholls then left the prison unit for a few weeks and went back into police custody. When he returned in November, his account had changed. On this occasion, he said that he had taken two men to the scene in his car and another three men had arrived in the Range Rover. He never said who had travelled in which vehicle, whether it was the gunmen or the deceased. We must also remember that in-between these meetings Nicholls gives his final statement to the police on the 14th October. But when he comes back to the unit, he has effectively got rid of a mystery passenger.

Nicholls also told Couzens that police knew everybody's movements because they had traced their mobile phones to various transmitters or relay stations, and that his statement had to fit the mobile phone evidence. Couzens was not aware of the full facts of the case until he left prison a few years later. During that time, he believed that Steele and Whomes had been convicted on other evidence, such as forensics and eye witnesses. Shocked at such a blatant miscarriage of justice he contacted the police, who did nothing. Couzens continued to seek justice, and made a statement which eventually became part of Steele and Whomes appeal in 2001.

Another man on the Witness Protection Programme, known for legal reasons as Mr P, said Nicholls told him early in 1997 that the story he was supposed to tell in court was "a pack of lies". Nicholls asked Mr P if he should go through with it, and he replied: "If you're telling lies you better not get caught". Mr P said he assumed Steele and Whomes were guilty and was not unduly bothered. "I thought there were forensics, witnesses. I could ignore Darren's perjury because I thought it was just the cherry on the cake. Now I realise Darren wasn't the cherry on the cake - he was the cake,"

A third man on the programme, Mr Oganciogw, stated, "We (Nicholls) talked many times about his case, and once we became close, he told me that he had made up the story about the shootings to Police. He did not say that he had lied to the police, but did say he had made the story up. My understanding of what he meant by the fact that he had made the story about the shootings up was that he had not told the truth to the Police." And here we have the problem with this whole case. "He did not say he had lied to the police, but did say he had made the story up."

The murders have not only become part of British history, they have joined the ranks where the crime has become part of British mythology. These myths surrounding a cocaine robbery, London Crime Cartels, a bad cannabis deal where a third of it was good, threats to be taken up North, may not be lies. The problem is, no one knows if they are the truth anymore.

II

The blurring of boundaries between crime cartels and police continued. The corruption was believed to be so widespread, that after the Brinks Matt robbery, Kenneth Noye was able to join the Freemasons when he was nominated by a serving officer. Operation Othona was set up in 1993, after the death of Stephen Lawrence, when it was revealed that numerous police officers had links with various criminals. One person whose name appeared in Op Othona was Billy Jasper. As the investigation was ongoing at the time of the Essex boys murders, much of the work done on Jasper was withheld from the public. Sadly, the enquiry into the death of Stephen Lawrence is still going nearly thirty years later. And as such, Jaspers links to the murders in Rettendon are still subject to restrictions.

In interview Jasper said that a London Crime Cartel had heard the Essex boys were going to rob them of a major shipment of cocaine; but we don't know if this was before or after the bad cannabis deal. According to Jasper, Tucker and Tate had arranged a deal a to sell 4 kilos of Cocaine for £132,000. This would fit Steele's story of taking 50k over, which would be about 4 kilos, and this would be a taster of the rest to come. The Essex boys wouldn't need their guns, it wasn't their drugs they were selling, and they were dealing with people they knew. Chances are they were going to get a cut for protecting Steele.

Jasper went on to say that the assassin stole the 4 kilos of Cocaine in payment for a debt owed by Tucker to a major South London criminal linked to the Brinks Matt robbery. Now we always thought that it was Tate who had a connection with Kenneth Noye; but let's not forget the half a million pounds worth of cannabis lost before Tate got out of prison. Was Tucker the one that took O'Mahoney and Tate to Rettendon to look for any of the missing cannabis because he knew that's where the drop was meant to happen?

Jaspers account seemed very credible. So, it is surprising that the police chose to ignore it. Well, perhaps it wasn't. Jasper was looking at sixteen years for an armed robbery. If he had gone on the Witness Protection programme like Nicholls, he would have had to confess the whole of his criminal past, and name names. Not only would these include some serious offences and some serious faces, but perhaps a lot of corrupt police officers as well? This is still the time when a lot of people were angry about the death of Stephen Lawrence. If there was any truth in detectives deliberately failing to investigate the crime, it would have caused a national outcry.

Operation Apache, the investigation into police corruption in Essex, had only just started. Operation Deenside, the investigation into a detective Chief Inspector passing on information to the Bowers family in Canning town, was also still in progress. Perhaps it would be better if Billy didn't become a hero and just served his time. When he was finally released from prison, Jasper was shot. He survived, but declined to talk any further about the Essex boys after that.

After the killings there was an investigation into members of the Camp family, headed by Kevin Camp, who owned a large area of farmland in Essex, and ran Topguard Security, which took over many of the clubs formerly controlled by Tucker. As well as employing door staff to nightclubs, they did security for boxing events and concerts. They were also involved in large scale drug importation and protection rackets. It is believed the legal, and illegal, revenue for these activities was worth around three million pounds a year. During a drug search a list was found with the details of serving police officers. The names of those Essex officers involved have never been disclosed to the public.

In 2001 the police went to carry out a review of Op Othona, but found a lot of information had been shredded in order to save space. It was decided by the Home office that all operations into police corruption in London and surrounding areas were to go under the name of Operation Tiberius. Luckily, among the items that had been saved was a secret recording involving the leader of a London Crime Cartel and a high-ranking police officer. On the 16th November 1995, they had a conversation regarding Leah Betts. Knowing that her death would spark a national outcry and lead to the government spending millions in order to crack down on drug dealers, the crime boss offered a simpler solution and said he would "take out" the suppliers who sold the pill. It is interesting that the word "suppliers" is used, rather than an individual. Whoever was speaking those words was talking about taking down a team. But again, the government has stopped any names from being made public in order to safeguard anyone who might be at risk from retribution. Operation Tiberius continued until 2016; and by then it had grown so large that the paperwork eventually reached over three thousand crates of material.

At the start of this century, Steele and Whomes put in their appeal to have their murder convicitons overturned. It was refused.

III

After the trial, forensic scientist David Bristowe, conducted a series of tests using Whomes' own mobile phone. Of the 20 calls made from the Wheatsheaf pub car park more than a third connected via the Hockley transmitter, as Whomes phone did on the night of the 6th, but none from Workhouse Lane did so. Mr Bristowe stated: "The new tests suggest Jack Whomes was telling the truth, and Darren Nicholls wasn't." The jury had been told at the time that Whomes must have been in an area overlapped by the two transmitters, and Workhouse Lane was in that area. But Mr Bristowe said his research showed that only one of the transmitters – at Ingatestone – was within range at the scene. Mr Bristowe commented, "I made about 60 calls at various places and heights up and down the lane, and not one of those calls was routed through the second cell site at Hockley, which the prosecution said was within range. I just don't think Jack Whomes could have been in Workhouse Lane when he made that call."

Bristowe carried out further tests that showed Steele was in the Bulphan area at the time of the 6pm calls. Whether he was at the farm owned by Billy Blundell, on his way to the Halfway House pub, or the cottage owned by Jack Whomes uncle, we cannot say. Bristowe also commented on the phone lists. "If you take Tate's billing as an example, Essex police request the billing days after the murder. They clearly received it. They then request it again in January but this time limit it to 18.59 hours, the time that they say was the last call. They have never disclosed the earlier schedule to the Defence. Which means Tate could have made calls after the prosecution state he was dead. More disconcerting is the schedules of calls have been manipulated and changed. A simple example is that the Tate 18.26 call to a well-known major criminal linked to a major crime Family is not on the schedule, neither are earlier calls to that person by Tucker and Rolfe. Why was that call not disclosed? Why was that person never interviewed or arrested?"

I have no proof of who this criminal is, but Mr Bristowe, who had been at the trial, certainly seemed to feel that the evidence had been biased in the prosecutions favour. To be so accurate on the time of calls he must have seen something, and been made aware of who that criminal was. Also, there is mention of the criminal calling Tucker and Rolfe. More importantly, he mentions Rolfe's phone, but we don't know if he is talking about a mobile or a landline. Bristowe also claimed Essex Police failed to do any investigation into Jasper's phone, or those he said were responsible. Their cell site and call data may have proved or disproved his account. They were certainly still in the time frame when that information could have been recovered. We will never know why the police did not feel this was necessary. We should also note that Mr Bristowe carried out all this work in his own time and with his own money. He is not saying that Steele and Whomes are innocent; only that the evidence presented to the jury was seriously flawed; which leads us nicely onto our next subject.

In 2001 the police pathologist Paula Lannas stood before a medical tribunal after her work in some cases was described as "appalling." She had been suspended after a murder trial she had been involved in collapsed due to what was described as a "series of blunders" by her. Issues with her work were already being questioned at the time of the Rettendon murders, but she was allowed to continue to practice for another five years. During the hearing Dr Lannas was accused of "demonstrating a continuing pattern of inadequate and unsatisfactory examinations and breaches of accepted forensic pathology practice." Basically, she was crap. The tribunal heard that "the sheer number and nature of the professional deficiencies alleged against her, give rise to concerns that are sufficiently serious that she should be sacked or suspended."

But then the panel decided it did not want to bring the Home Office into disrepute, and did not prosecute her. If they had, it would have meant that hundreds of cases in which Dr Lannas had given evidence in, including the Essex boys murders, could appeal for a retrial. The tribunal case was dismissed, and Dr Lannas, had her suspension suspended. Tellingly, she was told she could not return back to police work.

The Macpherson Report, which started in 1997 and completed in 1999, changed the way police would be held accountable for any miscarriages of justice. Much of it was based on institutional racism and the lack of convictions in the murder of Stephen Lawrence. But the report also looked at corruption in the police and the way large criminal gangs had managed to infiltrate most forces. An independent government agency would now investigate police corruption, rather than other police officers; and the Freedom of Information Act would allow people to review criminal investigations (unless any disclosure would bring exceptional harm to anyone still living).

Unfortunately, history as a way of biting back. The Macpherson Report was fully implemented in the Criminal Justice Act of 2003; which stated that all details of an investigation should be retained for a number of years, ideally on computer. But many cases prior to this date, such as the Rettendon murders, found that police officers notes and original paper documents had been moved, mislaid, or even shredded as police stations closed and storage rooms made way for hard drives. It is only the murder cases that are classified as unsolved that the police have a duty to keep all of the investigation material. Those cases that have conviction, such as Steele and Whomes, are liable to have things disappear.

Led by Jack's brother, John Whomes, numerous appeals were put in, and public demonstrations were used to keep to keep up the idea that a miscarriage of justice had taken place. He was not alone. Remember the defence barristers closing speech during the trial: "It is extraordinary that not one piece of evidence, let alone a combination of evidence, was found at the murder scene to connect the two defendants. The scene does not support the Crown's case and there is no evidence to confirm the account put forward by Nicholls." A man who was an expert in law did not believe there was enough for a jury to believe Steele and Whomes were guilty beyond all reasonable doubt.

But the Court of Appeal, which was reformed in May 2000, now included that any appeal must have "a real prospect of success." In order for Steele and Whomes to be successful; the Government, the police, the Crown Prosecution Service, the Criminal Justice System, the Witness Protection Programme, the Crown Court, and the Appeal Court, would all have to accept the Nicholls may have lied. If the killings had taken place ten years earlier or ten years later, the outcome at court may have been totally different.

Although there is one thing we haven't yet considered, which some people are not going to like. And that is...A small group of good detectives actually did a brilliant job in solving a triple murder. Forget the horseshit about the police doing the killings themselves. Just because some chump in a Stone Island top who got a speeding ticket ten years ago and now thinks he's Columbo says that the old bill did the shooting is mental. But I do accept that the police may have been watching the Essex boys before the murders, and that there is always a possibility that an individual officer could have changed the investigation after the murders were committed. So, let's knock on the door, ask if Ronnie Reality is at home, and go in.

The old school coppers from the murder squad didn't need

a shit load of data and a rainbow sticker to tell them who did it. There is the principle called Ochams razor, "the simplest explanation is most likely the right one." Steele believed his life was in danger, he took out the problem. Detectives must have known that Steele was involved in some way from as early as January when they get the phone records back. The clue is the payphone in Ipswich, and the call to Nicholls straight after the call to Tucker.

As soon as police check on Nicholls phone list they find Mick Steele. And you don't physically need the mobile phone to carry out call data and cell site locations. As long as they had Steeles mobile number, they could follow the trail. The next name that appears in Steele's phone records is Whomes. Again, you don't need his mobile in your hand. You start doing cell site locations. His number shows him on the night of the murders making a phone call from Rettendon to the man linked to the payphone in Ipswich, Darren Nicholls. An hour before this, Steele, who lives fifty miles away, was also near the Rettendon area. There is your real triangulation.

In January they start Operation Waterski, the surveillance on Steele, along with Customs and Excise. More importantly, they also start Operation Apache. If there are any links to the murders and corrupt detectives, it would be better to wait until you find out who the wronguns are before you bring in the right guys for the killings. The decision to use the Irish Mullock brothers on Steele in February was another reason the police believed that he was their man. Let's not forget, this is all before the official statement from Donna Jaggers and the arrest of Nicholls. It becomes a bit tricky trying to advocate pretending to be the IRA to try and get Steele to slip up, but this is the same time that Nicholls suddenly appears on the radar as a registered police informant.

At that point it probably sets the investigation back a few months before you can arrest them. Luckily, you finally get the statement from Donna Jaggers. In it she talks about the bad cannabis deal. This links Nicholls again, as he has recently been given four hundred pounds reward for telling DC Bird where a load of cannabis had been dumped. She also gives a clear motive for Steele, and the reason why they are in Workhouse Lane. All this before Nicholls has spoken one word about what happened that night.

When they are nicked, it's a sweet deal, as you not only catch the lot of them pretty much red handed with a load of drugs, you also bring in the two corrupt detectives who had been working with Nicholls for the last couple of months.

Ironically, it is when everyone is in custody, when everything should be done by the book; that the police leave themselves wide open to accusations. The numerous welfare visits, no challenges when Nicholls changes is account, the failure to investigate all lines of enquiries, the trips into London to see a book publisher; it all feels as though once the government made the decision to put Nicholls on the Witness Protection Programme, the establishment closes its eyes to all other possibilities, and officers in the case are told to stop acting like detectives and start behaving like social workers.

This decision must have come from the very top; but those people were never required to attend court to explain their actions. Something clearly happened between going "No comment" after being arrested for the murders in May, to giving a long and detailed statement nearly six months later. The numerous changes in Nicholls story simply cannot be explained by just remembering stuff.

It's not surprising that when the jury returned a verdict of guilty, Steele and Whomes shouted back that they were innocent. It's now been twenty-five years since the Essex boys drove down workhouse Lane. A quarter of a century; two eighths in old English drug money. We should have moved on; but somehow those unanswered questions that had followed the case from the very beginning have never gone away.

Chapter 22.

Conclusion.

"Now it's all over. And that's the hardest part. Today, everything is different. There's no action. I have to wait around like everyone else. Can't even get decent food. Right after I got here, I ordered some spaghetti with marinara sauce, and I got egg noodles and ketchup. I'm an average nobody. I get to live the rest of my life like a schnook."
Goodfellas.

I

Well, it's been emotional. I will repeat that the information from this book has come from the public domain, and all opinions are just mine alone. So, let's take one last trip even though I don't even think we've covered even half the investigation. In 1995 there were six hundred and sixty-five murders in the UK; nearly two a day; and yet the investigation into three men found dead in a car that December has gone on to have its own website, spawn numerous films, and cause arguments on social media. They have become part of that same fictional past like Jack the Ripper, where everyone seems to have an opinion on what really happened, who the real suspect is, and who was part of the cover up.

Those that remember 1995 will say you could walk down the high street and see someone you knew. You spoke to people in the pub rather than on the internet, everyone watched the same television programmes, you paid for things with cash, and you knew who the villains were. Today, the shops have turned into takeaways, you hear ten different languages in the supermarket, no one looks like what they do in the pictures they post on-line, a criminal in a different country can now hack into your accounts, and on the telly some cunt is getting praised just for baking a cake. If this is the modern world, you can fuck right off.

Many of the coppers involved in the Essex boys' murders have long since retired. They talk about how the drugs game has been taken over by foreign criminals, and how everyone accuses the police of being racist. Whenever they try to arrest someone, his muggy mate starts to film it. After events in 2001, the government told us that nobody will ever really feel safe again. In 2020 it wasn't even safe to leave your fucking home. Essex has become an urban sprawl of speed bumps and blocks of flats. Teenage boys have forgotten how to wear trousers. Pubs have been turned into restaurants, cars are electric, and even the old gate has gone.

The class system is still around. The current conservative prime minister Boris Johnson graduated from Oxford University. The current opposition leader, Kier Starmer, also graduated from Oxford university. Meet the new boss, same as the old boss. Since Steele and Whomes have been inside, the Human Rights Act became part of British law under the EU; and then the British people voted to leave. The white working class have been demonised into far-right benefit scroungers, complaining about illegal immigrants whilst getting another tattoo. The media abuses them as there is no political group on their side anymore.

The liberals and the left have gone into identity politics, where they can offer various minority groups loads of promises on the basis that it's all government funded; which really means it's really taxpayer funded. But the backbone of England continue to survive. As my dear old nan used to say, if you've ever taken a piss when you're in the bath; you're working class.

The middle class are working so hard to pay off the bills

and send their kids to the right school, they only get to social-
ise in front of a screen. And the police are so busy dealing with
comments on social media, they haven't got time to go on pa-
trol. The only news on the horizon is that Jack Whomes may be
eligible for parole in the near future. Mick Steele might be in a
while. He has always refused to take part in any rehabilitation
programmes, as he has always said he is innocent of killing the
Essex boys.

Much of the investigation is available to the public. But not
everything. A lot of information still remains hidden under the
Official Secrets Act and Public Interest Immunity, and it could
be kept locked away until 2045; when Steele would be over a
hundred years old. This secret information would include the
undercover operation on Steele and Whomes, everything Nicholls did as a registered police informant, the operation into
corrupt police officers, and if any of the Essex boys themselves
had passed on sensitive information to the police. If the establishment believes that just one small item could link to other
things more serious, then it will never release anything. Who
makes that decision; the establishment does. That leaves us to
continue with this guessing game of what really happened that
night. Could there have been a hitman invovled?

In a country where three hundred people a day are reported
missing, and at least ten of those disappear without a trace
never to be seen again, you could argue that the number of professional killers out there could be a lot more than realised.
Let's not forget all those other deaths that may not have been by
natural causes. Tucker and Rolfe were a couple of wurzels when
it came to murder, but they still managed to make Whitaker's
demise seem like a drug overdose.

In 2003 Dave King, a former business associate of Tucker,
and a well-known drug dealer, went to carry out his daily body-
building routine at his gym in Hoddesdon. Roger Vincent from
Essex and David Smith from Elstree in Hertfordshire, were told
that King had become a police informant after he was arrested
on suspicion of smuggling 14 kilos of heroin from France, and

miraculously got bail. They drove up to King in a white escort van and shot him using a machine gun. It transpired that Vincent and Smith were gangland hitmen. In 1994 they had carried out a similar attack, where Robert Magill was shot in a country road, and they escaped in a BMW. The car was recovered. In the boot was a handprint on a plastic bag. The print belonged to Kevin Lane. All three men were arrested and charged. Vincent and Smith were acquitted before the trial began, for unknown reasons. And so, Kevin Lane stood trial alone. He admitted to using the car a few weeks prior, but knew nothing about the murders. There was nothing else to link him, but he was found guilty and served 18 years in prison.

After Vincent and Smith were convicted for the murder of Dave King, it was revealed they had a very close relationship with a Detective Inspector Spackman of Hertfordshire police, who at some point had been in charge of the Magill murder investigation. This included him meeting both men whilst the investigation was live, even though they were both considered suspects. Spackman was later convicted of theft after stealing a hundred and sixty thousand pounds in cash that had been seized from drug dealers. Two other people who had been convicted of offences whilst Spackman was in charge of both investigations have been freed on appeal.

I am not saying Vincent and Smith were involved in the Essex boys murders, but it shows there are people out there who are available to carry out a killing if and when required, and these two were in business for nearly ten years. It is quite possible a hitman was involved in the Essex boys killings. Tucker, Tate and Rolfe were either in the lane to sort out an issue with the Bundells, to take out a rival; or because they were planning to take a million pounds worth of cocaine by pointing a gun at a member of the cartel when the plane landed. They missed on all three counts.

Darren Nicholls does not exist. The name has gone, he doesn't even have a birth certificate. When he went to give evidence at the Old Bailey, he was already a dead man walking, but he knew enough to be able to get the jury to believe him, and start a new life once the trial was over. He admitted that he had changed his account about a lot of things, but he must have done enough for the jury to make that ultimate decision.

But let's fast forward. We now have more information. We are now aware of Nicholls talking to book and television companies before the trial. We have statements from people who were on the Witness Protection programme with Nicholls in prison. There is the new phone evidence. We can now look at the investigation with a fresh pair of eyes to try and see the truth. So, over twenty-five years later, who killed the Essex boys? The answer is...Steele and Whomes did.

II

To be more precise, they conspired with others to murder the Essex boys. If either Steele or Whomes had managed to produce just one independent witness for anytime between 5pm and 8pm of the 6th December; that's either Steele or Whomes, then Nicholls whole account would have been discredited. If any independent witness had positively identified Tucker Tate or Rolfe after 7pm, that's Nicholls account discredited. If Steele had told police to go look for CCTV at the petrol garage or Tesco's; or Whomes, having not bothered to call Nicholls to tell him he was picking up the VW Passat, had also not bothered calling him to say he had collected it, they would be safe. But once those pieces of the jigsaw puzzle start slotting into place, the picture becomes clearer.

Steele and Whomes were in the Rettendon area that night, a round trip of over a hundred miles from where they live, to pick up a trailer, and a broken down car, just as three people they knew were killed. Their defence, for what it was worth, wasn't enough. We had the missing letterbox, the petrol receipt that didn't quite match, the meeting with an in-law who couldn't remember the date she visited Steele's bungalow.

The prosecution was right in saying that Steele and Whomes, who were arrested in May 96, could have given that information to the police then. Instead they wait until June 97, over a year and a half since the murders to give their alibis. If you had not been accused of murder the situation would have been farcical. They conspired in the murder of Tucker, Tate and Rolfe. The tragedy is I don't know if I can say they pulled the trigger; and isn't that the basis of Nicholls evidence?

The first option is that there was a threat to Steele's life, until someone spoke to him. Steele, a man who could tell the IRA to go fuck themselves, would no doubt give it straight to anyone who was asking questions. If that same person then spoke to people such as Barry Dorman, they would know that it definitely wasn't Steele who was trying to rip them off. Leaving Tate well and truly in the shitter.

The second option is that Tucker was the target. Somewhere along the line, whether it's the cannabis drop that landed in the nearby reservoir, a robbery that's gone wrong, or the death of Leah Betts, a crime cartel wants him gone. They become linked to the cocaine robbery, which also implicates Steele; and if Tucker and Tate go for it, they can both be ironed out.

The third option is the simplest. By now Tucker and Tate are such loons that they couldn't be trusted to put two bits of Lego together, let alone carry out a decent job. Whether it was smuggling cocaine, cannabis, or fucking coconuts, these clowns would still end up shooting someone if they weren't careful. Steele knew Tate was never going to pay back the money he owed to people who had put money into the syndicate. He knew that Tate would probably kill him before there was a showdown rather than lose face. He spoke to others and got them down the lane. It doesn't matter if he was in the car or not. It doesn't matter who was going to do the killing. But the judge was right. Steele and Whomes were guilty of conspiracy; and it didn't matter who pulled the trigger, conspiracy to murder still carried the same sentence as if you had killed them yourself.

My personal view is that Steele and Whomes conspired with at least two others to get the Essex boys murders, and one of the men in this conspiracy was Darren Nicholls.

II

At the start of this book I asked the question, can you prove beyond all reasonable doubt that they did it? Perhaps the real question should be, has a miscarriage of justice taken place?

Its has reached the point that if Steele and Whomes now admit their guilt they could go free. It is probably too late for them to name others. The court and justice system will say this is just playing the blame game; and the police could say there is no evidence they can produce to back up their claim. The Witness protection programme is never going to admit they fucked up. As far as the Government is concerned the case has already been solved. And even though the murder investigation has more holes in it than Fred West's back garden, it would take something very powerful for their convictions to be overturned.

So why write a book about two people I think were involved? I grew up around men similar to Steele, Whomes, and the Essex boys themselves. When people speak about white privilege, they are not speaking about my world. I knew from a young age that there was an upper level of white privilege that I would never be allowed access to. Your chances of escaping the bottom of the ladder would be constnatly stopped by those at the top.

Pretty much every politician has gone to the same three schools or two universities; is that justice? To me, there is not something quite right about this whole investigation. From the moment the prime minister declared a war on drug dealers after the death of Leah Betts, the establishment took over. At the point of being sentenced both men pleaded with the judge that they were innocent. Three members of the jury broke down crying as they were led away. They were too late. Steele and Whomes have now served over twenty years in prison for a crime they continue to say they did not commit. It goes back to Lord Blackstone in the 17th century, and that guilt has to be proved beyond all reasonable doubt. I don't think that level of proof was reached.

But didn't I say they were guilty? Yes, of conspiracy. So why do I think there has been a miscarriage of justice? We all know that money talks and bullshit walks. They say that if a politician thinks a billion pounds is a lot, they are in the wrong game. Today's illegal drug market is worth around two billion pounds a year. In 2001 Steele and Whomes lost their appeal to have a retrial. After that, Operation Apache was closed down. DC Bird and DS Stimpson, who had been arrested the same time as Nicholls, were never charged with any offences. This is strange, as police had phone recordings of drug dealing, setting up an amphetamine factory; and attempting to steal a hundred and fifty thousand pounds worth of drug money; all with the help of Darren Nicholls. Both officers retired from the police after being suspended on full pay since 1996. On top of six years salary, both detectives were given two hundred and fifty thousand pounds each in compensation for the stress caused to them because of the police operation, as well as their police pensions. They also signed a confidentiality clause contract. What the conditions are I don't know; but both have refused to speak about Nicholls or the murders ever since.

This amount of money is peanuts compared to the real costs involved. If the case went to the court of appeal and Steele and Whomes won, what would be the outcome?

Let's say they get a million pounds each in compensation. A new investigation would have to take place to see if there was any evidence to arrest and charge anyone else. That is going to cost about three million. Currently, there are three thousand people in the UK on the Witness Protection Programme. They are still monitored on a regular basis. The running cost must be in the region of over ten million pounds a year.

If it was proved that Nicholls had lied, then every other

case which involved the use of a protected witness would also be put in doubt, and the cost of retrials and compensation would run into billions. The police would have to have another internal investigation. The justice system would require another major overhaul; and the public would lose faith in judges, and the idea of being a member of a jury.

You see, the truth is, it's not the three dead men in the Range Rover that are important, nor is it the two men currently serving life in prison. It's the one man on the Witness Protection Programme that is keeping the Titanic that is the justice system from sinking. His authorisation to go into the programme was signed off by the chief constable of Essex, then various members of Parliament, and finally the Home Secretary at the time. Nicholls currently holds the key to billions of pounds worth of secrets. As such, there is no way the establishment is going to start looking into this case. I think they knew the police got the right men; they just didn't get all of them.

And here comes the sucker punch; Nicholls knew both the defendants and the victims, he was involved in a criminal activity, he was in the area, he did get a phone call at 7pm, and he must have known what Steele and Whomes were also doing that night. Somewhere in his story there are elements of truth. Perhaps he was just the driver. Perhaps there was also someone else involved. Are you ready for the gut punch? The only reason he was able to get on the Witness Protection programme and be able to change his story, not once, but over twenty times, must have been because someone in power wanted it to happen.

There must have been a point when the police wondered if Nicholls should have been charged with conspiracy to murder as well. But if he changed his mind and refused to speak, the whole investigation would collapse. The establishment wasn't going to have that. Instead, Nicholls, and possibly others, was allowed to go free because it meant Steele and Whomes could be charged. Even if this was done for all the best reasons, even if only a tiny detail was changed to fit a witness statement, even if they thought it was the only way to get justice; as soon as you stop telling the truth, the whole truth, and nothing but the truth, you are not giving evidence, you are making up a story.

From then on it is impossible to prove the facts of the case beyond all reasonable doubt. It's the details that matter, and so many are missing. Perhaps the real question is not who killed the Essex boys; but was the establishment knowingly involved in a miscarriage of justice in order to secure a conviction? That is something only you can answer.

III

Steele and Whomes have appealed their convictions every year since 2001. The government has so far refused to re-open the case.

It is not known if Sarah Saunders ever returned to the home that Tate took out a life insurance policy on.

After the murders, Donna Jaggers had a long-term relationship with an Essex police officer.

Jesse Gale, the man named by Billy Jasper as being involved in the shootings, was killed after being hit by a car in 1998.

After being released from prison Billy Jasper was shot. He survived, and moved away from East London.

Darren Nicholls and his family were given new identities and moved away from Essex.

Mark Murray, the drug dealer believed to have spoken to Billy Blundell about shooting Tucker, moved to Spain just before the murders.

Bernard O'Mahoney has continued to write and appear on television regarding the Essex boys and other matters.

Despite numerous requests from various parties, the now retired Supt Dibley has refused to speak about his investigation into the murders.

Billy Blundell passed away in 2020

At the time of writing, Linda Millard is still listed as missing.

No one has ever been arrested and charged for the murder of John Marshall.

Although it ran for three years, and cost hundreds of thousands of pounds, no police officer was ever convicted for corruption during Operation Apache.

Printed in Great Britain
by Amazon

53898334R00154